Miracles

Leisure Entertainment Service Co., Inc.
(LESCO Distribution Group)
And
Dorchester Media LLC.

For Paul J. Gross,
a man who turned good ideas
into great things. Sorely missed
and deeply loved by family and
friends

Leisure Entertainment Service Co., Inc. (LESCO Distribution Group)
65 Richard Road Ivyland, PA 18974   www.leisureent.com

Published by special arrangement with Dorchester Media, LLC.

Printed in the United States of America.

A Special LESCO Edition

FIRST TIME IN PAPERBACK

Dorchester Media is
a consumer magazine publisher.

Our Women's Romance Group of
eight titles includes the world's
largest and best selling women's
romance magazine, *True Story*.
True Story has a great history
(1919) and heritage and continues to
touch the heart, mind and soul of
readers by sharing everyday
experiences of romantic life.

In addition to *True Story*, sister
publications include *True Confessions*,
True Romance, and *True Love*.
Special collector magazines from
the substantial archive include
True Story Remember When.

For more information on all of
Dorchester Media publications, write
to Publisher, Dorchester Media,
333 Seventh Avenue, 11th Floor,
New York, N.Y. 10001.

We hope you enjoy the book.

Table Of Contents

This book consists of true stories. Names, characters, places and incidents were changed. Any resemblance to actual events, locales, or persons, living or dead, is entirely coincidental.

An *Original* Publication of Dorchester Media, LLC.

ISBN:
First LESCO Edition Printing: February 2006
1-60016-005-0
Printed in the U.S.A.

Leisure Entertainment Service Co., Inc.
(LESCO Distribution Group)
65 Richard Road Ivyland, PA 18974
www.leisureent.com

MIRACLES

THE POWER
OF PRAYER

When I walked down the aisle on my wedding day, I thought I was the luckiest woman in the world. I walked slowly, enjoying it, wanting to make the moment last. I had no way of knowing that in only three short days I wouldn't be able to walk at all. In three short days I would be lame.

Greg and I awoke early that third morning and decided it was the perfect day to hike to the other side of the lake. After a quick breakfast in our cabin, we put some cheese, ham, and bread in a backpack and started down the trail. The trail wound through trees and across stretches of pebbly beach, sometimes close to the water's edge, sometimes many yards away.

I was walking ahead of Greg through a grove of trees when, suddenly, he yelled, "Stop!"

I whirled around to find him standing still, looking at me, his eyes twinkling.

"What's the matter?" I said.

"Don't you know what kind of tree that is?" he

said, pointing to a large tree that was next to me at the edge of the trail.

It looked like an ordinary oak to me.

"No," I said. "Is it something special?"

"Special! I'll say it's special. That just happens to be a kissing tree. Whoever goes past it has to stop and kiss the person who's behind."

I started to laugh. "Only if the person in back can catch the one in front!" I said, and I turned and raced off down the trail, knowing full well that Greg could easily overtake me. Of course, I anticipated the pleasure I would have when he did catch me.

The fall leaves crunched under my tennis shoes as I ran, and I could her the thud of Greg's feet, too. I looked back over my shoulder to see how close he was getting and, somehow as I looked behind me, I failed to see the tree that had fallen and rested across the trail.

I heard Greg yell, "Watch out!" but it was too late. I remember trying to catch myself, but my feet went completely out from under me. Then I landed on my head. I had hit a sharp rock on my way coming down.

Later, I learned that I was unconscious for more than twenty-four hours. Greg, realizing I'd hit my head, had been afraid to move me in case there was a spinal injury. He'd run back to camp and called an ambulance. Then he'd run back to be with me until help arrived.

I don't remember any of it—being carried out of the woods on a stretcher, taking the eighty-five mile ambulance ride to the nearest hospital, being prepared for the exploratory surgery that the doctors eventually decided was necessary. All I remember was falling— and waking up in the hospital the next afternoon.

THE POWER OF PRAYER

I opened my eyes slowly, not knowing where I was or what had happened. My head ached, and I was terribly thirsty. There was a glass of ice water on a stand next to the bed, and I reached for it. Or, rather, I tried to reach for it. My hand lay stiffly on the blanket, ignoring the messages that my brain was sending it. I blinked and stared at the glass of water. Again, I tried to reach the glass, but my arm didn't move.

I tried to move my other hand and was relieved when it responded normally. Then I tried to wiggle my feet. The left foot worked fine, but the right one didn't move at all. I couldn't even move my toes on the right foot. I turned my head in the other direction, knowing by then that I was in a hospital, and I saw Greg slumped in a chair, sleeping.

"I'm awake," I said.

He jumped as if I'd jabbed him with a needle.

"Thank God!" he said. "Are you all right? I thought you'd never wake up. I fell asleep waiting. I have to tell the doctor."

He hurried out of the room but was back in only a few seconds.

"Are you all right?" he asked again.

"I can't move my right arm or leg," I said. "I tried to reach the glass of water, and I can't do it."

Greg nodded, not seeming too surprised. He didn't say anything, but he picked up the ice water and held the straw to my lips while I had a drink. Before I finished, a doctor came into the room.

"This is Dr. Moore," Greg said.

Dr. Moore examined me thoroughly, telling me as he worked what had happened in the hours since I'd fallen. He explained that I had a skull fracture and a brain concussion and said that my headache would probably persist for several days.

"But what about my arm and leg?" I asked when he finished. "I can't move anything on my right side."

I don't know why I was telling him. He'd just spent twenty minutes trying to get some reaction from the right side of my body.

"Head injuries are strange," he said. "We never know what the results might be. Actually, we were afraid you might have a vision or hearing problem in addition to the paralysis. It doesn't look now as if that's going to happen."

"How long will this last?" I said. "Will it go away gradually, like the headache?"

I saw the look of pain that had crossed Greg's face. In a flash of insight, I knew what the doctor was going to say before he said it. And I knew that the news was not going to be good.

"It may go away gradually," he said. "And it may respond to treatment, but—"

"But it may not?" My question was almost a whisper.

"It may not," he said. "Probably, it won't. I have to be honest with you. Most likely, the paralysis is permanent. I'm sorry."

Greg reached for my right hand and closed his fingers around it. When I tried to squeeze back, to respond to the pressure of his hand, I couldn't do it. I turned my face into the pillow and began to cry.

Then Dr. Moore was explaining something in technical terms, but I couldn't understand anything he had to say. I was too upset. Paralysis. I couldn't be paralyzed. I had just gotten married. And that was the dream of my life—to be married to a man who loved me as much as I loved him.

THE POWER OF PRAYER

Why was God punishing me in this way? I tried to tune into the doctor's words, but I couldn't. My brain just wouldn't accept the words that were coming out of his mouth. Finally, I concentrated more so that I could pay attention to what he was saying.

Through my sobs, I heard Dr. Moore say, "I'll leave you two alone for a while. I'll be back later."

I felt Greg's hand on my shoulder, rubbing me lightly, offering comfort.

When I finally quit crying, Greg pulled the chair up close to the bed and we talked.

"At least, you're alive," he said. "I was afraid I would lose you. When you stayed unconscious for so long, I was so scared. I thought. . . ."

I forced a smile. "You can't get rid of me that easily," I said.

"And Dr. Moore wasn't kidding when he said they were afraid the damage would be worse. Not only sight and hearing—they were afraid the brain damage was severe enough that you wouldn't be able to think right, either. When you realize the possibilities, semiparalysis seems like a lucky break."

Lucky break. It was a lucky break that I was paralyzed? Maybe some doctor thought it was a lucky break, but that doctor didn't have my life. He was going to go home to his wife and family, probably while I laid in this hospital bed.

Yet, after I thought about it for a few more minutes, I agreed with the analysis. At the time, I said Greg was right, but, as the weeks went on, I began to wonder how lucky it was. The headache faded, as the doctor had predicted, but the paralysis definitely remained.

Although a program of physical therapy was started, at the end of six weeks, there was no improvement at all. I was able to sit up in a wheelchair and had learned to feed myself left-handed without spilling too much food, but Dr. Moore and the specialist he called in for consultation both agreed that the paralysis was permanent. They suggested that I drop the physical-therapy exercises, go home, and start learning to live my life from a wheelchair.

The day I left the hospital, Dr. Moore came to my room for a talk.

"I want to warn you," he said, "not to waste your money going from doctor to doctor, hoping for a cure. There are a lot of quacks around who will be happy to give you hope in exchange for your cash, but they can't offer you a cure. Dr. Brennan, the one I called in for consultation, is one of the top men in the country. If there was a way for you to be helped, he would know it."

I nodded, appreciating his concern.

"So often," he continued, "people with an incurable disease or a condition such as yours that won't improve with treatment would rather search for a miracle than to accept reality. Don't bother chasing the impossible. Remember there's no such thing as a miracle."

"I'll remember," I said.

Greg was waiting to take me home, and I was curious to see what that home looked like. The apartment that we'd picked out together before we were married had been a walk-up, on the third floor of an old Victorian house. It was perfect for us as long as both of us could climb the stairs.

After the accident Greg had looked for a different place, one with ramps or an elevator so that I could get around in my wheelchair. He'd finally found one in a modern, new apartment building. The rent was more than we'd hoped to pay, and it didn't have nearly the charm nor interesting features of the old Victorian place, but he'd leased it for a year.

I tried not to show my disappointment when I saw the sophisticated high-rise building, but Greg sensed my feelings.

"I know it isn't exactly your style, Gloria, but there just weren't many places available that would work for us now," he said.

Somehow, in the weeks that followed, that apartment came to symbolize my whole life—nothing was as good as I'd anticipated. Everything I did seemed to be a compromise of some sort made because of my handicap.

I love to cook and had looked forward to preparing special meals for Greg, but one-handed cooking was slow and difficult. Anyone who has tried separating an egg with one hand will know what I mean. Even opening a can one-handed can be a problem. Instead of gourmet meals, I served mostly foods that were simple to prepare, or I bought frozen dinners. We had enough to eat, but it wasn't at all the way I'd planned it.

Other areas of my life were even more disappointing. There was no way that I could go back to my job as checker in a supermarket. My boss was sorry to lose me, and I did receive some disability payments, but I was unable to work. Our expenses were higher than we'd thought and we had just one paycheck instead of two.

My sex life also fell far short of my expectations. On our honeymoon I'd discovered how great sex with

Greg could be, but after I got home from the hospital, he acted as if he was afraid to touch me. He was considerate and affectionate, but every time a kiss threatened to become more than just a friendly peck, I could almost feel him back away. Naturally, I wondered if my condition turned him off—if he found me unattractive now that I was confined to a wheelchair.

Finally, after more than week of living that way, I took the initiative one night in bed, making it impossible for him to turn away. Greg responded with the same passion he'd shown on our honeymoon, but found that my own desire was smothered in frustration about halfway through our lovemaking.

Although I wanted Greg, it was terrible not to be able to move as I once had. I felt as if half of me was sensuous and responsive and the other half was a wooden doll.

Instead of feeling fulfilled when it was over, I felt deprived. Naturally, that didn't make Greg eager to approach me again, and so the area of our life together that we'd both looked forward to with such pleasant anticipation became instead just one more difficulty to adjust to. Our life together was terrible.

Within a few weeks, I began to be continually depressed. I tried to keep busy, to increase the number of things I could do with my left hand, to find ways of being useful, but I was bored at home alone. And, of course, I couldn't help comparing my life with the ones my friends had to live. More and more frequently, I began to wonder if Greg wouldn't be happier without me.

Then one evening, Greg came home from work so excited that he could hardly stand still. One of the men in the plant where he worked had talked all day about a "miracle cure." The man's sister had been suffering from a rare nerve disease and had been given only a few months to live.

"Three days ago," Greg said, "she went to a prayer lab right here in town, and she was healed! Her pain disappeared, and her symptoms are gone. Yesterday, she went back to the doctors who've been treating her, and they couldn't find a trace of the disease. They couldn't explain the cure, and when she told them about the prayer lab, they didn't argue that it had caused her to be healed."

"What is it?" I asked. "I never heard of a prayer lab. How does it work?"

"I don't know why they call it that. Actually, it's a prayer group, and there are more than two hundred members, people from churches of all denominations as well as some unaffiliated people who still believe in the power of prayer. They meet weekly, and they pray for anyone who needs their help.

"The person they're praying for doesn't even have to be there. They healed a man in another state who had Hodgkin's disease, and they cured an elderly woman in a nursing home who had a tumor." He paused and his eyes glowed as he said, "Maybe they could help you."

I stared at him. Dr. Moore's words echoed in my mind: *Remember there's no such thing as a miracle. Don't waste your time chasing the impossible.*

"I don't know," I said. "I've never had anything to do with faith-healing."

"Neither had this guy's sister. She didn't even go to church. It worked for her just the same. Besides, what do you have to lose?"

I hesitated. I did believe in God, and I belonged to

a church, but I'd never been really active, and I never thought of prayer as a way of asking for help. For me, prayer was more a way of giving thanks for my blessings. Or, at least, it used to be—I hadn't felt too thankful lately.

"I—I'll think about it," I said.

I knew Greg was unhappy that I didn't show more enthusiasm, but so much of my life was turning out to be a disappointment that I was afraid to get all excited about his prayer lab and then just be disappointed again. I found, though, that I couldn't forget about it.

The next day, it kept popping into my mind when I least expected it, and I kept wondering if there just might be a possibility that it would work. Dr. Moore had warned me about quacks who were out to make a profit because of someone else's misfortune, but the members of the prayer group made no charge. They asked for nothing in return for their service, not even publicity. They said they already had more requests for prayer than they could handle.

In midafternoon, I called the pastor of my own church and asked him if he ever heard of the prayer group.

"Many times," he answered. "Twenty-five or thirty of our own congregation participate in it. I've been to several of the sessions myself."

"Then you think it really works?" I asked.

"Only God can heal," he replied, "and God sometimes moves in mysterious ways. I believe He intends to heal us through the knowledge and skill of our doctors and through our own good sense in following their directions. But, sometimes, doctors run into a problem they can't solve, a disease they can't cure. When that happens—well who's to say that there aren't other ways?"

"Do you know anyone personally who was healed this way?" I asked. I hated to sound so doubting, but I knew how stories could be embellished as they were retold.

"I know a woman in her sixties who was losing her vision due to a circulatory problem. Her doctors had warned her that she'd be blind in less than six months. That was eight months ago. But this week, she passed the eye exam for her driver's license. She says the group is responsible, and I believe her."

When I hung up the phone, my hand was trembling. For the first time in months, I felt there was hope that I'd be normal again.

I told Greg my decision as soon as he got home. He immediately called the contact person for the group and was told that the members would be happy to pray for me at their next meeting. Their next meeting was only two days away.

I was more nervous during those next two days than I'd ever been in my life. A hundred times a day, I questioned the wisdom of what I was doing. Over and over, I told myself not to get my hopes up too high. Not everyone the group prayed for was healed—the contact person had stressed that. They had no way of knowing in advance who would be helped and who wouldn't.

No matter how much I tried to keep my emotions under control, deep down inside, there was an intense core of excitement that grew and multiplied until, by the time we left for the meeting, I was totally convinced that, within a few hours, I'd be stepping out of my wheelchair forever. Maybe it was wishful thinking—or maybe it was faith.

The group met in the basement reception hall of a large church. There was no ramp, so Greg had to carry me down the stairs while someone else brought my wheelchair. My pulse raced as I saw that there were already seventy or seventy-five people gathered, even though we had arrived fifteen minutes early. We were warmly welcomed and told where to sit. People continued to stream in, rapidly bringing the folding chairs that were arranged in circular fashion. Additional chairs were brought and added to the outside, making one more circle.

It's difficult to describe the atmosphere of that meeting. There was lively talk and the laughter of good fellowship, but it was something more than that—a closeness and a sharing of purpose that seemed to provide a unity, even though the participants ranged in age from late teens to quite elderly. Some were formally dressed in suits and ties; others wore jeans and tennis shoes. A few carried Bibles; most came empty-handed.

Yet the love I felt in that room was warm and unwavering. I had never been in a group like this one. Oh, I was a regular churchgoer. I grew up in the church and had gone for years. I had even encouraged Greg to attend with me. He really wasn't much of a churchgoer before we started dating. However, he enjoyed going to church.

Yet our attendance at church regularly didn't translate to prayer. Although our minister talked about making time for prayer in our lives, we really hadn't done that. I always had planned to, but somehow, we never made the time.

Now this prayer group was giving me a new outlook on life. I had never seen so many different people willing to pray at the same time—and for people that they didn't even know. I felt something special was going to happen to me.

The leader opened the session with a brief prayer, and then he spoke about a man in another state, Allen Tilton, who had requested that the group pray for him. Allen Tilton had broken his leg skiing, and the break hadn't mended properly. He was left with an awkward limp, which wouldn't have been so bad except he earned his living as the manager of a ski resort. Now his limp attracted attention and served as an uncomfortable reminder to patrons that they could injure themselves on his ski slopes. As a result, the owner of the resort was looking for a new manager.

The leader repeated Allen Tilton's name several times, and then a hush fell over the room as everyone in the group bowed his head in silent prayer. I closed my own eyes and offered my prayer for the recovery of that man whose name I knew but whom I had never met.

Please, God, I prayed, *heal Allen Tilton. Take away his limp, and make him well.*

The praying lasted about twenty minutes, and then, almost as if they'd received some silent signal, the members of the group stirred and began to talk among themselves. They relaxed briefly, and then the leader called them to order. The leader introduced me and told the group about my accident and the paralysis that had resulted. When he mentioned that the accident had happened on my honeymoon, just three days after my marriage, a murmur of sympathy rippled through the group.

I was then asked to wheel my chair into the center of the circles of chairs, which I did, and, once again, all heads bowed and all eyes closed. As I looked at the people who surrounded me—rows of chairs, each containing someone who at that moment was praying for me—I was overwhelmed with gratitude, and, bowing my own head, I offered my prayer of thanks.

Dear God,

Thank you for all these people who want to help me, I prayed. *Thank you for showing me that even strangers can care about each other. Help me be worthy of their love for me. And, God, if it be Thy will, please let me walk again. Amen.*

I remained still, with my head bowed, but inside, I was churning with excitement. My heart was pounding, and my mouth felt dry.

I'm being healed! I thought. *God is healing me tonight, right here in this room, before all of these people. When their prayers have ended, I'll be well again. I'll stand up, and I'll walk around the circle, and I'll thank them for what they've done.*

The sudden jangling of the telephone broke into my thoughts. I looked up and saw a man in the back row hurry out of the room to answer the phone. It rang twice more before he got there, and the distraction served to end the prayer. All eyes opened, and I saw the people smiling at me, looking hopeful and expectant.

I smiled back, my eyes filled with tears. "Thank you," I said. "Thank you all for what you've done."

I felt whole and happy, and I knew it was time to stand up, time to demonstrate my healing. I put my left hand on the arm of the wheelchair to steady myself—but my right hand remained stiffly in my lap.

THE POWER OF PRAYER

I swallowed and looked down as I tried to move my right foot. Nothing happened. I willed my foot to lift up, but there was no movement at all. My right side was just as paralyzed as it had been when I arrived.

Disappointment washed over me, and I wondered what I should do, what I should say. Just then, the man who had gone to answer the phone rushed back into the room and shouted, "It's Allen Tilton on the phone. His limp is gone!"

A great cheer went up, and everyone stood and began talking excitedly. Shouts of "Thank you, God!" and "It's a miracle!" rang out, and people hugged each other, laughing.

I felt a hand on my shoulder and looked up to see Greg standing next to me. I knew how much he'd been hoping that I'd be healed and how disappointed he must have been. With my good hand, I reached for his hand and squeezed it.

"My paralysis is still here," I said, "but I've been healed inside. I'm happy again. I feel as if I can cope with this disability now."

I waved my hand around the room. "All these people," I said, "they all love me and care about me. Somehow, it just doesn't seem so important anymore that I can't walk."

Before Greg could answer, some of the group came over to join us.

"Come back again next week," a young man said. "Sometimes, it takes longer than one night."

"We'll keep praying for you," a white-haired woman told me.

I smiled at all of them, said "thank you" over and over, and when I looked at Greg, I saw that he was smiling, too. I had not received from those people or from God what I had come seeking, but the inner peace I felt at that moment seemed like an even better gift. A miracle had indeed happened that night. No, two miracles—one for Allen Tilton and one for me.

We stayed and talked with people for about half an hour, rejoicing with them that Allen Tilton had been helped by our prayers. I told them that I had been helped, too, and how glad I was that I had come.

When it was time to leave, several of those new friends walked with us as Greg carried me up the stairs. Eager hands opened the car door for us. My folded wheelchair was put into the backseat. Then my scarf slipped from my shoulders. Greg closed my door and came around to get in the driver's side. As he put the key in the ignition, I looked out the window at the people who were waving to us, and my heart filled with love.

Greg and I went home that night and talked for the first time in a long time. We talked about our love for each other. I think we needed to hear that from each other.

Although I didn't walk, our lives did improve. Greg and I regained the closeness that we had shared before we married. And that closeness also improved our sex life. I couldn't move much because of my paralysis, but we adjusted to accommodate that. And the love that we shared for each other grew and grew.

Although Dr. Moore didn't think I had any chance of recovery, he liked the change in my attitude. He felt my positive attitude would improve the quality of my life.

"You may not walk again, but you can certainty learn to enjoy your life," Dr. Moore said. "I'm so happy that you and Greg are weathering this crisis together. Sometimes newly married couples are unable to deal with problems of this magnitude. I'm glad you haven't allowed that to happen to you."

"Well, we're learning more about God's love and love for each other," I said.

"Yes, we know that love is the strongest force in the universe. And as long as we love each other, we'll be able to handle any problems."

We went home that night feeling content. I had never expected to feel happy or content again. Yet, I felt love and happiness in Greg's arms that night.

And we continued to go to the prayer group. Although a miracle hadn't happened for me, miracles were occurring for other people. I still believed that a miracle could happen for me one day.

After attending another prayer meeting, the people had helped Greg get me to the car. Lyle and Victor lifted me into the car. Then Greg helped me with my seatbelt, and we were preparing to leave.

Then without trying, without thinking about it, without planning anything, I raised my right hand and waved back. I didn't even realize what I was doing until I heard Greg gasp and the car keys fall to the floor. My hand stopped in midair, and I looked at it, looked at Greg, and looked back at my hand.

Hardly daring to breathe, I tried to raise my right foot. It came off the floor with ease.

I turned to Greg and said, "I'm going to get out of the car."

He opened his door and leaped out, shouting, "It's happened! It's happened! Gloria's been healed!"

Slowly I moved my hand to the door handle and pulled up. The door swung out, and someone held it open for me. By then Greg had run around to my side and was standing there with his hand extended to help me. I reached for him with my right hand, and then I swung both my legs out of the car and stood up.

The people who were still inside heard the shouting and ran out to join us.

The tears streamed down my face as Greg and I moved slowly through the crowd. My legs were shaky, and I had to lean on him for support, but I was walking. I was really walking!

The next day, I visited Dr. Moore. He was astounded when he came into his office and saw me standing there, and he was even more amazed when I told him how it had happened. He examined me right away and agreed that there was no sign of any paralysis.

"I take back what I said about miracles never happening," he said. "You've proved that they do."

When the news of my healing got out, I received dozens of letters and telephone calls from people who are suffering from various ailments. I've told all of them the same thing: Get the best medical advice you can, and follow it. Don't ever think that prayers can be used instead of medical help. That would be expecting God to do for you what He wants you to do for yourself. But if you're doing what the doctors say, if you're doing all you can to help yourself, there's no reason you can't ask God's help, too.

Every week now, Greg and I join the other members of the prayer group to offer our prayers for those in need. Sometimes, our prayers help; sometimes, they don't. No one knows why or how a cure such as mine happens. I certainly can't explain it. All I can do is be thankful for it.   THE END

MIRACLE OF FAITH . . .

WE PRAYED FOR
OUR DAUGHTER'S LIFE

My marriage started out as a typical 1970s marriage. My husband and I were much too young, and the babies came right away. The old saying about "babies having babies" really applied to us.

Both my husband and I had a hard time adjusting to being parents and making a living for ourselves.

Right after we got married, my parents moved across the country, leaving me to fend for myself completely. Having only my husband's family for comfort proved to be a lonely thing for me, as I never fit in too well with them. So there I was, just living from day to day, working and taking care of my babies.

My husband soon bored of this lifestyle. He looked up his old drinking buddies and started hanging out with them. I never knew when or if he would be coming home. There were many dinners that were put into the garbage after being on the stove for too many hours. The kids hardly knew their dad, and too much money was being wasted in bars— money we could have used to pay our many bills.

Then the fights began. They were always the same—yelling and crying and my husband storming out the front door. I couldn't believe that we were the same two people who were so loving and caring just a couple of years ago. In my heart, I knew that I still loved my husband, but I also knew we just couldn't live this way.

It was then that I started going to church again after not having attended for many years. The kids and I would go while my husband slept off his Saturday night drinking. The kids loved church and looked forward to dressing up and going each Sunday. I don't think I really listened or took the things the minister was saying too seriously until one Sunday when he spoke on the power of prayer. He told us that it didn't make any difference if we were in church or at home or wherever, just as long as we opened up our hearts.

Soon after this, my little girl got really sick with a liver infection. The bills mounted up and so did my fear. One night while at her bedside, the pressures got the best of me. I just dropped to my knees and prayed my heart out. Crying and praying aloud, I stayed there for hours until I could no longer stand the pain in my legs.

As I started to rise, I felt a hand on my shoulder, helping me up. There was my husband with tears rolling down his cheeks. Together we prayed and cried and just held each other. Afterward we talked like we never had before and renewed our love. To this day I believe that if he hadn't come in and seen me like that, our lives would never have changed.

My daughter recovered and grew into a beautiful woman. My marriage did a complete turnaround, and I found true happiness. We will be married twenty-three years this year and plan to be for many more. After all, we have the first six years to do over again. The power of prayer has made a big difference in our lives. I thank God every day for the happiness I found in Him and my family and husband.

THE END

৲ⱰⱰ

A SPECIAL LIFEGUARD

Owen was in the Army in Canada when we got married. But soon after he got his release, we moved to the United States. He got a job installing power lines for an electrical company. It meant climbing high poles and working with high-voltage wires, and it was dangerous. But Owen said the money was excellent.

One day Owen's pal had a bad fall and injured his back. Then we decided to return to Canada. Worrying that the same thing might happen to Owen was no way to live. And, by then, we had a baby daughter, Maripat, to think about.

We went to live near his folks in a little town at the mouth of a wide river in Canada. There were good fishing and marshes and woods for hunting. Owen started working with a construction company and was away all week. When he did get home, he'd go hunting or fishing with pals.

One particular Saturday, he'd gotten up at five and left to go fishing with his friend Eddie in Eddie's boat. He promised faithfully that he'd be back in time for the party we'd been invited to. But when evening came and he hadn't returned, I found myself getting angrier by the minute.

Owen's mother came over to baby-sit and calmed me down some, but my anger grew. I didn't like the way Own disappeared for hours and hours. I even thought about walking out with Maripat just to give him a good scare when he came home.

Darkness fell and it grew late. I knew there'd be no party for us now. My mother-in-law stayed, and we made pot after pot of coffee. Owen's mother made some phone calls, but no one had seen Owen and Eddie. I didn't worry until Owen's mother told me that my husband couldn't swim.

The awful fear I knew so well began gripping me, twisting my stomach into a knot. Owen's mother said all we could do was pray. I'd never been a strong believer. I'd attended church, but not regularly. I said I had no right to ask help from Someone I'd spared so little time for, but she said that didn't matter. God was always there when we needed Him most. All we had to do was pray and have faith.

We knelt together by the kitchen table. We prayed and prayed. I found words I never knew I had inside me, phrases I hadn't uttered since childhood. The long night dragged on slowly. By now we knew some terrible accident must have happened. Owen's mother fell asleep with her head on the table, but I dare not sleep; I had to keep praying.

When dawn broke, people went out in boats searching for Owen and Eddie. Before long, we heard they'd found Eddie along the coast, and the boat had drifted ashore after it had capsized. There was no sign of Owen yet.

Still, my newfound faith didn't waver. I kept praying. I knew they'd find him, and, at last, they did. He was stranded on a small sandbar. They brought him in cold and shivering, suffering from exposure. He could barely speak. But he was in my arms again, safe. God had answered my prayers.

"I was drowning," Owen told me afterwards. "I was going down for the third time. I couldn't see anything except the waves. And, you know what? It was okay. It was just like going to sleep. I didn't want to struggle anymore. Then I heard this voice say, "Hang on, Owen, don't go to sleep. Hang on, and the next thing I knew I was washed onto this sandbar."

God knew. He didn't fail me in my hour of need. And it came to me then about fear. How I'd been scared when Owen was in the Army, then on those high-voltage wires. I thought for sure he'd be safe here in his hometown, but fear is everywhere. There's no place to hide from it—except in the Lord. He is our only refuge, and our strength. I know that now. My new faith has reshaped my life.   THE END

PRAYER SAVED MY MOTHER

The letter from my mother was very disturbing. My Aunt Sabrina, with whom Mother had gone to live soon after Dad died, had fallen and broken her hip. *Things look very bad,* Mother wrote. *Sabrina is in*

*a coma, and the doctors are afraid that she might
not pull through.*

My first thought was one of panic. *What will happen to Mother if Aunt Sabrina dies?* I'd been so
happy that their living arrangement had turned out
for the best, not only for the two women now in their
eighties, but for me as well. Mother had no income
of her own beyond the small monthly rental fee she
received from the house she and Dad had owned
and a stipend from Social Security.

Aunt Sabrina had hated living alone after Uncle
Darrell died and had begun asking Mother to move
in with her almost immediately after Dad passed
away.

I was an only child, and I felt a special concern for
my mother that was in part purely selfish.

Although I loved her very much, I was burdened
by the thought that if ever she needed a home, it
would be up to me to provide it. Now it seemed the
time might have come when that possibility was
about to become a fact.

But I couldn't see any way that my husband,
Jayson, and I could take Mother to live with us now.

Jayson was out of a job, and we were struggling
to hang on to our first home on just my small salary.
Then, too, our house was in the mountains where
we were without inside plumbing in the winter when
the long pipeline to the well below the hill couldn't
be kept from freezing. It was no place to bring an
eighty-year-old woman with arthritis.

Besides, things weren't going so well between
Jayson and me right then. His unemployment made
him irritable at times and even led to his drinking
more than was good for him. I couldn't let my moth-

er see how bad things were with us, both financially and emotionally. She was always so proud of how well I managed, and I knew the present situation would hurt her.

But where could she go, except to come to us? She didn't need a nursing home, even if there'd been money for one. She couldn't live alone in her big old house, even if her tenants moved out, and there was no live-in help available in that small town four hundred miles away from where Jayson and I lived.

With Jayson's moods and his difficulties in dealing with the unworthiness he felt from being out of work, I couldn't talk it over with him and add another burden to his shoulders.

This had been a particularly bad day, with another interview ending in a turndown because Jayson was "overqualified." After a dinner eaten in heavy silence, I was almost glad to see my husband put on his coat and leave for the village bar a quarter of a mile away.

Left alone, I kept going over and over in my mind the problem my mother's situation presented.

There was an old pump organ in the house, left to us by the previous owners. On my last visit home, when Mother had moved her furniture and things to an upstairs room so she could rent the rest of the house, I brought back with me the old hymnals I'd loved as a child so I could play my favorite hymns on the organ. I had often found peace sitting there by the hour, playing the old songs and even singing the words. So it was natural that in my troubled state on this evening, I turned again to the organ and the old hymns.

Sitting on the old swivel stool, I leafed through one of the books. When I found hymns that seemed to reflect my emotions, I played them and sometimes I sang the verses: "Be not dismayed what-e-'re betide. God will take care of you," and "Just when I need Him most, Jesus is near." All the while, an unspoken prayer repeated itself over and over in my mind:

Dear God,

Please take care of Aunt Sabrina and all of us. You know how scared I am about this.

A great peace began to fill my heart. When I had played the last hymn, my mind was at rest. I went up to bed, feeling that all my troubles were safely in God's hands and that He would indeed take care of us all.

A few days later another letter came from my mother.

Aunt Sabrina rallied and is doing well, she wrote. *At ten o'clock on Friday night, she came out of the coma and the doctors say she will be all right. She'll have to be in a wheelchair, of course, but she can come home next week. Thank God, we can still be together and help one another.*

I laid the positive letter on the table, and the memory of Friday night came back to me.

I'd looked up at the clock as I'd put the hymnals away and closed the cover of the organ. It was just nine o'clock. But back in the Mountain Time zone where Aunt Sabrina was coming out of her coma was eleven o'clock.

The two sisters had a few more years together, and when the time did come when Mother needed to live with us, Jayson and I were ready to welcome her to a better house and a happier time of our lives. God understood that we needed those years to grow into the maturity that enabled us to handle that responsibility when it came.   THE END

MY SON IS TRAPPED BETWEEN 2 WORLDS

I wasn't surprised when I started to hemorrhage in my fifth month of pregnancy. After five miscarriages, I had learned that being pregnant doesn't always mean having a baby. For me, it meant watching the light go out of my husband's eyes as I started cramping and hemorrhaging.

Several doctors had warned me not to get pregnant. They told me there was something wrong with my uterus and I would never be able to carry a baby to term. They also told me that this pregnancy had to be the last. The doctors told me another miscarriage would surely kill me. So this was my last chance to give my wonderful husband a child of his own to hold.

As the ambulance rushed me to the hospital, I felt numb with despair. There would be no baby—ever. How could I live with that? I think I still had a tiny grain of hope left until the doctor said the baby had dropped and the fetal heart tone was a very low sixty. A miscarriage was imminent and there was nothing anyone could do. In that moment, I hit rock bottom. Then I remembered the one person to whom nothing is impossible—our Lord and Savior,

Jesus Christ.

I closed my eyes and began to pray. I didn't ask the Lord to save my baby because He knows our every need. I just thanked him for the baby I knew was going to be born when the time was right. When I said amen, I very clearly saw a pair of hands holding a tiny baby. Suddenly, I was calm. I knew Jesus was watching over my little one, and I had nothing to worry about.

When I went into the labor, the doctors were very concerned about the delivery of my child. They were preparing for a complicated delivery. They told me if my child survived delivery, he would have to be in an incubator awhile because of some developmental problems. My baby's lungs were not developed fully and there was some heart trouble.

I prayed when I was in labor. The doctors delivered my baby and whisked him off to be placed in an incubator. I had already known that my baby would be a boy. It had been revealed to me in a dream.

My husband and I went to see the baby every day. He was so small and tiny. Many days I believed he wouldn't survive. I brought my fears to the Lord once again.

One day as I was praying, another vision came to me. It seemed that an angel was holding my baby. The angel held my baby lovingly and said that the baby belonged with him. Tears began to roll down my cheeks. Suddenly, the angel's expression changed. Tears rolled down his cheeks, too.

I thought the vision was over, but it wasn't. Then the angel returned and said, "You have been faithful. You have prayed and kept the faith throughout.

You have been a good and faithful servant. To you, will be granted the desire of your heart. Your baby will be returned to you."

I was happy but tired from crying. I fell into a deep sleep. The doctors were concerned about me. They thought I had lost the will to live. I was sleeping because I knew that I would need my rest for my new son.

Several hours later I awakened. A nurse came into the room smiling. "I'm so glad you finally woke up. There's a little guy waiting to see you downstairs."

I smiled wearily. The nurse helped me into a wheelchair, and I went to see my son. The doctors told me that my son's recovery was miraculous. I nodded my head. I knew that Jesus had saved my little boy.

Samuel is twelve years old now. He is a constant joy to me and my husband. And he fills our home with wonder and love.

I know some people don't believe in miracles, but I know better. I know that Jesus saved my son—and that's a miracle I'll never forget.　　　　THE END

PRAYER CHANGES THINGS

My husband and I each attended Sunday school and church regularly as children, but somehow after we were married it was easy to find excuses for not attending. We lived on a farm, and morning chores for our dairy herd continued well into the time the Sunday-morning services started. The same thing was true at night—milking was never finished until the evening services were half over. As a result, we just drifted away from going to church. I supposed we could have been called nonparticipating believers. We did see to it that our six children attended Sunday school, were baptized as Protestants, and took part in church-sponsored youth activities. They made up in religious activity for what we lacked.

When our eldest daughter went away to college, she brought home any number of boyfriends. We accepted them all with no thought of her ever getting serious about any of them. So it came as a great shock when she asked us one day what we would think of her becoming a Catholic. One of her boyfriends was of that religion, and he would not convert to hers. My answer to her was that it really didn't matter to me which church she attended as long as she did attend. After all, hopefully, we are all going to the same place. My childhood faith was liberal enough to accept other religions.

However my husband became furious and blew up. No child of his was going to join another church, he said, or even worse, marry a man of a different faith. When tempers had cooled down, my daughter went back to school, but continued to visit us on Sundays. She always brought the same young man.

One day after they had visited with us for an hour or so, she spoke up quietly. "Cecil and I want to get married," she said. Her father stormed out of the door in a rage. She would be disinherited if she married Cecil, he said, but worse yet he would have nothing to do with her for the rest of her life. I prayed that his attitude would change. I didn't want to lose my daughter, but I didn't want to lose my husband, either.

When a letter came a few days later from our daughter with wedding plans and an invitation for us to take part in them, my husband insisted that his word was law and that none of our family could take any part in it. We could go into a period of mourning for her as if she were dead. I prayed to God that my husband would change his mind and see that different kinds of believers could all be good people, and that we would become a family once again. It seemed that the more I prayed, the more stubborn he became, and I could not get him to change his mind. It was tearing our family apart.

A month after the wedding, my daughter and son-in-law came home to visit us. My husband happened to be in the house when they drove up. By the time I went to open the front door, he had disappeared out the back door. They visited us off and on during the first year. Each time they came he would leave, although he didn't fuss about the rest of us seeing her. "Thank you, God, for softening his heart," I prayed. "Help him to see that he is hurting himself more than her and help him make his way back into her life."

However, my husband was very stubborn and always managed to be somewhere else when she came. I was a bundle of nerves, wanting to see her, yet not wanting her to come because it upset him so much. When she wrote letters, he wouldn't read them or listen if I tried to read them aloud. He would get up and walk away. It got so I'd just leave them on the table where he couldn't help but see them, and although he wouldn't read them in my presence, I knew he was secretly reading them. I would fold the paper in a certain way and come back later to find it folded differently. He really did love his daughter.

Years went by. Babies came—first a little girl, then a second, and the next year a third, with no grandfatherly love given to any of them. I never prayed so hard as I did before each baby came. "Make their grandfather able to experience the joy those babies could bring him," I'd ask God.

I'm not a nagger, so I said nothing to my husband to try to change his mind, but I prayed constantly. The other children were all friendly with their sister, but they had to see her secretly—no family Christmas parties and no mention of her name in conversations with their father.

Eventually our youngest son went off to college. When it was time for him to come home for the summer, my husband was busy with fieldwork, so I had to drive to the college town to bring him home. When we got home, I saw a car in the yard with an out-of-state license plate. There also were three little girls picking dandelions in the yard. My heart jumped to my mouth. My son and I went into the house. My husband was having a great visit with our daughter and her husband in the living room. I never found out what happened. But it was an answer to my prayers that I wasn't home when they arrived unannounced, because my husband had to come in from the field when he saw a car in the yard.

That was the first of many happy visits. Eventually he visited them in their own home.

Yes, God does answer payers, even for those who do not attend church. Sometimes it may take Him years, but in the end He is there. When I see my grand-daughters, I thank God that they had a chance to get to know their grandpa before he died. They had three years to make happy memories of him.   THE END

✒

WHISPER HIS NAME

In 1963, it was discovered that my second son was severely brain damaged. He was four years old at the time and up until this point he had been fine. I couldn't believe it! To this day we have no idea how it happened, but right then—even though my father was a minister, as were both my uncle and my brother—I turned my back on God.

My life had always been perfect. *How could He do this to me?* I wondered with despair. And finding no answer, I quit going to church and began drinking.

My dad had always told me, "When you find yourself in a fix and there's no time to pray, just whisper the name of Jesus." I forgot my father's advice until the summer of 1969. My eldest son—who was eleven at the time—had taken both swimming and diving lessons, and we were swimming together in a small lake my father owned. We'd swum across several times before, so on this day we decided to swim over and back as usual. But on our way back, my son gave out and panicked. He wrapped himself around me in a strangling grip and we couldn't move. I knew if he went down, I was going with him—we would both be drowned.

Then I remembered what Dad had told me so many times before. With a great effort I managed to pull my son off me while still keeping us both afloat, and then I said to him, "We must whisper the name of Jesus."

We were only in the middle of the lake and both of us were already worn out, and all we could manage to gasp was, "Jesus, Jesus," over and over again. But it worked. We both calmed down and made it safely back to the opposite shore.

That was the turning point for me—when I went back to the faith in which I'd been raised. It's been fifteen years since that near-tragic day, and when I look at my handsome son who will soon be twenty-six, I know I'll never forget my miracle or cease to praise the compassionate God that gave both of us the strength to make it across that lake.   THE END

THE MIRACLE OF THE TREE

It happened one Christmas Eve. My husband and I were going through difficult times then; he was out of work, and I had a job working evenings at a hospital nearby.

I tried to get the night off so that I could do the things that so many of us leave for the last minute, but since I had the least amount of seniority, I had to work.

One of the things I needed to do was buy a

Christmas tree. We always left that for Christmas Eve, because most places that sold real trees lowered their prices that night.

My husband promised me that he would take care of things while I was at work, and that when I got off at 11:00 P.M., everything would be done—including buying and decorating a tree. I called home around 9:00 P.M. to see how everything was going, and became a little nervous when he hadn't gone yet to get the tree. He spoke with much confidence, though, and assured me that he'd have the tree before I came home.

When I arrived home a little after 11:00 P.M., the house was neat and tidy—but no Christmas tree was in sight! My husband was sprawled out on the couch and fast asleep. When I saw the dispirited expressions on the faces of my two older children, I could hardly contain myself. I marched down the hall and knocked on my friend's apartment door. I had to talk to somebody.

She tried her best to calm me down and get me to see that it wasn't the end of the world if we didn't have a Christmas tree. She said that I should appreciate whatever we did have, considering the circumstances. She finally convinced me to go to Midnight Mass with her, hoping it would make me feel better about everything.

In church, I prayed harder than I ever did before. I asked God to forgive me for my anger, and to help me be thankful for what I had.

As my friend and I were walking home from mass, a truck loaded with Christmas trees came speeding by. Suddenly, as we stared in amazement, one of the trees fell off of it and landed in the middle of the street. The truck didn't even stop. You can imagine our excitement as we ran and picked it up. It was one of the most beautiful Scotch-pine trees I'd ever seen—one that I couldn't have afforded even if we had gotten to the store on time.

I'll never forget that night. It serves as a reminder to never lose faith, for God is always there when you need Him and always on time.   THE END

GOD IS IN MY HEART

I had never been a religious man; in fact, I never attended church, or even really pondered the existence of God. I was too busy trying to earn a better living, get ahead, and acquire nice things. I felt I was stronger than most, and that I had to rely on myself; no one, including God, would help me. I was wrong. A few years back, a drunk driver changed my outlook on life forever.

My wife and our fourteen-year-old daughter had been out grocery shopping. On the way home, less than three blocks from our home, a drunk driver ran a stop sign and smashed into the passenger side of my wife's car. The police estimated that he was traveling at sixty miles per hour. The drunk driver was declared dead at the scene from massive head injuries. My wife escaped with minor injuries, but our daughter had received the brunt of the impact.

The passenger door window had exploded in her face. Sixty-six stitches were required to close the cuts on her face, neck, and scalp. Her right arm and collarbone were broken. As the bucket seat collapsed toward the car's dashboard, my little girl's breastbone was cracked. Four ribs broke, causing a punctured lung. Her head struck the side of the steering column, fracturing her skull.

She was in surgery for more than six hours. My wife prayed throughout the evening. I just kept telling myself that she was young and strong and a fighter.

When my daughter finally came out of surgery, the doctor informed us that her head injury was even more serious than they had first thought.

The following day, she lapsed into a coma, and her brain began to swell. Our doctor told us there was nothing left to do but pray. For the first time since I was a child, I prayed. I wept as I prayed to God to spare my daughter's life.

Three days later, she opened her eyes and told the nurse she was thirsty. The swelling had receded! Our doctor told us it was a miracle.

My daughter had a long road to recovery: several more operations and months of painful therapy. That was seven years ago. This year, she'll be twenty-one, and will graduate from college. I hold God in my heart every day now, and that's where He belongs! You see, He has not only given my daughter a second chance, but myself as well.   THE END

෪෨෪

THE GIFT OF PRAYER

My son and his best friend were a mismatched

pair. Everyone said so. They came from different worlds and had nothing in common. But somehow our studious, well-mannered son, a shy and sensitive boy who never once got into the scrapes other teenagers did, became fast and inseparable buddies with a notorious boy. Needless to say, my husband and I were as upset as we were bewildered.

We'd known this boy by reputation since he was a youngster. We'd heard of his childish pranks and, more recently, of his brushes with the law. Usually, these were minor offenses like trespassing and petty theft, but we heard whispers of worse things: fights and public drunkenness, disorderly conduct, unruly gatherings of his motorcycle gang.

My husband and I would wince every time a carload of rowdy boys screeched to a halt outside the house. We tried to explain to our son about bad company; warn him that even good, sensible people can be lured into wrongdoing if they associate with a bad crowd.

Our son would just put us off with smiles and vague reassurances. "He needs a friend like me," he'd say. He was never disrespectful or defiant, yet no matter what we said to him, he'd go to join that howling mob. It was usually after midnight that our son would finally come striding in, calm as always, flashing a grin to show us that all was well.

Then it came. That which all parents of independent teenagers dread the most, happened: the late-night phone call, the flat voice of the police officer, the news so hard to understand and accept through the fog of sleepiness and disbelief. "Your son's been in a serious accident . . . tried to run a railroad crossing, was smashed by a locomotive . . . car totaled . . . he and a companion are in critical condition, still alive. . . ."

My husband and I were at the hospital in twenty minutes. There we learned that, as we had expected, his rowdy friend had been driving. The doctor told us that both boys were out of immediate danger; they had suffered similar injuries, however, and both were unable to move their legs. Only time would tell if the paralysis was permanent.

At our son's bedside, looking down at my son so small and vulnerable, I could no longer control my tears. He fixed his eyes on me, eyes that fought through fear and anesthesia and pain, and flashed a faint but plucky smile, a dimmed version of the soothing everything's-okay grin he'd given us the previous evening as he went out the door.

I put my hand on his arm. "I'm praying for you, honey."

He shook his head slightly. "No, Mom," he whispered with difficulty. "Pray for my friend. Pray for him."

I prayed all right. I prayed harder and more fervently and more humbly than I ever had in my life, but it was all for my own son. I couldn't pray for his friend. I couldn't push my way through the anger I felt at the irresponsible troublemaker whose recklessness had possibly ruined my son's life forever. I didn't have a single plea of mercy in my heart for this boy who had hurt my son, not a shred of pity, only a cold and unyielding bitterness.

So when it was this boy who recovered full use of his legs, to the astonishment of the doctors, while my son's paralysis remained and the prognosis worsened daily, I could feel no pleasure, no sense of victory. "How could God be so unfair?" I asked. "How could He reach down to heal the wicked and the guilty, while leaving the good and the innocent to suffer?" It became an obsession with me; the injustice of it made me nearly insane. The next time I saw my son, I exploded, weeping and pacing the room, pouring out my resentment and envy in a torrent of harsh and unkind words.

My son listened to my tirade quietly, and he reached out to grasp my hand. His face was pale and thin, but without a trace of strain or turmoil.

"It's as it should be, Mom," he said.

"But after all the praying I've done for you," I whimpered.

"I've been praying for my best friend." He smiled, his eyes lighting up with a strangely peaceful joy. "Don't you see, Mom? If God had one miracle to spare here, He spent it well by using it on the one of us who needed it most. My friend needed to be reminded of God's existence, power, and mercy. I didn't. I already knew. You and Dad have seen to that."

I suddenly felt as though I were burning with shame. Compared to our son's dignity and resignation in the recovery of his friend, my complaints seemed incredibly petty.

It took some time, but I was eventually able to share in my son's delight. Slowly, at first, reluctantly, we came to know his best friend, seeing in him what our son must have seen all along: the qualities of intelligence and sensitivity he had so carefully hidden under an exterior of sullen toughness. We helped him through his rehabilitation, and he now is a changed young man with a future.

Some would think our son wasn't so lucky, but thanks to his example, I know better now. Confined to a wheelchair, almost certainly for the rest of his life, he hasn't slowed down a bit. And in every important way he hasn't changed at all. Active in church and soon to enter college, he plans to earn a degree in psychology and devote his life to working with the handicapped. He'll be good at it, too, because he possesses a natural and intuitive wisdom rare and unteachable. After all, it was he who, all by himself, sensed that God is most likely to hear our prayers when we make them for the sake of others and not for ourselves.   THE END

A CAKE WITH SPARKLERS

When I was turning eleven, I wanted a pretty dress for my birthday more than anything else in the world, and I wanted to take a cake to school to share with my class like the other kids did—a cake with sparklers on it. Sparklers on cakes is an old Southern custom, and we were from Louisiana.

But my mother said, "Sweetheart, you know your daddy hasn't sent us a check in almost a year. We just can't afford a new dress—not even sparklers." Mama turned her back to hide her tears, but I could hear the tremor in her voice.

At Sunday school that week, Miss Raston, our teacher, showed us a picture of Jesus healing a blind man. "Jesus told us," she said, "that we must put our faith in God, and that we must believe.

Jesus said, 'Ask, and ye shall receive.'"

Miss Raston went on with her lesson, but to myself, I thought: *God has deserted us. Mama and I believed in God and prayed to Him that Papa would find work and send for us, but it hasn't happened. God has forgotten us, and Papa has forgotten us, too.*

The Fourth of July came and went, a quiet one for us. Mama could not get a job, but pawned her watch when our money was almost gone. My birthday was only a week away and I felt miserable, but I tried to hide it from Mama.

God, I prayed on my knees, *please, oh, please, let me have a party dress for school. And, God, sparklers for my cake, too. Please, God. Please hear me.*

But I never believed my prayer would be answered. My faith was gone. First we were deserted by Papa, and now it seemed that God had deserted us, too. I began to sob, and ran down to the creek behind our house. I couldn't let Mama see my tears.

There by the creek, I began to cry again, but silently. Tears were streaming down my face as I began to make a castle in the sand—a big castle, where we could all be together and Papa would be king, and Mama the queen. I would be a royal princess and have nice things, and party dresses . . . and sparklers on my birthday cake.

My daydream ended as my fingers, deep in the sand, touched something—a stick, I thought. I dug deeper. Sticks, eleven of them, were there—the bottom ends of sparklers in their battered box!

My heart swelled to bursting and I jumped up and

rushed home to tell Mama the wonderful news. She met me on the porch, her eyes shining, and spoke first.

"Baby, you won't believe it! We've heard from Papa! He's found work and has sent us a check! Oh, darling, you'll have your beautiful dress!"

God had heard my prayers, and He'd answered them. I knew then that He hadn't deserted us—and never would—as long as we believed!   THE END

⌖⌖⌖

MYSTERY ELVES

In late October of 1982, my cousin and I decided we had to move to within commuting distance of a large city. We'd spent the previous six months looking for jobs, which would bring in enough money for our families to live in relative comfort. She had two sons and two daughters. I had two daughters and a son. We agreed that we would try our hardest not to go on public assistance.

Still, the move was a scary proposition. We buoyed each other's courage by pointing out our great health, our youth, and our skill at commercial cleaning. We methodically wrote down our assets. We had between us one old station wagon, which ran well, several changes of good clothes, and almost a thousand dollars, besides whatever we could get from selling our furniture. Surely, it would be enough.

We made careful plans. First we'd talk to our kids about our decision, and then we'd explain to family and friends. In late November, I would drive the hundred and fifty miles to the city of our choice to rent a house, get the utilities turned on, and stock up on groceries. Then I'd return for the others.

All went well at first. We sold everything except the old black and-white TV, but we decided I'd take it and everything else we could fit into the car on the first trip. That would give us more space during the actual move. My cousin bought a car-top carrier, and we happily contemplated the extra room it would give us.

My trip to the city was fruitful beyond my wildest hopes. By six o'clock that evening, I had rented an old, somewhat drafty, two-storey house with six bedrooms, a stove, and a refrigerator. I then bought groceries and called my cousin from a pay phone to tell her and the kids the good news. I decided to sleep over at the new house and leave early the next day to bring them home.

We moved in on a Sunday. My cousin and I enrolled the kids in school on Monday and purchased the few supplies they needed. After the school bus picked them up the next day, we congratulated each other on our progress and decided we would fix up the place, scout out secondhand stores for furniture, then go out and find jobs.

That proved to be more difficult than we had anticipated. We applied for many jobs, but there were more people to compete with here. Our money quickly dwindled, and the second Wednesday in December, we realized we had no choice but to apply for public assistance. We had twelve dollars between us, so we had to apply for food stamps, too. The social workers saw no problem in our getting the help we needed, but they told us it could take up to thirty days before we got a dime.

Back home, we called all the places where we had put in job applications, then talked to our landlord, who assured us he'd let us pay the rent when we could. My cousin and I then discussed our seemingly insurmountable problem. Christmas was a few days away, and we had no money for gifts or a holiday dinner. We cried and agreed we'd have to tell the kids that night.

After dinner, we explained to them how bad our financial situation was, and we told them how it would get much better in a month or so. Then I dropped the bomb. Through tears, I told them there was no way we could celebrate Christmas the way other families did because we had no money.

To my surprise, my eight-year-old son came over and hugged me. He told me not to worry because Christmas was Jesus' birthday, and He wouldn't need any help to make Christmas come. He said Jesus hadn't had much money, either, so everything would be all right.

I prayed hard that night for God to help us reward the child's faith and somehow make Christmas special for all of them, even without money.

The next week, the telephone brought some eagerly awaited news. My cousin and I were both hired by the same janitorial company. She'd be working days, and I'd be working the graveyard shift. We'd need only one car, and one of us would always be with the kids. We gave thanks for what we felt was our salvation. There would be no paycheck before Christmas, but we were productive wage earners again. The kids were overjoyed.

Late in the evening on December 22nd, the doorbell rang. As I walked to the front door, I heard a car start up and drive away. I opened the door. There was no one on the porch, but when I looked down, I cried out in surprise and joy. There by the door were three boxes of food, including a turkey and all the trimmings. Written in black marker on all the boxes were the words MERRY CHRISTMAS. The message was an understatement.

The next evening, the doorbell chimed again. My cousin and I both went to the door. Standing on the front porch were two young women dressed in red-and-green elf suits, complete with pointy shoes. One of them put an envelope into my hand and said, "Merry Christmas." They hurriedly left as I mumbled my thanks.

I stepped back inside and opened the envelope. It contained five crisp new twenty-dollar bills. My son, who was standing in the doorway, grinned and said, "Didn't I tell you, Mom?"

Through the years since that Christmas, not one of us has ever lost faith in God. That year proved to us that there is nothing He can't do. THE END

MY RECOVERY FROM LOSS

Wiping my hands on my paint-smeared jeans and pushing a straggling piece of hair from my face, I answered the doorbell. My eyes beheld five neighborhood children under one large umbrella. Mischievous grins lit their faces, and I could tell that they were hiding something behind their backs. "Happy May Day," they said in chorus and handed me a "basket" full of construction-paper flowers they had made. Of course—it was May Day. I had forgotten. But the children hadn't.

Going back to my work with a lighter heart, I thought about my special relationship with children and how it had come about. I had two young sons and was expecting another baby when the church that I attended decided to take part in a program called "Fish." I thought at first that I wouldn't volunteer, but I couldn't refuse.

I decided that even with a new baby I could visit shut-ins. They probably would enjoy seeing a baby. I signed the sheet to visit shut-ins and promptly forgot about it as things got even busier in my life. I had two false alarms before the real thing. Yes, it was a daughter! But not a healthy, normal daughter. It was off to the children's hospital for surgery. She died two weeks later.

My heart grieved for my baby. I didn't eat, and I didn't sleep. I didn't want to be with my friends anymore. And, especially, I didn't want to go to church anymore.

Finally, in my darkest days, I packed away the baby clothes, thinking it might help if I didn't have to look at them. I was carrying the box down to the cellar when I dropped it. Something came over me, and suddenly I was sobbing and stomping all over those clothes. When I finally became aware of what I was doing, I sat down on the floor, still crying, and asked God to help me.

No flashes came from heaven to let me know that He had heard, but as I went back upstairs, the phone rang. The call was a reminder of my promise to visit shut-ins. I didn't want to, but something told me I'd better. After all, I had volunteered. And maybe, just maybe, it would take my mind off that terribly empty, aching spot in my heart.

The two ladies I was assigned to had both lost children. But while one still grieved fifty years later, and had become a bitter, self-centered recluse, the other had devoted her life to making children happy.

It was as if God were saying, "There they are. Which one do you want to be like?" Which one, indeed! I realized which way I had been heading and quickly reversed my course. And so now I stand, with my May Day flowers in my hand, realizing how lucky I was that I'd asked God for help on that dark day so long ago.   THE END

A WIDOW'S RETURN TO LIFE

Last year my neighbor lost her husband from a sudden heart attack. They had just celebrated their twenty-fifth anniversary and had been planning a long-awaited cruise. The neighborhood was stunned. I think at first no one wanted to believe what had happened. But we learned to accept it— everyone but my neighbor, that is. She was emotionally destroyed by his death.

She and I had always been very close. We had often shopped or had lunch together, and our children, now either married or away at school, had been playmates. After her husband's death, however, she stayed secluded in her room and refused to see family and friends. She had always depended heavily on her husband for all major decisions and had never even learned to drive a car or handle their finances. And now, when she needed us most, she just turned us away.

At first, I respected her wishes and left her alone. But then the situation began to eat away at me. Why was I abandoning such a good friend in her hour of need? It certainly wasn't the Christian thing to do! So I turned to God in prayer; I knew He would show me the way.

Two months passed without any change. One evening after supper I went for a drive to think about the problem. As I drove through a small town, I noticed a little white chapel. On an impulse, I stopped and went in. The late evening sun streamed through the stained-glass windows, and candles glowed softly around the altar. I knelt there and prayed earnestly for my neighbor's recovery and for a way to help her find a new way of life.

When I left I felt stronger, confident that God would help her realize that her life wasn't over, that her husband wouldn't have wanted her to suffer so. After I got home, I told my husband about the church and my prayers. He agreed that it had been the right thing to do. He added that my neighbor was certain to snap out of her depression now that I'd asked God for help.

My phone rang the next morning, and my neighbor asked if I had time for a cup of coffee! I was shocked at her grief-ravaged face and loss of weight. She confided that she had awakened during the night suddenly feeling much stronger and no longer so completely alone. She said that she had just made an appointment for lessons at a driving school, and she asked if I could help her practice. I was so happy! God had answered my prayers! I knew now that she would make it.

Three months later, her new driver's license sat propped against the sugar bowl as we had our coffee. Since then, she's been taking bookkeeping and money-management courses and has put her gardening skills to use by working in a florist's shop.

Best of all, she has formed a support group for other widows. She's made new friends and discovered that she has unexpected strengths and talents.

I am convinced that her sudden recovery was more than mere coincidence—it was indeed a miracle of faith. Remember, God hears all our prayers—and answers them! THE END

GOD HEARS ALL PRAYERS

I stood in front of the glass in the Isolation ward of the pediatric unit, my heart filled with dread. Behind the wall of glass that separated me from my baby, the doctor was busy giving her an extensive examination. It seemed like an eternity before he finished and came through the door toward my husband and me. What he told us made my legs turn to jelly, and I began to shake uncontrollably. My beloved baby girl had salmonella poisoning and her fever was 105 degrees. If it didn't break soon, permanent brain damage would occur.

My husband stood beside me as the doctor delivered the news, his arm around my waist. If he had not been there, I am sure I would have sunk to the floor.

After the doctor had left, my husband and I stood and watched our eight-month-old daughter through the glass. Her beautiful hair had been shaven off, so the intravenous needle could be inserted into her temple. Another needle had been inserted into her tiny ankle. Ice bags and sand packs surrounded her to keep her from moving.

I began to weep hysterically, knowing in my heart that our only child was dying . . . and we weren't even allowed to be near her. A nurse approached and informed us that we should go home. There was nothing we could do. She told us that only time would tell if our daughter would survive. "All I can tell you to do is pray," she said.

We were not churchgoers, though my grandparents were very religious. The idea of really praying had never occurred to us. The nurse's words seemed to be just a figure of speech.

Later that night, the doorbell rang and when I opened it, there stood my grandparents' minister. I invited him in, and he told us that my grandmother had asked him to come by and pray with us. My husband and I looked at each other, remembering the nurse's words. We allowed the minister to pray with us, and then he left, saying he would check with us the next day. "I'll be praying for her," he said as he left.

For the next two days, there was still no change in our baby's condition. Our doctor met us the second evening around seven o'clock, at the hospital. "If there's no change by midnight, I'm afraid there is no hope. Even now, I feel she cannot survive without permanent brain damage. All I can tell you to do is pray."

Once again, my husband and I looked at each other. We'd been hearing a lot about prayer lately. I went directly to the phone in the hospital hallway and called my grandmother. "Can you and Grandpa come to the hospital right away?" I asked. "Call your pastor and ask him if he can come, too, please," I continued.

In twenty minutes, my grandparents and the minister were at the hospital. The nurses directed us to a small waiting room so we could have some privacy. Soon, other members of my grandparents' church began to come in, until the small room was crowded with people. We all joined hands and the minister's deep voice led us in prayer.

We were still praying when the doctor entered the room. His face was creased with worry, and my heart once again filled with dread. "The baby's fever has broken," he told us. "She seems to be out of danger, but we don't know yet if any permanent damage has been done."

After he left, we once again began to pray. We thanked God for His mercy and for healing our baby. We asked Him to make it a total healing so she wouldn't suffer any permanent damage.

Our baby daughter is twenty years old now, with no signs of the illness of so many years ago. She is as beautiful now as she was then, and when I look at her, I still thank God for healing her. What beautiful memories I would have missed, had she died that night that we prayed. I thank God for answering our prayers, and I thank Him for giving me the wisdom not to underestimate the power of prayer. THE END

୨୧

A LITTLE BIT OF FAITH . . .

After three years of trying, my husband and I had finally conceived. Throughout the first seven trouble-free months of pregnancy, I felt great. Every day was filled with dreams and plans for our future with the unborn miracle I was carrying.

As time wore on, however, my body began to swell and in my eighth month, I had to be admitted into the hospital. I was informed that my labor must be induced immediately or I might risk losing my baby. With my husband by my side, twenty-two hours later, I gave birth to a six-pound baby boy. His head was terribly distorted, and he was a deathly blue. Within moments, my son was rushed into intensive care. By evening, his temperature had soared, and his life was hanging perilously.

My son had an infection, which is fatal in fifty percent of the cases. He was paralyzed on one side, and as with most cases, within twenty-four hours he had developed spinal meningitis. His head was still distorted by the forceps, and it was discovered that his brain had actually been bruised by his violent entrance into the world.

There was a tube inserted into my baby's nose and a tiny needle embedded into the skin of his forehead. He had patches connected to his chest to monitor his heartbeat, and to my horror, in the places where the patches had been moved, his thin skin had been torn away with the tape, leaving painful, open sores.

For eight months, he had stayed curled up, safe, warm, and free from pain and suffering. Now he lay in constant pain from the needles and from the sores. And the doctor had said that he was surely experiencing severe headaches due to the brain bruise.

In my room, I begged God to end my baby's suffering. I must have stayed on my knees for over an hour. But when I rose, I rose with new strength and a serenity that I had never known before.

I rushed into my son's hospital room and I assured him that everything would work out. I knew that he didn't understand the words, but I liked to believe that he understood the peace that I felt.

My son was healed. But then, our faith took us even further. My son's doctor said that my boy would never be right. He said that we should prepare ourselves for years of special classes and special teachers and not to expect too much of him.

Obviously, he didn't know the Great Physician. My son is now in the third grade. He has continuously remained on the Honor Roll. He reads everything he can get his hands on. Math comes quite easily to him and he spells better than I do!

We have learned that there is nothing you can't accomplish with a little bit of faith and a whole lot of love.

THE END

᠅

THE GRACE OF GOD

When I was a young mother and wife, I was so

happy, I thought I had it all. We had God and each other and we thought that we didn't need anything else. I was about to give birth to our third child when one night, a week before our son was to be born, I was lying in bed, unable to sleep. It was near midnight, and everything was quiet. I had a vision of myself in a hospital room. The doctor was telling me that I had just given birth to a son, and that my son was about to die. For the rest of the night, I couldn't sleep.

The next morning I went to the doctor, who told me everything was fine. But what I didn't know at the time was that my water had broken that night I had the vision. One week later I gave birth to a little boy. Before the doctor spoke, I knew what he was about to tell me because I had heard him that night. Then he said that my baby was dying. My son would die before the night was over because when my water broke, he was without protection.

When my baby died, part of me died with him. I no longer knew the God that I loved and trusted. I wanted no part of my husband. I turned away family and friends, and I went into my own little world.

One year later, I found out that I was pregnant again. I still couldn't handle the loss of my son, and I considered suicide. I thought it would be easier than going through another pregnancy. I had everything planned. My husband was at work and I was preparing to go through with my plan. Then I heard a voice saying, "My grace is sufficient for you, for my strength is made perfect in weakness."

Those words saved the lives of me and my unborn child. I found the faith in God that I had lost with the death of our son.

I had my baby—a perfect baby girl. She is now eighteen years old, and I thank God for her and the rest of my children. I'll never forget our son, but by the grace of God, I can accept His will.   THE END

A CHILD'S FAITH

It had snowed, and it was so cold in the bedroom of our log cabin, my fingers were numb as I hurriedly dressed. I could hear my husband trying to get that stubborn old stove to give more heat. No matter how hard we tried, it was just too old to adequately heat our small cabin.

I looked over at our five-year-old daughter, sleeping. We had brought her home from the hospital the previous day. She had survived another bout of pneumonia, one of many she'd suffered that miserable winter. She opened her eyes and smiled. I quickly dressed her in warm clothes, and we hurried to huddle around the feeble heat.

We ate breakfast sitting around the stove. We had given up trying to eat our meals at the table. Money was so short this year, since our daughter's hospital stays had taken every cent we could make above necessities. My husband repeated the words he had said to me so often. "I sure wish we could buy that heater our neighbor has for sale. It would really keep this house warm."

Our daughter asked, "Daddy, do you want a new stove?"

My husband looked down at her and smiled.

"Well, it would sure be a godsend, but I'm afraid we can't afford it right now." She told him not to worry, that she'd just ask God for the stove.

She knelt beside her bed. Her hands were folded beneath her chin, and her lips were moving. In a short while, she came out, kissed each of us, and said, "We will have a new stove soon."

That day, a lady we had met at church was at our door. She brought blankets, and warm clothes for our daughter. I opened the stove to put more wood on the struggling fire. Our guest said, "That stove doesn't throw much heat, does it?" I told her that we would like to get another as soon as we could. She asked me if the one our neighbor was selling was the right kind. When I told her that was the stove we were planning on getting, she wanted to go take a look.

Our neighbor showed us the stove. To me it was beautiful. The woman from church asked me if I liked it and I told her it was the nicest stove I had ever seen. She immediately paid for it, over my protests. She said that God told us to help each other.

After work, my husband brought the stove home. In no time the new stove was burning brightly. At dinner, we were able to sit at the table and enjoy our meal. We thanked the Lord and our friend from church for the stove.

Our daughter said, "I'll be right back. I've got to thank the Lord myself." As she knelt beside her bed again, the thought raced through my mind, "And a child shall lead them." It only proves once more that God does indeed work in mysterious ways.

THE END

GOD'S MIRACLE

Three years ago, late one Sunday night, we received a call that my grandparents' house had exploded. They lived thirty miles from us and it was a nightmare driving over, not knowing if they had made it out alive.

When we were three miles from their place, we could see the flames and expected the worst. At the house, the firemen sent us to the neighbor's house. My grandmother and uncle, who lived with them, were there and they were both okay. My grandpa, who was eighty, didn't make it out of the house. The fire chief said it was a miracle that my grandma and uncle had made it out because the explosion was so bad.

The firemen tried to save everything they could. They were able to save only a box. My dad took the box and put it in his pickup until later when things settled down. My grandma and uncle were upset over grandpa dying, and they were homeless and broke. All of their money had been in the house and they had no insurance.

Several days later, my dad remembered the box the fireman had given him. Most of the items in the box were burned, but at the bottom of the box was a picture of Jesus, untouched. Underneath the picture, there was six hundred dollars. Miraculously, the money hadn't burned.

That night as I held the picture of Jesus, I understood why my grandpa died. He was sick and couldn't take care of himself anymore. Grandpa was independent and was afraid of having to go to a nursing home. Even though the fire was terrible, I know God took Grandpa quickly and spared him from having to face his worst fear of losing his independence. It still hurts to lose him, but even through a tragedy, God worked a miracle.   THE END

THOSE IN NEED

Around Christmas of 1976, my husband was hospitalized and was subsequently out of work for several weeks. Living on my salary was rough, and we were almost touching bottom.

My father is a Baptist minister, and every year at Christmastime we always got a list of needy children at the Miracle Hill Children's Home in Greenville. Many children are housed there, and it is a faith-based operation. Some children are orphaned and others are abused or neglected. The list gave the children's ages and sizes so we would know what to buy them for Christmas. We had always tried to help, but this particular year I didn't see any way we could afford to.

Several weeks passed, and it was one week before we were to go and carry the gifts to the home. I still felt strongly that we should sponsor a child, but I kept putting it off. Then on Wednesday night, during a prayer meeting, my father announced that there were still some children left without sponsors. The gifts were to be taken to the home the following Sunday afternoon. I felt the Lord speak to me, and I pledged that night to sponsor two of the children, not knowing how my husband and I would pay for it.

That Friday, my husband and I went shopping and bought outfits and a toy for each of the children we had agreed to sponsor; the total bill was seventy dollars. I tried not to worry about the money, but I could not seem to help it. But the joy on the children's faces on Sunday made the sacrifice worth it.

The following Monday, my husband went back to his job. Then the following Friday, when he picked me up at work, he was wearing a huge smile. I asked what he was so happy about, and he pulled some money out of his shirt pocket. You know how much it was? Seventy dollars! His co-workers had taken up a collection to help him out, and that's how much they ended up with. Our sacrifice was rewarded, and those children were made happy. God does reward us for having faith and trusting in Him.   THE END

THE POWER OF PRAYER

One night my son was coming home from a party and he fell asleep at the wheel, flipping his truck over. My second son came and got me and we rushed to the hospital, only to hear the terrible news. Upon examining him, the doctors told me that my son shouldn't have survived. He'd broken his neck in five places and twisted his lower spine. The hospital wasn't equipped to handle his injury, so he was moved to a larger city hospital. The doctors there gave me the same diagnosis and didn't know if they could help him.

The doctors said they would try surgery, but nothing was guaranteed. They said my son could die, or he could come out of the operation paralyzed from the neck down.

By this time, I was so upset. I hadn't left the hospital once, for fear of my son dying while I was gone. I was pacing the floors, wringing my hands, and trying my hardest not to cry and fall apart. All of a sudden, a powerful feeling told me to see my pastor. I tried to push it aside because I didn't want to leave the hospital. But I knew it had to be done.

I went to see the pastor and we prayed together. He promised me he would say a prayer for my son in church on Sunday. I left there with a weight lifted from my soul, and somehow I knew my son would be okay.

My son went in for surgery and the doctor said he'd be in the hospital for a year of therapy. Amazingly, he was only in there for three months. He left the hospital on his own strength and without the help of any aide.

I'm very grateful for the knowledge and hard work of the doctors, but I know that it was the power of prayer that truly healed my son. I believe in God's miracles, and no one can tell me any different. THE END

RESCUE ME

My husband has always worked in noisy shops,

and over the years he suffered a severe hearing loss. It had gotten so bad that he couldn't even hear me call from the second storey of our house.

Two years ago my husband and I were working in the backyard. I was up on a ladder cutting away a vine that had become entangled in our cherry tree. My husband was running the lawn mower in the far corner of the yard.

Suddenly, the ladder gave a big lurch to the right, causing me to lose my grip. I caught on to a piece of the house, but every time I shifted my weight, the ladder moved a little more.

Slowly, fear started creeping into my mind as I thought of all the horrible things that could happen if I fell. I knew that calling out to my husband would be futile, because he'd never hear me over the noise of the mower. Tears formed in my eyes as I realized that my greatest fear had become a reality. As my throat closed up from fear I called out to the Lord for help.

All at once the mower stopped and I heard my husband calling to see if I needed help. I was so shocked he asked, because I was hidden from his view behind the cherry tree. There was no way he could've known I was in trouble.

Later, after my husband rescued me and we were discussing the incident, my husband told me that he thought he'd heard my voice calling him. It was then we knew that a miracle had taken place. We gave our thanks to the Lord for being the voice in my husband's ear.

Since we have always trusted in the Lord to help us in our times of need, He couldn't have shown us more clearly that He is there to hear and answer our prayers.

THE END

PREMATURE MIRACLE

I was only six months pregnant—I couldn't be having my baby. This can't be happening, I thought to myself as another pain hit me. Suddenly, I felt my water break and realized that I was in labor.

The rest of the night was a blur. The trip to the hospital and the emergency surgery seemed like a nightmare. My baby was three months premature and weighed only two pounds. He had two holes in his heart and his lungs were filled with fluid.

A week after his birth the doctors came and told me that my baby had no chance of living. His veins had collapsed and they could no longer feed him. They wanted to remove the life support systems.

That night my husband and I went to the nursery to say good-bye to our son. Just one look at him and we knew he was dying. We got down on our knees and turned our son over to God.

We asked him to heal our baby if it was His will. If not, we asked that he go painlessly. But whatever God's will was, we were prepared to accept it. Miraculously, God heard our prayers!

The next morning the entire hospital was talking about the "miracle baby." My son was actually crying! He continued to improve and, many weeks later, we brought him home.

Today, as I look at my nineteen-year-old son who stands tall and strong, I thank God for this miracle. I truly believe that God answers prayers. All you need is faith! THE END

DON'T TAKE HIM FOR GRANTED

I was raised in a Christian home, but I always took God for granted. My family went to church every week, but God was never a part of my everyday life. I only prayed when I wanted something, but God never seemed to answer those prayers.

Even when I married and left home, I never thought about God. When my first child was born, I thanked God that she was healthy and then forgot about Him again.

We moved away from our city to a smaller town. My husband got a job at a resort, washing dishes, but we managed to make ends meet.

One day, my husband came home from work early. When I asked him why he was home, he said the resort was closing down for the winter and he'd been laid off. Times became hard for us. There were no jobs available, and we had to live on welfare and food stamps—they never stretched far enough.

We moved into subsidized housing and tried to prepare for winter. Our daughter was a year old and we were worried that we wouldn't be able to provide for her. My husband started spending his time in the bar.

One night, after I tucked my daughter into bed, I began to pray. I looked up from my prayers and saw my old Bible. I hadn't prayed in two years, but I decided to give it another try. I felt very peaceful that night and believed that God would answer my prayers.

Two days later, I saw some women looking around our apartment building. They knocked on a door down the hall, but no one was home. I told them they wouldn't be home until later. They told me they were from a church and they were here to give food out. They asked if I knew anyone who needed help. I told them that I needed help, and they gave me eight bags full of food, some clothing, and a Bible.

From that time on, they came every month and brought us basic necessities. I began going to church again, and felt peaceful, even in the face of an alcoholic husband. After four months, my husband began to realize what he was doing and went through rehabilitation. He even went to church with us.

It's been three years since then, and we're expecting our third child. I'll never forget the kindness of the church and how that one act changed my life. My husband has been sober for two years and he has a steady job that pays well. I realize now that God really does answer prayers, and I'll never again take Him for granted.   THE END

MY BROTHER, MIRACLE MAN

It was a beautiful spring day in May 1980. I was just sitting outside, enjoying the weather, when a car came flying into the driveway. It was my uncle, and I knew then that something was wrong.

He and my brother worked together at a sawmill in a nearby town, and my brother wasn't with him. I followed my uncle as he ran into the house where my mom and dad were.

He was very upset as he told my parents that my brother had been badly hurt. On the way to the hospital, he explained what had happened.

My brother and one of the other boys were tying down a load of timber with chains and a bucker. It seems that they had put a pipe on the bucker handle to get better leverage, and the pipe slipped off and the bucker handle came up and hit my brother in the face.

By the time we got to the hospital, the doctors had already begun surgery on him. When the surgeon came out to talk to the family, he said the bucker handle had crushed the right side of my brother's head, shattering his skull. The doctor had picked pieces of bone out of his brain. If he survived, the doctor said, he would not know anything or anyone, and he would be a vegetable; he would never be able to walk or talk again.

I couldn't imagine my brother that way. He was always strong, physically and mentally.

After two weeks, he was still unconscious. I was so afraid that he would never wake up. I'd go in and sit by him, talking and praying day after day.

One night I overheard my dad asking our preacher to have a special prayer for his son. When the preacher went into my brother's room, I closed my eyes and said a special prayer for my precious brother. I didn't care if he didn't remember me; I just wanted him to open his eyes, so I'd know if he was responsive. Sixteen hours after I said those prayers, my brother woke up.

It's been nearly twelve years since my brother was hurt. He is a walking, talking, loving miracle. He's blind in his right eye and can't hear with his right ear, and forgets small things at times, but there is absolutely nothing else wrong with him.

I know that God is the reason my brother is still here today, and I thank Him every day.　　THE END

THE TRUE MEANING OF CHRISTMAS

During one sad summer, I went through a shattering divorce. At twenty-three, with no skills or education and three small children, I felt my world falling apart. My aunt wanted to help us out, so she invited the kids and me to move in with her. Then in October, my cousin and her family were having financial problems and needed to move in.

I had enough money saved to find my family a place to live, but very little left over. The children and I were soon down to any meal I could make inexpensively.

I realized I had to apply for welfare; at least then I could get food for my children. I was given a hard time at first because I was from out-of-state, but then they sent me to a church for a ten-dollar food voucher and said I'd have to wait a few weeks for my food stamps.

As the holidays approached, each night the children and I would take an evening walk to look at all the houses decorated for Christmas. One night during our walk, we went into a church. I sat and poured out my problems and tears to the Lord, and asked him to help me take care of my children. Then I spoke to the pastor. He listened with empathy as I cried, and said he'd mention my situation the next day during services.

A few days later I was returning home from another day of job hunting, and I suddenly stopped and stared at my front porch. It was covered with grocery bags filled with turkeys, vegetables, baked goods, fresh fruits, and even canned jam and fruit— from people whom I had never even met!

Then two nights before Christmas Eve, I noticed some more bags and a Christmas tree on my porch. The bags contained wrapped gifts, toys, and candy.

Fifteen years have passed since then. I've received my high school equivalency diploma, and in six months I'll be graduating with a degree in criminal justice and sociology.

Though things have changed, I'll never forget where I once was, or the people who cared and gave with their hearts and prayers. That year I learned the true meaning of Christmas. It's not about making out our Christmas shopping lists or receiving the fancy new coat or the new dress and shoes.

Christmastime is the time to make lists of all the things we so very much take for granted and should be thankful for; but most important of all, it is the birth of Christ, who makes all things possible.   THE END

A HEAVENLY GIFT

I didn't scream or moan. I just sat staring at Dr. Haversham, and my husband, Will. When something that bad hits you, you're so numb you can't talk. Dr. Haversham had just told us that our daughter, Erin, was going to die.

"We thought we could remove the tumor, but the malignancy has spread too far. We think removing it will only hasten her death," he said quietly. "So, we just closed the incision. At least she'll live a few more months, three, maybe less. We'll keep the pain under control as much as possible. You don't have to worry about that."

Worry! I fought back hysterical laughter. Torment was more like it. Surely this was a nightmare from which I would soon awaken. Only, I knew I wouldn't.

It had started two weeks ago when I'd taken Erin to see Dr. Haversham. She hadn't seemed very sick—just not as lively as usual. The horror had reached its peak when all the lab tests were completed and the doctor gave us the results. Erin had cancer of the kidney.

It was so hard to believe! How could a cancer reach that stage in our child without our knowing it? The symptoms had been such slight ones. Sometimes her tummy got upset, and she complained of pain there. But that wasn't very frequent, and all kids had tummy aches. Will even had scolded me for being too concerned over her. He said I was acting like a fussy mother hen with one chick.

A few times Erin told us her back hurt, but we didn't worry about that, either. Will had bought her a pony—Lacey—for her birthday, and she'd spent every hour she could riding him. She knew no fear, and, though she bounced around a lot, she never fell off. We decided the bouncing had caused the back pains, but I hated to forbid Erin to ride Lacey. Then the pony developed a saddle sore and couldn't be ridden for a couple of weeks, but Erin's back pains continued.

I took her to see Dr. Haversham, who, during his first examination, had felt the tumor mass. He hadn't been sure, of course, until all the tests had been made.

Again and again Dr. Haversham told us we weren't to blame for neglecting her. The kind of tumor she had could occur in children from birth to five years, and symptoms came late. Sometimes, when it was far advanced, there was bleeding from the kidneys, but the pain was neither constant nor severe. Often when it was discovered, it was too late for surgery to help. It was too late for Erin—that was what I had to face. How could I? I started trembling violently. Will reached out and closed an icy hand over mine.

"You'll have to be brave for Erin's sake," Dr. Haversham said. "Right now she isn't afraid, and she won't be if you don't show your fear. The operation didn't cause her much distress, and, in about a week or ten days, you can take her home. Of course, you will have to bring her back again, because we can control the pain far better here. But we'll handle that when we come to it."

"Will there be quite a bit of pain?" Will asked in a strained voice.

"Well—eventually, there will be," Dr. Haversham admitted. "As the tumor spreads to adjacent nerve trunks, it will cause neurologic pains—but we can greatly alleviate them." He stood up, sighing. "It's always hard to tell parents such news. In your case, it is extra hard because she's your only child. Believe me, I know how rough this is for you, and I suggest you go get a cup of coffee and pull yourselves together before going up to see Erin. She's awake now and waiting for you."

In the coffeeshop, Will and I were too steeped in misery to speak. Why Erin? Why, out of all the children in the world, did this have to happen to Erin? We had waited so long for a baby, and she was the only one I could ever have.

I hadn't married in the first flush of youth. At twenty-five no man had found my tall, willowy figure, and average appearance irresistible. Both my older sisters had married and moved far away—one to the state of Wyoming, the other to Montana.

I taught second grade and continued living at home with my parents, who rejoiced in my singleness. They were pleased to have me at home with them. Both of my parents were old and ailing. I was too happy teaching school to worry over becoming an old maid—until my parents died within a few months of each other. Alone and lonely, I drifted through the rest of the school term through a hot, boring summer, and started the fall term in September with little enthusiasm for it.

On opening day, the principal introduced me to Will Braxton—our new sixth-grade teacher. Instantly, life became exciting. I floated to school on winged feet. The drab, old school building became a lush paradise because Will was there. And if I failed to invent an excuse that took me near him during the day, Will sought me out on some flimsy pretense.

To me, Will was the best looking man in the world. He wasn't typically gorgeous, but he had the nicest eyes and smile I'd ever seen. Somehow, his face looked friendly and comfortable—like you could tell him anything. He had been fatherless since he was twelve.

"We were great pals. My dad's death was a terrible blow," he said. His mother had died a short time before he transferred to our school. Because of his recent bereavement, he knew exactly how lost and lonely I was, now that my parents were gone.

Loneliness may have drawn us together, but soon we were deeply in love. Will and I wanted exactly the same things out of life—companionship, a home, and children. We were married at the end of the school year, and no two people were ever happier.

I was twenty-six and Will was thirty when we married. We planned to start a family right away, but we were married five years and had almost given up hope when I finally got pregnant. Then I walked around in a kind of glory, and Will felt the same way.

I had an easy pregnancy; although, I worried a bit because I was having my first baby when I was past thirty. And there were complications when I went into labor; although, my doctor assured me, afterward, that it wasn't because of my age. However, he also said I could never have another child.

Once Will and I would have minded that, but we'd waited so long for our little one, we just felt blessed. Erin had her daddy's hair and eye color. Her turned-up nose and little chin was something she'd inherited from me. Maybe she wasn't beautiful, but almost from birth she had a wonderful, sparkling personality. Nobody spending more than five minutes with her could help being charmed.

Erin was bright, too, and had a terrific imagination. All her dolls became real people to her, and somehow she made us feel they were, too. Will rigged up a little playhouse under a big sycamore tree, and our little daughter spent many happy hours there. There weren't many children in our neighborhood, but she played alone contentedly, often inventing imaginary playmates, giving them names and talking to them as if they were alive.

Like all kids, she was naughty at times, and, of course, we spoiled her. Sometimes when she couldn't have her own way, she would scream and stamp her little foot. Then, five minutes later, she would be her sunny self again.

Now this unbelievably terrible thing had happened. We were going to lose our only child, the very center of our lives. Like Erin in a rage, I wanted to stamp and scream; but I was too frozen even to cry.

A HEAVENLY GIFT

Will and I finished our coffee quickly and took the elevator to the pediatric wing of the hospital. We found Erin lying in bed, pale, but not frightened or unhappy. She had decided her operation was like having her tonsils out—only in a different place. She hadn't liked the idea, and she'd cried when they pricked her finger for blood tests, but, all in all, she'd accepted it.

"Hi!" Erin greeted us with a smile that was almost as bright as ever. "Things are real funny around here. A nurse gave me a shot and I cried, but I fell asleep right away. She did it in this room"—pouting a little—"and I didn't even get to see the operating room."

Erin had seen a PBS show about hospitals, and she was fascinated. She constantly begged me to let her stay up late to watch "E.R." Of course, I didn't want her to watch that show. Some of the story-lines were much too adult for her, plus the show came on very late. I wanted her asleep by ten o'clock. Erin said she'd wanted to be a part of the real thing!

It's funny what parents can do when they have to. Will and I appeared as cheerful and matter-of-fact as if we weren't being torn to pieces. We discussed the chances of Erin having ice cream soon and assured her that she wouldn't have to stay in the hospital long. She asked me to bring her some new books and her favorite doll and a "surprise."

She was comfortable because they had given her medication for pain, but when it started to wear off, she whimpered pitifully, saying, "I hurt, Mama."

With my heart breaking, I rang for a nurse who gave her a shot at once. Erin yelled at the prick of the needle but, in a few minutes, started to go to sleep. I stayed with her while Will went out to get something to eat. When he came back, I went home to sleep.

We took turns at her bedside the next few days. After she appeared stronger, Dr. Haversham said it would be better if we came only at regular visitors' hours. "We mustn't let her think she is sicker than the other little patients here," he told us, "or different in any way. She knows the children's parents come in the afternoon and evening only, and she's starting to wonder why you two are allowed to stay here so much."

Thus started our secret life. Oh, tears did come— wild storms of weeping to me when I cried aloud in my agony. Once I found Will crying in our bedroom. Neither of us slept much, and we could hardly eat. Sometimes we simply clung to each other. At other times we each would go into a private world of grief that the other couldn't share. One thing beat at us, night and day. We were going to lose our only child—we were going to lose Erin!

Two weeks later, she was allowed to come home, and we had to hide our feelings from her. We were almost able to lull ourselves into a false sense of security, because she was up and around, eating well, and acting almost like her old self. It was hard to believe anything was seriously wrong with her. Then, little by little, she slipped downhill. As Dr. Haversham had predicted, the pain started mildly, at first, but grew ever stronger.

"I hurt so much, Mama," she said once, puzzled. "All over me. Why?"

"Maybe you were active too soon after your operation, darling," I hedged. "Try to play more quietly now."

Finally, the time came when she whimpered and moaned all night in spite of the medicine we gave her. And one morning there was bright blood in her urine. My heart almost stopped when I saw that fatal sign. Trembling, I held her to me to make sure she wouldn't be frightened, then carried her into her bedroom where I laid her on her bed.

"Rest here a moment, dear," I said, "till Mama comes back to dress you." And I rushed to the telephone and called Dr. Haversham. Sighing, he told me we'd better bring her back to the hospital.

I had wondered a million times how I would tell her she was going back without scaring her, but to my surprise she didn't ask a single question. "Okay," she said. "Then the nurses can care for me at night when I cry, and you won't have to stay awake, Mama."

"Why, darling, I'm sure they'll fix it so you won't hurt at night. Anyway, after an operation, people often have to go back to the hospital for a check-up."

She nodded. "Like Wendy, who had her tonsils out, then got an infection," she said, like a wise little woman. Wendy was a slightly older child who lived a few blocks away and played with Erin sometimes.

"That's right," I said, relieved. "Just like Wendy."

Our child had been home with us exactly six weeks. When Will carried her to the car, we both knew she never would come home again.

She settled into the hospital routine happily enough. She liked the nurses, and they loved her. The head nurse, Miss Palmer, was a tiny woman, hardly bigger than a child herself, and Erin took a special liking to her. Miss Palmer was so busy, and she couldn't spend much time with my little girl, but she was charmed with Erin—just about everybody was. Once she called me into her office for a brief talk.

"You're a born mother, Mrs. Braxton," she said. "I'm going to speak bluntly. I know how you feel, and yet you never show it in front of Erin. With her you're as bright and cheerful as any child could want, and that, more than pills, is making things easier for her. Now, you probably feel that you're too old to have another baby, but I think you should. It's safer, medically, than it used to be, and it will help you more than anything else."

"I can't have another baby!" I told her what had happened at Erin's birth.

"I'm sorry," she said gently. "Then I think you should consider adoption. You may think this is no time for me to bring up the subject, but you and your husband need children. You also need something to look forward to and applying for an adoptive child would give you that. I don't mean you should decide right now—but keep it in mind. No child could ever take Erin's place, but you would find it easy to love another one for itself, and it would keep your lives from being empty."

Miss Palmer meant well. She was trying to give me something to think about so I wouldn't fall into complete despair—as if anything could prevent that! An adopted baby? Right now I couldn't even think about it.

Luckily for Will, school started again, and he had his work to take his mind off our trouble—at least for part of each day. I wondered if it was hard for him to teach other children now.

A HEAVENLY GIFT

I devoted all my time to Erin. I didn't have to observe regular visitors' hours anymore. I could stay with her from morning till night. But that was becoming a torture, too, for she was losing so much weight. She seemed to be melting away in front of my eyes.

Although the medication did keep our child from suffering too much—for which I thanked God every day, it also made her groggy, and she dozed a lot. Other times she seemed almost like her old self and played and talked and glowed like a little candle that flickers brightly just before going out. She never once asked about going home, accepting her hospital stay in a matter-of-fact manner that amazed us both.

"I'll just have to be here till I get well," she said once. "But, Mama, it sure is taking lots of shots!"

How she hated those shots! She almost always cried, and sometimes when she begged the nurses not to give them to her, I had to leave the room.

I guess it was that, on top of everything else, that caused my blinding headaches. The first one hit suddenly one afternoon at the hospital. Erin was asleep, and I mumbled an excuse to the nurse on duty and took a taxi home. After that, they happened frequently. When I was in their grip, there was nothing I could do except collapse on my bed. Dr. Haversham said they were brought on by strain and gave me tranquilizers and painkillers, but nothing helped except rest in a darkened room with an ice bag on my head.

I resented those headaches with a helpless fury because they kept me from my baby. I couldn't let her see me so ill. When one struck, I just stayed at home. I told her I had to catch up on my cleaning or cook for Daddy or go out to the farm to see how Lacey, her pony, was doing. Erin accepted my excuses like a little soldier.

"Don't worry about me, Mama," she said, comforting me. "You can't stay here all the time. I won't get lonesome, honest." Her thin little face became serious. "Only you might get lonesome for me."

"Oh, I will, darling! I do! It isn't even home without you!" I very nearly broke down and regretted the words immediately. I had forced myself to act cheerful, so I had to continue.

Erin's eyes clouded at first but then she smiled. "Oh, Mama"—being cheerful for my sake now— "you can see me anytime!"

Shortly after that her drug dosage had to be increased, and she became much quieter. Her eyelids fell over her eyes. But even though she seemed like a sleepy child, kept up past her bedtime, her mind was clear, and she continued to say things beyond her years.

One day she said, "You feel bad, Mama, because you think I'm lonesome. But I'm not—even a tiny bit."

"Well, you have the nurses," I started.

"I know, Mama. But they don't have time to play with me. I have some children to play with now."

"What do you mean, sweetheart? What children?"

The drugs, I thought, *probably bring on dreams till she can no longer distinguish between dreams and reality.* Yet if my little girl felt like talking, I would listen. I would remember every word she said for the rest of my life, I was certain.

"I have a brother and sister now, Mama," she

went on. "Their names are Paul and Dawn, and they come to see me every day. We play games and we have fun."

I patted her little hand. "Why, of course, Erin. I remember the imaginary friends you had in your playhouse. Let's see—there was Amy and Princess Diana and the twins Sam and Sammi. Have they come to see you here, too?"

"No, Mama," she said patiently, "and Dawn and Paul aren't like them. They're my real brother and sister. Paul's a big boy, eight years old. He has red hair and a million freckles, and sometimes he teases me. But he's not a bad boy. He was just lonesome till he got Dawn and me for sisters."

"Well he sounds like a very nice big brother." I said lightly. "And what's Dawn like?"

"Oh, she's a real sweet little girl. She's only four, and she's got long black hair and black eyes. She looks like she's tan, like me in the summer, but she says it's the real color of her skin. She's kind of shy, and the other day she cried. She wouldn't tell Paul and me why she was crying, but he stood on his head and made her smile again. She's the nicest sister, just the kind I've always wanted."

Erin's eyes drooped, and I knew so much talking was tiring her. "Know what, Mama?" she whispered, rousing. "I wish Paul and Dawn could be with you sometimes so you wouldn't get lonesome. They'd like to be with you, too, 'cause you're their mother—but I guess they have to stay with me right now. . . ." Her eyes closed then, and she drifted off to sleep.

I looked down at her, blinking back tears. My wonderful little girl could make an imaginary brother and sister seem so real! She evidently had minded being an only child and dreamed up these children out of her need for companionship. If she could only live, what a future she'd have! What a writer she would make with her sensitivity and marvelous imagination! But there was no future for my talented child. I stumbled out of the room, blinded by tears.

During dinner, I told Will about Erin's Paul and Dawn. He sighed.

"It's not unusual. She has always dreamed up playmates, and now she needs someone closer— like a brother and sister. Well, if they give her comfort, I thank God. It may be a life blessing He is giving our child."

My hands clenched. I didn't believe in God's blessings anymore.

After that Erin talked a lot about Dawn and Paul. It worried me because it now seemed as if she were drifting into dreams that would end in death. Still, they made her happy. And that was the most important thing.

Only a few days later Erin stopped talking about her imaginary sister and brother and everything else. She slipped to a deep coma from which she had never emerged. Twenty-three months later, she gave a spasmodic jerk, upheaved a long, sighing gasp for breath—and died.

I don't know how we got through the funeral. I remember very little about it except the overwhelming smell of flowers and my dazed grief at how small the white coffin was.

Empty months followed—long, torturing months when I felt I had nothing to live for. I knew Will was suffering, too, but I couldn't seem to break through my shell of agony to reach him. He tried—how he tried—to get through to me, but I was like a woman carved out of ice.

On Erin's birthday, I went into her room—which I'd left exactly as it was—and spent the whole day there. When Will came home, I heard him calling me. I didn't answer. Finally, he opened the door of the room and saw me sitting in the rocking chair where I had lulled Erin to sleep when she was a baby. But I wasn't rocking now. I was sitting stiffly, just staring into space.

He grabbed my hand, jerked me up, and almost dragged me into our bedroom. "You're going to go crazy," he said fiercely. "You can't keep on this way. Look at you!"

He wheeled me around and made me face the wall mirror. I saw my tangled, unwashed hair, my not-too-clean housedress, my old, scuffed slippers. *I look like a witch,* I thought dully.

"I love you!" he cried. "I won't let you destroy yourself. Start teaching again. You must do something to keep busy."

"No," I said flatly.

"Then let's adopt a baby. I know you're in no shape to care for one now, but you're a mother through and through. A baby would help you pull yourself together, and you would learn to love it. It's the only answer, Alana. And if you won't try to help yourself, I'm clearing out. I've suffered, too—believe it or not—but I'm not going to stop living. I'm sorry, Alana, but I can't go on this way."

I'd known I was cut off from Will—now terror struck me. I had lost Erin; I couldn't lose Will, too. Slowly, painfully, I started the hardest struggle of my life—to rejoin the human race.

At first I did mechanical things. I cleaned my dirty house and started taking care of myself. I had my hair set and my nails manicured. I bought a new dress—that was a real triumph. I planned good meals for Will and attempted to talk to him while we ate.

It took months, but finally I was back to normal—at least on the surface. I was even able to respond to my husband's lovemaking again. If I still felt dead inside, nobody suspected.

Finally, I agreed to apply for a baby. Will had been urging me to until I couldn't hold out any longer. Maybe a baby would help, but could any child make up for losing Erin? Then I remembered what Miss Palmer, the head nurse at the hospital had said.

"You would find it easy to love another child for itself." And Will was so sure adoption was the right answer. I just went along with the idea.

We expected an investigation and a long period of waiting when we went to the agency—but we hadn't expected to be turned down flat.

"I'm very sorry," Ms. Hallie, the social worker there, told us. "We have a law in this state that says adoptive parents that are your age are generally not considered. I also noticed on your application that you have certain medical problems. We generally don't allow parents to adopt who have severe medical problems."

"But my problems aren't serious. I have medication to help me deal with the illness, and I haven't been ill since college."

"It is really for the child's sake," she said, trying to cushion the blow she'd dealt. "When he or she would be twenty, you, Mr. Braxton, would be sixty-one. You would be retired from teaching. Are you sure you could handle the expense of a college education on a teacher's pension? Of course, natural parents have babies when they're even older than you folks, but we want to give our babies the best possible future. Frankly, parents have too many problems—especially if one parent has a potentially life-threatening illness."

Maybe the law was right—maybe it wasn't. But there would be no baby for us. I was hurt but somewhat relieved, too. A baby might have constantly reminded me of the daughter we'd lost. But I felt terribly let down, too. I could hardly face the life that stretched ahead, barren and empty.

"I guess we're out of luck," I said, sighing wearily.

"Would you consider an older child?" she asked.

I shook my head. I felt the only way I could love an adopted child would be to get one as an infant—that way I would feel it was really mine. An older one could never be close to us.

I hid my hurt and tried to comfort Will when we got home. "We have each other—that's the important thing. Lots of married couples never have babies and get along all right. Next year I'll start teaching again."

"Why are you so against taking an older child?" he asked.

"Their characters are already formed, and they have memories, and there'd be a difficult period of adjustment. I just can't face that somehow."

"Maybe you're right," Will said. "We'll forget about it."

I decided to go back to teaching without waiting

for the new term and took a substituting job. But after only a month, my headaches came back—more severe than ever. I had no choice but to stop working. That, too, was a relief, but the headaches didn't let up. Sometimes I moaned for hours with pain.

"Even if it is just nerves, you're sick," Will told me finally after a sleepless night. "Tomorrow you're going to see Dr. Haversham."

The doctor admitted I had a problem. "I'm going to put you in the hospital under sedation for several days," he said. "You aren't having a nervous break-down, but you've strained yourself to the limit, try-ing to be normal. You need rest—lots of rest. Yow body is exhausted from your emotions. When we get you over that exhaustion, I think you'll be able to carry on again."

I checked in that night. At first I felt disturbed at being in the same hospital where Erin had died, but soon the strong medication erased even that from my mind. I slept and slept and slept. The doctor gradually reduced the heavy sedation, and I awoke one morning, refreshed and calm. I began to take an interest in what was going on around me.

Miss Palmer dropped in to visit with me. She had come to my room several times before, but I'd been too groggy to talk, she said. With her usual blunt-ness she plunged right into the subject she wanted to discuss.

"If you would only adopt a baby, you would find a new life," she said. "I told you that once before, but I guess you didn't listen."

"We did try to adopt a baby and were told we're too old."

"I never thought of that," she said, frowning. "But what about an older child?"

"Don't start that! An older child would never be like my own."

"Don't be silly. You've got a mother's heart, and your frustration is causing most of your trouble. What you need is a child who needs you. The greater the need, the more you would respond, and pretty soon you'd be pouring out the love that's locked up inside of you."

"Stop it!" I cried.

"I'm not going to stop. In fact, I came here today for a purpose. We have a four-year-old girl from the children's home in the hospital now, who's been operated on for club feet. She'll be able to walk almost normally, but she'll always have a slight limp. Her chances for adoption are not good. What's more, she's of mixed blood. Her father was Cherokee and her mother has some Latina blood.

"They were very poor but decent people. The mother died of pneumonia when the child was two years old, and the father couldn't support her, so he signed her away to the home. If no one takes her, she'll be in an institution until she's eighteen. She's a gentle little thing who needs love more than any child I ever saw."

"Spare me your sob stories. I'm sorry for her, but I wouldn't accept an older child if she were the most beautiful, appealing little girl in the world."

Miss Palmer bit her lip before answering. "She is neither beautiful, nor appealing. In fact, she's very plain. She has coarse, black hair and copper-colored skin. And she's so lonely and starved for love she hardly ever talks. She needs a mother's love and care, and somehow I got the idea you were a tenderhearted woman." She stood up to go. "I guess I'm fighting for Dawn's happiness, too. It seemed to me you were the only chance she had."

"Dawn?" I stared openmouthed. "Did you say Dawn?"

"Yes." She looked bewildered. "Why?"

I couldn't answer for the memories rushing through my head, memories of my darling Erin saying she had a sister named Dawn—a sweet, shy, dark-skinned little girl. A coincidence—of course—but suddenly I knew I had to meet this child.

"I might as well walk over and see her," I said, reaching for my robe and slippers.

I wish I could say Dawn took one look at me and held out her arms. She didn't. She just lay there, a tawny wisp of a child with big black eyes, lost and lonely. We were strangers, but suddenly I had the feeling that I was seeing Dawn through Erin's eyes—and, to Erin, Dawn had been a sister. Of course, it wasn't this same girl. Erin's Dawn had originated in her mind. And yet, her imagined sister and this very real, deserted little girl were so much alike!

Erin had seen into the future. She had talked about her sister, Dawn. I just humored her when she spoke about it—but now there was a Dawn. God must have granted her a special ability since her own future was limited.

Neither Will nor I had the answer to that, but the same compulsion gripped us both. We had to take Dawn. All my arguments against an older child didn't mean a thing anymore. My heart told me Dawn was Erin's sister, just the same as if she had been born to me.

A HEAVENLY GIFT

Things weren't easy at first. Dawn was so shy and seemed almost sullen. Sometimes she cried and screamed for no apparent reason. And one part of Erin's imaginings was wrong; Dawn didn't feel I was her mother—at least, not at first. But Will and I lavished our love on her, and that was what she needed most. Slowly she responded to it, and now she's a completely changed child, happy and affectionate, accepting us fully as her parents.

Some will say that there was a logical explanation to the things Erin told me. Erin's sister, Dawn, was a drug-inspired dream, and the fact that I found another Dawn who answered her description was an odd coincidence, nothing more.

But I know the truth. God let my little girl see into the future. And He let her see into the future to help me. He knew that I would need some other child to love but that my heart would be hardened against caring and loving another child. After I lost my precious Erin, I felt as though my world was coming apart. I had hardened my heart toward life and love.

The only way I would accept another child in my life was for Erin to tell me about her. I know some of you may think I'm crazy. But I'm not crazy. God—the One who I thought had deserted me—had a plan all along. Although He was allowing Erin to leave me, He was going to bring another child to love into my life.

There are things in heaven and on earth that we can never fully comprehend. Now Will and I are looking for a freckle-faced redhead named Paul. Somehow, we are sure we'll find him.   THE END

"MOMMY, I TALKED TO THE ANGELS"

Adrienne was so excited. How could I tell her there wouldn't be a Christmas this year? She was such a sweet little girl. She didn't deserve to be forced to live this way.

I should have known it wouldn't be easy. We hadn't had one easy day since Kenny had walked out on us eighteen months earlier. And it was still hard to believe that he'd left me.

Thank goodness I had good kids who never caused me any trouble. They had been confused about their daddy's absence. Although I'd originally told them he was looking for a new job in another city, I finally decided it would be best to tell them the truth.

It was a hot summer night about two months after Kenny had gone away. We were sitting outside our trailer because it was unbearably hot inside. We couldn't even turn on the fan since the electricity had been shut off for nonpayment.

Vincent, my son, was a very grown-up twelve-year-old, and Adrienne, my daughter, was like a little baby doll. She was three years old with pale, delicate features that made her seem like a very fragile porcelain doll.

The children sat on either side of me on the rickety steps leading to the trailer door. Adrienne leaned against my arm, her soft curls damp from the heat. Vincent looked up at me seriously with his big eyes. I decided to be direct.

"Listen, kids, when I told you that Daddy had to go look for a job, there was a little more to it than that."

I paused, searching for the right words. "Actually, Daddy didn't want to be married to me anymore. Sometimes, after a lot of years, a man and woman find they don't love each other like they once did."

"Don't you love Daddy anymore, Mom?" Vincent looked at me directly.

Oh, how could I answer him? Truthfully, I decided. "Well, honey, that's the funny part. I still do, but Daddy doesn't feel the same kind of love for me."

Adrienne got the saddest look on her little face. "Daddy doesn't love us anymore?"

"Oh, yes, honey. Daddy loves you and Vincent very much. Moms and dads never stop loving their children." I hugged her tightly.

"How much does he love us if he hasn't even come back to see if we're all right?" Vincent asked.

"Hush now." I spoke softly to him. "Let's not upset Adrienne right now."

"He hasn't even sent money for food, Mom. The electricity is shut off. What're we going to do?"

Vincent's growing up too fast, I thought. "Well, Mr. Smartie, as a matter-of-fact, I'm going to work, starting Monday."

He looked and sounded surprised. "Doing what, Mom?"

"I'm going to be a waitress down at Hilton's café in town, and you're going to be Adrienne's baby-sitter, okay?"

"Yeah! Vincent's going to baby-sit me," Adrienne said as she started bouncing up and down.

"Sure, Mom, I guess so. But wouldn't it be better if I got a job, being that I'm a guy and all?"

I tried to stifle my laughter. "And just what would you do, big fella?"

"I could deliver newspapers or work at Mr. Myzinski's grocery store."

I gave him a big hug, even though he thought he was too grown-up for that stuff. "Honey, I really appreciate that, but I think with salary and tips, I can probably do a little better than that. But, you know, I won't be able to do it unless I can count on a dependable sitter here with Adrienne."

"You can count on me, Mom."

"I know I can, son."

So, the summer passed. I worked eight to ten hours a day and never complained. The longer days meant Hilton's was extra busy and that meant better tips for me. I got the electricity turned back on, and the kids were eating good food. The rent was caught up at the trailer park, and, by the end of July, I even had enough to take the kids on an all-day trip to the big amusement park outside of town.

I still missed Kenny terribly, but Adrienne and Vincent seemed to be adjusting well.

By the middle of August, though, I realized we had more problems to deal with, and soon. Vincent would be starting school again in September. I couldn't find a baby-sitter in the part of town we lived in. I managed to walk to and from work but nobody else was going to walk clear across town to where we lived. At least not for what I could afford to pay.

I also realized it wouldn't be easy to walk once the snow and bad weather came. And to think I used to love living in the country.

I put the trailer up for sale. Vincent helped me clean it inside and out. We scrubbed and polished until the old place didn't look half-bad. I even splurged on frilly, new kitchen curtains that made it look real cozy.

I knew it would be hard to leave. It had been home for a lot of years, the only one Vincent could remember and the only one Adrienne had ever had.

We had moved in when Vincent was almost two years old. Kenny and I had been so happy then. I remembered how he'd picked me up at the bottom of the steps and carried me through the door. "Welcome to our first home, honey," he said. The kiss we'd shared then had been so special, so full of promise.

We had been living on the second floor of his grandmother's house, and although I loved her a lot, I was finally glad to have our own place. There was even a second bedroom for little Vincent. It was as if we were newlyweds again. It was great not having to worry about Grandmom hearing us or about Vincent waking up in his crib next to our bed. Life had been good to us.

Our relationship seemed to start going bad right after Adrienne was born. At first, Kenny had been thrilled with his new baby girl. But then, he started complaining about the price of formula and diapers and all the things babies seem to need.

Vincent had been almost nine years old when I got pregnant. We'd thought that Vincent would be the only child we'd have, so we had given away most of his baby things. Trailers don't have a lot of storage space.

Bit by bit, we accumulated a lot of bills for Adrienne's crib, playpen, and other baby-related items. I bought some things, pretty pink dresses at a discount store, a first aid kit at the grocery store. But even though I tried to conserve money, the purchases still put us in the hole, and I was even guilty of charging some of those pretty little dresses and frilly, little-girl socks on our credit card. Kenny was pretty mad about that. Then, Adrienne went through a bad spell where she had colic, and she kept us both awake at night. I finally started sleeping on the couch while she lay in the playpen, so Kenny could get some sleep.

Before Adrienne turned two, they started laying off at the mills where Kenny worked. Six months later, he got his pink slip. He didn't tell me about it for almost a week. I had asked for grocery money and he blew up.

"There isn't any grocery money, Beth! There's no money for anything."

When he settled down, we talked about our situation. There would be unemployment checks. "But those checks come only for twenty six weeks, Beth. Then what'll we do?" he asked.

"You'll find something else, Kenny. I have faith in you."

"MOMMY, I TALKED TO THE ANGELS"

Luckily, the trailer was paid off and the rent at the trailer park was low. I managed to cook low-cost, filling meals, and I didn't spend one extra cent on anything unnecessary. But, by the end of the twenty-six weeks, Kenny still hadn't found a job. There were just too many steelworkers out of jobs and not enough other jobs to go around.

I had suggested looking for a job myself, but Kenny got angry and began throwing things and slamming doors. He was a very different person from the man I had fallen in love with.

"No wife of mine is going to work!" he shouted. "Don't ever mention it again."

We hardly spoke during the next two weeks. I'll always regret that. The day Kenny walked out for good, I found a note in our bedroom with fifty-five dollars inside.

Here's half the money we have left, he'd written. He also wrote: *It's better this way, Beth, and I'm sorry.* But the really tough part was where he'd written: *There's nothing left here for me.*

Nothing left? I thought, *What are we, Kenny? Are the kids and I nothing?*

I believe, somewhere deep inside me, that I expected him to realize what a mistake he'd made and come back to us. I think I was waiting for that day, the day we would be a family again. Six weeks later, that dream was shattered when I opened an official-looking envelope—divorce papers! There were lots of legal words, but it boiled down to the fact that if I didn't contest it, a "no fault" divorce would be final in ninety days. The letter said just to sign on the dotted line.

What it didn't say was how you sign away thirteen

years of loving a man and the two kids that came about because of that love? It didn't say anything about all the sacrifices we'd made to make a go of our marriage. It didn't say how I was supposed to stop loving him.

I had nobody. Kenny's grandmom had died before Adrienne was born. I was an only child of parents who split up before I knew who my daddy was. *Adrienne's going to be just like me,* I thought. *She won't even remember her daddy.*

My mama had died when I was eighteen, a couple of months after I married Kenny, so I'd never been on my own before he walked out.

Well, Kenny had been gone since April, and I'd proved that I could be on my own. After two months at Hilton's, I knew I could handle a job and a home. Selling the trailer seemed to be the right thing to do. We would have enough money to get an apartment and find a baby-sitter for Adrienne. The divorce would be final in September, and it would be a new beginning for us. Life would be good again.

My dreams faltered when I found out that ten-year-old trailers weren't selling for much money, especially in our depressed community. We only had two serious potential buyers after three weeks of showing it. I finally let it go to an older couple.

After paying all our debts and closing costs, I came away with a few thousand dollars. To me, it was still a small fortune. I thought that with that much money, we could get an apartment and some furniture—so many things were built into the trailer I hadn't realized how many things we'd need. But I made good tips at Hilton's, so I thought we'd be able to manage.

"MOMMY, I TALKED TO THE ANGELS"

I opened a checking account in my own name—for the first time. Beth Cahner—it was printed right on the pretty blue checks.

I had one week to find an apartment before the new owners moved into the trailer, so time was not a luxury of mine.

I asked my boss, Louis, for a few days off so I could look for a place. He wasn't too happy about it. "Three days, Beth. If you're not back, I'll have to hire somebody else."

After two days, I figured I'd looked at every apartment in town. They were either too small, too dirty, or too expensive. At last, on the third day, I found the perfect place. It was a two-bedroom apartment on the first floor of a lovely old house in a quiet section of town. It was more than I'd planned on paying, but I decided I'd use the money from the trailer for the security deposit and the first month's rent, and replace it when I got back to work.

I had an ad in the paper for a sitter, so I went back to Hilton's. I'd worked three days and was getting worried about a baby-sitter. Vincent was due to start school in a couple of days, and I didn't have a sitter for Adrienne. Only two women answered my ad. One had breath that smelled of whiskey. The other seemed responsible but didn't even smile when I introduced her to Adrienne. I decided if that sweet little girl couldn't get a smile out of her, she wasn't worth hiring.

Several teenage girls stopped by when they heard I needed a sitter, but they couldn't start till after school hours.

Vincent would be home by then, so I really didn't need them. I appealed to Louis again. He wasn't happy about giving me more time off, but I was a good worker and I counted on him knowing it, too.

"Beth, you just had three days off."

"I know, Louis, and I appreciated it. I just haven't found a sitter yet, and Vincent starts school the day after tomorrow."

"Okay, just a few more days, Beth. I mean it. You know we've been extra busy." He softened a little and smiled. "I need you, but if you're not back, I'll have to hire somebody else—in a week."

I smiled, realizing my two days had jumped to a week. I always knew Louis was softhearted. Finally, he said, "I know you need the job and I'd hate to lose you, but it's business, you know?"

"I do know, Louis, and I'll do my best." Then I added, "Thanks for the week."

He looked at me for a minute, then said, "Listen, did you check that bulletin board at the grocery store? Sometimes they list people looking for work."

"Thank you, I will."

I checked the bulletin board, I checked ads, I even went door-to-door in our new neighborhood, but I had no luck. The week was running out. I called Louis, wondering if there was any chance of working the evening shift. It would be hard on the kids being alone all evening, but it would at least be something.

"Beth, you know I hired you so fast because I needed a daytime waitress," he answered. "I have women begging to work nights. Ellen and Naomi have had that shift for years, and I hired Tara six month before you started. She's supporting four kids."

"MOMMY, I TALKED TO THE ANGELS"

I knew all that because my shift usually went a couple of hours into the dinner shift, when we were busy. I had gotten to know all the waitresses.

"Couldn't I try switching with one of them, Louis?"

"Beth, Ellen and Naomi have preschool kids. That's why they work at night, so their husbands can baby-sit. Tara's husband can't get work. She's working as a cashier during the day and then working here nights."

Here I was feeling sorry for myself when other people were even worse off than I was. At least we had some money in the bank, and I'd find someone to watch Adrienne soon.

Louis started talking again. "It's been rough without you, Beth. I've even had my wife, Ivonne, filling in a couple of hours a day, but her mother's at our place and she's got her hands full." He paused for just a second then said, "Her mother's pretty sick. She has cancer, Beth."

"The café's your business, Louis. You have to do what's best. I understand, honestly, I do." I tried to hold back the tears. *I'll find another job,* I thought. "I appreciate all you've done for me, hiring me with no experience and being so good about the time off and all."

"There's not much I can do, Beth. I've had two women coming by every day this week. They heard you might not be back," he said. Louis stopped briefly, but when I didn't say anything, he continued. "I told them to stop back tomorrow. They're so desperate—their husbands are out of work, too. They're even willing to split the shifts. I've never done that, but I know those ten-hour shifts weren't easy on you."

We were both silent then, and finally I said, "Louis, thanks again, for everything."

"Sure, sure. Listen, you come down and see us sometime. Bring the kids. There's always free pie and coffee for former employees, okay?"

"Okay, Louis."

"I'm sorry, Beth. I really am."

"I know. Bye."

The weeks passed into months. I hadn't worked long enough to collect unemployment checks, so we lived off of the money in the bank.

I left applications at every restaurant, bar, and store in town, trying to get a job on a late shift anywhere I could. I never realized how lucky I'd been to get the job at Hilton's so quickly, especially considering that I had no experience.

My "fortune" was going fast. With rent, utilities, and food taken care of, I figured we would be all right for a while yet. Of course, the unexpected always happens.

The flu bug was going through town in October. Adrienne got it right before Halloween. It was the middle of the night when her high fever scared me enough to call a cab and go to the emergency room at the hospital. Funny how you don't think about money at a time like that—you just care about your child, so you act.

Adrienne had a difficult twenty-four hours, but once the antibiotic took hold, she improved dramatically. I was overjoyed. Two days later the bill arrived. I could hardly believe it! It came to over four hundred dollars. *And that doesn't include the forty dollars for the taxi and the forty-six dollars I paid for the medicine,* I thought.

A week later, Vincent came down with the same symptoms. This time, I called a local doctor and explained that Adrienne had just gotten over the flu and that Vincent had the same symptoms. He told me he'd rather not prescribe any medicine by phone, especially since he'd never seen Vincent before. I really couldn't blame him.

It was the third of November and the first snow was falling. I couldn't pack up a sick kid on the bus, so I called a cab again.

At least Doc Gary, as everyone called him, was closer than the hospital, and he only charged ninety dollars for the visit.

In just ten days, our medical bills soared to almost a thousand dollars. With everything paid for in November, we had less than nine hundred dollars left in the bank. I prayed that I wouldn't get sick, and swore, if I did, I would lie in bed with aspirin and cold cloths.

Thank goodness it didn't happen, and November slipped into December. One night, in early December, I sat down to figure out our financial situation. A snowstorm was brewing, and the wind was howling. I used to love snowstorms, but now all I could think of was a higher gas bill. Figuring the lowest amount possible for utilities and food and the monthly rent, we would just make it through the month. There could be ten dollars to spare for Christmas, if we were very careful.

Total depression engulfed me as I realized little Adrienne would have no Christmas this year. I had been so sure I would get a job with the holidays approaching, but after double-checking all the places I'd left my applications, there still was no job for me. With the steel mills shut down, people just weren't buying. Some of the smaller shops had also closed down. That wasn't surprising. The smaller shops depended on the steel mill worker to support their businesses.

As the snow blew and swirled outside my bedroom window, I decided I'd have to try again tomorrow. I'd check the unemployment office to see if they had any jobs listed. I was willing to do anything.

My hopes were dashed; there were no jobs for me. I had been stopping at our neighborhood church almost every day, asking God to help me take care of my children. That day, I had no desire to stop in.

But Adrienne tugged at my hand as we walked by. "Mommy, aren't we stopping at church?"

So we went inside. Adrienne knelt with her head down on her folded hands, looking so sweet and innocent. She looked so peaceful.

Suddenly, she looked up at me and whispered loudly, "Mommy, is it all right to pray for Christmas presents?"

I smiled, remembering the talk I'd had with her and Vincent about our funds and how little we would be able to have for Christmas.

There was a stifled laugh behind us, and I turned in time to see a priest who could have passed for St. Nicholas himself if he'd dressed in red instead of black. He came up to us and scooted down in the aisle next to Adrienne.

"Why don't you just write a letter to Santa Claus?" he asked.

"Oh, I did, Father, but my big brother said that since we just moved to town he may not find our new apartment."

"I see."

His kind eyes met mine, and I sensed his understanding immediately. After all, his parish must have been filled with unemployed steelworkers and their families. He'd probably heard our stories hundreds of times.

"What's your name, little one?"

"Adrienne Cahner, Father."

"Did your daddy work in the steel mill, Adrienne?"

I held my breath, but let her answer.

"Yes, a long time ago, but he's been gone a long time now." She sighed. "He didn't love Mommy anymore—but he still loves me," she hastened to add.

"I'm sure he does, Adrienne."

He stood then and extended his hand. His grasp was gentle, yet strong. "I'm sorry, Mrs. Cahner. Job loss affects men in so many different ways. Separation seems to be a common happening."

"He made it more permanent, Father—we're divorced."

"Then I'm even sorrier. It's sad, especially when there are little ones. Do you have other children?"

"Yes, a wonderful son. Vincent will be thirteen next month."

"Mrs. Cahner, I've seen you here often the past few weeks. Do you belong to our parish?"

I was a little embarrassed. "No, Father I've been away from the church for years, and we just moved to town in September. I've just felt the need for God in my life so strongly lately." I felt myself blushing. "I mean . . . I never stopped believing or anything. I guess I'm like a lot of people praying when the kids were sick or when I lost my job."

"Were you laid off?" he asked.

"No. I couldn't find a baby-sitter for Adrienne, so I had to quit."

"Oh, Mrs. Cahner, I wish you had sought us out. The women of the parish banded together and formed a day-care center here at the church for a very nominal cost."

The tears started then and I couldn't stop. I picked up Adrienne, and before he could say another word I ran out of the church. I heard him call my name, but I didn't look back. I didn't want or need his pity.

When we got home, I went into my bedroom and hibernated for a week. Vincent tried to fix meals, and Adrienne tried to get me to color in her books, but I wouldn't budge.

"Why?" I think I must have said it aloud a hundred times that week. Why hadn't I gone to the church sooner? If I had been able to keep my job, we would have made it, and Adrienne could have the kind of Christmas she dreamt about.

"A Christmas tree, a teddy bear, a turkey, and a pumpkin pie," she said anytime someone asked what she wanted for Christmas. But now it was too late. I didn't even have enough money to pay the day-care cost if I had a job.

"Mommy, Mommy, look!" Adrienne came running in and jumped on the bed. "Vincent found a box of Christmas decorations, and he gave me his old book to read. Look, Mommy." She pointed to a picture of a tree with beautifully wrapped gifts beneath it, and a little girl and boy hanging their stockings at the fireplace.

"See, Mommy, that's Christmas. A tree and presents and stockings." Then she added quickly, "And turkey and pumpkin pie."

"No, Adrienne, that's not what Christmas is about." And suddenly I knew it was true, but she looked so stricken I pulled her close and hugged her. "Adrienne, honey, you made Mommy remember what Christmas really means." I began to tell her the centuries-old story of Jesus and the nativity.

Vincent came in, too, and stood listening, then sat on the bed beside us. They both listened as I told the biblical Christmas story. When I was done, we all sat quietly for a moment, then Vincent looked up at me.

"That's really what Christmas is about, Mom. Could we put up the manger set, like we did at Grandmom's, remember?"

"But Christmas is almost a week away."

"No, it's only six days—five, if you don't count Christmas Eve. I think we should do it early, Mom, please," Vincent said.

"All right," I replied.

"Yeah!" Adrienne yelled, as usual.

They both went out to the living room and, after a few minutes, I followed.

Vincent had found the box where I stored the manger set. He looked up at me when I walked in, then whispered, "I've had lots of great Christmases, Mom. Adrienne hardly remembers last year. Let's try to make it happy for her."

I hugged my little man. "You're so grown-up, Vincent."

"Hey, I'm almost a teenager."

We gently unwrapped the figures from pieces of year-old newspaper. It seemed so much longer than a year ago. . . .

Kenny had been with us then. We had managed on his unemployment checks. He waited until late Christmas Eve and got a gorgeous tree at half-price. We stayed up most of the night decorating it, wrapping little gifts for the kids, and filling their stockings. Then, we'd unwrapped these same figures, passed on to him from his Grandmother. Adrienne had squealed with joy in the morning. It was the last truly happy time I could remember.

I set the old wooden stable on the table Vincent had set in front of the living-room window. He'd even draped a sheet over it. Kenny's grandfather had made the stable over fifty years ago. His grandmother had told the story often and now I told it to our children.

"It was a special treasure to your great-grand-mom, kids, so we have to take good care of it. Your great-granddad is an angel in heaven and he's looking down on us. I know he's glad we've taken care of the manger he built."

"Let's get finished," Vincent said.

Out came the three wise men, the sheep, and the angel with a broken wing. Adrienne asked, "Can an angel fly with a broken wing?"

"This one won't have to," I answered, "because it's going to sit on top of the stable."

We rummaged through the paper, and finally, at the very bottom was the tiniest figure of all. Adrienne laid him gently in the wooden manger, and we were all silent for a moment, looking at the scene we'd recreated.

I felt good again. "How about some hot cocoa, kids?"

"Mommy, shh." Adrienne held her finger to her lips. "Baby Jesus is sleeping."

"Sorry, then let's tiptoe to the kitchen and we'll have our hot cocoa."

"With marshmallows?" she asked.

"If there's any left," I replied. I had bought marshmallows as a special treat for Thanksgiving to broil on top of our sweet potatoes. There were two left in the bottom of the bag, and I assured them both that since I was watching my calories, they could each have one.

Vincent shook his head. "Mom, you don't have to watch your calories a bit."

"No, you're not fat," Adrienne added.

I couldn't help laughing and it felt good. "Thanks, kids, that's the best thing I've heard in a long time."

Vincent had been right. Seeing the manger scene the next morning cheered me up right away. By the time the kids got up the next morning, I had made my plans.

"Hey, you guys, since Vincent's school vacation started today, I think we should celebrate and go look at the Christmas store windows at Morgenson's."

"Yeah!" Adrienne exclaimed.

"Then we'll stop at Hilton's and have pie," I told them.

"Can I have pumpkin pie?" Adrienne asked.

"I'm pretty sure Louis will have pumpkin pie."

Secretly I hoped Louis's offer of free pie and coffee was still good. It had been almost four months

114

since we'd talked.

It turned out to be a terrific day. We got the bus into town and headed right for the big department store. The windows had been magically replaced by a winter wonderland. Adrienne was thrilled with the little forest animals decorating snow-laden pine trees, and even Vincent enjoyed the tiny chipmunks with red scarves around their necks, skating on make-believe ice.

We looked at every decoration in every window in town. At one point, Adrienne decided to tell a street-corner Santa where we lived. Vincent and I convinced her they were just helpers collecting money for the poor.

"Are we poor, Mommy?" Adrienne asked.

"Not like some people, honey. We have a place to live and food to eat," I said.

"And we have each other," Vincent added.

I gave them both a hug, but at that moment, I realized we would have to give notice to our landlord. We'd have to find a cheaper place—one we could afford on welfare.

"Come on, let's head for Hilton's and get our pie."

"Yeah!" Adrienne yelled as she skipped ahead.

Louis welcomed us with open arms. He insisted we have a meal on the house. I told him we'd just come for our pie, but he wouldn't take no for an answer.

Adrienne was delighted. She had never ordered in a real restaurant before. "A cheeseburger, French fries, chocolate milkshake, and pumpkin pie, please."

Louis laughed. "I like a lady who knows what she wants."

Adrienne crinkled up her nose at him and said, "I'm not a lady. I'm a little girl."

"Well, you're going to be quite a lady when you grow up," he said.

"Just like my mommy."

"Then you'll be a very great lady," Louis said.

Vincent leaned over and asked me what he should order. Louis heard him and said, "Vincent, you order anything on that menu, but I seem to recall your mom telling me you had a preference for roast beef and mashed potatoes. We have a great pot roast in the kitchen that I think you'd enjoy."

Vincent grinned from ear-to-ear, literally. "That'd be great, Mr. . . ."

"Just Louis, Vincent. Just plain old Louis."

"I honestly just wanted pie and coffee," I said, when he turned to me.

"You're as skinny as a rail. I'm bringing pot roast for two with extra mashed potatoes, lots of gravy, and fresh homemade rolls and butter."

It was a terrific dinner. The place was decorated with wreaths, hollies, and poinsettias. There were even red candles on all the tables. The other waitresses stopped by our table to say hello while we had our dinner. It was so good to see everyone again. Then we had pumpkin pie with gobs of whipped cream for dessert.

I couldn't help but give Louis a big hug when we were leaving.

"Thanks so much Louis. It was a great meal." Little did he know it was the best meal we'd had in over a month.

"It's the least I could do. I'm going to keep an eye out for a job for you, too."

"Bye, Louis," Vincent said as he shook Louis's hand. "Thanks, it was a terrific dinner."

"Bye, Louis." Adrienne hugged him around his knees. "Thank you very much, especially for the pumpkin pie."

He bent down and hugged her back. "That's okay, sweetheart. I hope you have the best Christmas ever."

"Oh, we will," she said. "My great-granddaddy is an angel in heaven, and I told him what we needed for Christmas."

"And what would that be?"

Her eyes sparkled as she spoke. "A Christmas tree, a teddy bear for me, a car for Vincent, and a new coat for Mommy, a red one." She thought for a minute, then quickly added, "And turkey and pumpkin pie."

"Isn't Vincent a little young for a car?" he asked.

"Not a real one." She giggled.

"And that's all you want for Christmas?" Louis asked.

She crinkled her nose again, thinking hard. "Well, some candy canes would be nice—and marshmallows," she added.

"Marshmallows?" he asked.

"We used the last two in our hot cocoa last night—"

"Adrienne," I interrupted, "I think that's enough. Besides, we've had our Christmas at home already, remember?"

That set her off. Then she began telling Louis all about her great-granddaddy's stable, the angel with the broken wing, the old brown cow, and finally the baby Jesus. ". . . and that's what Christmas is."

"That's right, angel," Louis said.

She giggled again. "I'm not an angel, I'm a little girl."

That night I tucked a tired, but happy little girl into bed, and I was ready to go to bed myself shortly after that. Vincent asked if he could take out a set of twinkling lights to put around the manger. "Adrienne would like it, Mom."

"You're right. Go ahead, honey, but don't stay up too late."

The next morning, I woke to hear little-girl squeals. Adrienne ran in the bedroom and jumped on the bed. "Is it Christmas, Mommy? Is it?"

"No, honey, not for three more days."

Vincent stood in the doorway rubbing his eyes. "What's going on?"

"Adrienne thought it was Christmas."

He grinned despite his words. "Adrienne, you're just a dumb little kid."

"But, come see. It looks like Christmas." She dragged me out of bed, pulling on my nightgown, and, sure enough, it did look like Christmas.

Vincent had left on the twinkling lights around the manger scene, bathing the figures with a soft light. He had found our wreath and hung it in the front window, and he had arranged hollies and red candles on the kitchen table. A tall cardboard Santa stood on the inside of the front door. Santa looked like he was on his way inside.

It took so little to make Adrienne happy. I decided right then and there that we had a right to enjoy this holiday. And I was going to make it as special as I could for my uncomplaining family.

"Vincent, you take care of your sister. I'm

going shopping."

"But, Mom. . . ." Vincent said. He was aware of our low finances.

"It's all right, honey. I have a little left. We can at least have a good Christmas dinner."

"Let's have turkey and pumpkin pie!" Adrienne said with excitement in her voice.

"How about chicken and pumpkin pie?" I asked.

She clapped her hands, and I knew she'd be fine.

It was hard to stick to my list and pass up all the goodies. I tried not to think of the wonderful stuffed turkeys we'd had at Kenny's grandmother's house. She was famous for her cranberry-orange relish, sweet-potato pie, and other treats.

A small roasting chicken will be just as good as a turkey, I thought. Trying to convince myself, I picked up ingredients for my homemade stuffing. A few potatoes and a can of cranberry sauce completed my dinner menu. I had everything I needed for piecrust at home, so I bought a can of pumpkin filling, canned milk, and eggs. We would stuff ourselves on pumpkin pie, I decided. Then, I saw two candy canes for the kids' stockings that I couldn't resist.

After I made my purchases, I was surprised to find I had seven dollars left. I bought a small metal car like the ones Vincent had been collecting since he was little. This one was a blue convertible, which I knew he didn't have.

I also bought a small teddy bear to fulfill at least one of Adrienne's wishes. *Let her believe her angel did it,* I thought. *It's good for a little girl to have some of her dreams come true.* Two chocolate candy bars and a foil-wrapped chocolate Santa for Adrienne completed my shopping.

I was near Hilton's, so I decided to stop in and thank Louis for the dinner.

As I walked into the café, Louis looked at my small bag. "Those are your kids' presents?"

"Just stuff for their stockings," I said, hedging. To change the subject, I asked how his wife's mother was doing.

"She died last month, Beth. It will be a tough holiday for Ivonne."

"I'm so sorry. I didn't know."

"That's all right, you didn't really know her. Besides, you're going to have a tough Christmas, too."

Could he know how bad off we are? I wondered.

"When you get a tree with that great piny smell, it's going to be—"

"No tree this year, Louis," I interrupted.

"Beth, the kids should have a tree. Let me—"

"No, Louis, no tree," I said.

I hoped I'd made it clear. Louis had done enough. I didn't want him to do any more for us than he already had. He had been more than kind to me and my family.

The day before Christmas Eve I got the kids up early and took them to mass. Adrienne talked to Father Ramsey for a few minutes after the service, while Vincent introduced me to a friend from school and his parents. We spoke briefly, then went home.

"Father Ramsey told me tomorrow's the night Santa comes, Mommy."

"That's right, honey. Let's hope he finds our house."

Vincent walked up ahead with her and I heard him

tell her that he'd read in the paper that Santa had a problem. The elves had had the flu and couldn't make very many toys this year. He turned and winked at me.

Adrienne came back and took my hand. She had put on her pouty face. "But, Mommy, the angels promised I could have my teddy bear," she said.

"Now, Adrienne, you didn't really talk to the angels, did you?"

"I did! And they told me there'd be a tree and a teddy bear and presents for you and Vincent, too."

"Well, baby, we usually get at least one wish on Christmas—wouldn't a teddy bear be nice?"

She nodded, smiling, then said, "And a tree."

I knew I couldn't scrape up enough money for even a bargain tree late on Christmas Eve. I just hoped she wouldn't be too disappointed.

Christmas Eve dawned even more gray and dismal than the day before. It was depressing.

I wrapped the little gifts I'd bought and hid them in my closet. I started the stuffing in preparation for Christmas dinner. We'd have to make do with scrambled eggs tonight. I'd have to go for food stamps next week.

I mixed the pumpkin and spices together and rolled out the pie dough. I started to feel a little Christmas spirit. Carols played softly on the radio, and Vincent was helping Adrienne draw a Christmas tree on a big piece of cardboard we'd found in the basement. The spices made it smell like Christmas even if it didn't feel like it.

We ate our scrambled eggs while the pies baked.

"It smells great in here, Mom," Vincent said.

"When do we get to eat the pies, Mommy?"

Adrienne asked.

"You pie monster," I teased. "They're for Christmas dinner."

"Oh, Mommy," they moaned.

"Well, maybe a little piece after church. It should be cool enough to cut by then, and after all, we have two pies."

The evening mass was a Christmas vigil. Everyone held lighted candles, the choir sang softly. Several people spoke to us after Mass, although we didn't stay long. The gray day had turned into a black night with a light drizzle falling steadily.

As I turned to leave, Father Ramsey pressed an envelope into my hand.

"What's this, Father?"

"A Christmas gift, so don't you dare open it until tomorrow. Just put it under your tree."

I didn't bother telling him there was no tree. I put up a little decorative pine, but it wasn't a tree.

"See, Mommy. Father Ramsey knows there'll be a tree!" Adrienne pulled me close and whispered, "The angels must have told him."

She had so much faith! What would I say to her tomorrow?

Our house wasn't far from the church, but it had become colder and the dampness lent more of a chill to the air.

"Let's hurry, kids. It's freezing."

A truck half full of Christmas trees rumbled by us.

"They must be the ones that didn't sell," Vincent said.

How sad, I thought. *And Adrienne wants one so much.*

"Wonder what they do with them?" Vincent

asked. I knew he was thinking the same thing.

"I don't know, son."

We started down our long, dark street, one lone streetlight guiding us home. It stood halfway down the street directly in front of our house. As we walked, I began to notice the change. The rain had turned to snow, and by the time we reached our house, they were huge, wet snowflakes.

"It's going to be a white Christmas," Vincent yelled.

"It's a Christmas miracle," I said. I smiled in remembrance. "That's what my mother said every snowy Christmas Eve."

We were in front of the house now, and I was fumbling in my purse for the key, when Adrienne started jumping up and down, screaming, "The angels came! The angels were here!"

Vincent had to grab her to keep her from running into the street.

"Mommy! Mommy! Look, the angels brought our tree, just like they said." There, in the middle of the street, smack in front of our house, was a huge, bushy pine tree!

Of course, I'll always believe that tree fell off the truck that passed by us, but then again, as Vincent said, "The angels could have knocked one off the truck right in front of our house."

Knowing we'd never find the owner of the truck, we dragged it into the house. Adrienne had her Christmas tree. We decorated it with more of Grandmom's treasures, then had a piece of pumpkin pie. I tucked a happy Adrienne into bed that night.

Vincent gave me a big hug before he turned in.

"MOMMY, I TALKED TO THE ANGELS"

"It's going to be a merry Christmas, Mom."

After the kids were in bed, I filled the stockings, hung them on the window ledge, and sat for a few minutes in the glow of the Christmas lights, letting the true peace of Christmas settle in. Then I turned out the lights and went to bed.

Adrienne was up bright and early. She bounced on the bed. "Mommy, it's Christmas!" she exclaimed.

She raced to the living room, stood in front of the tree, and clapped her hands in delight. "I didn't dream it! It's our Christmas tree!" She turned toward the window. "Our stockings are filled!" She ran back down the hall. "Vincent, come quick! The angels filled our stockings. Hurry!"

She was dragged him down the hall, while he tried to wipe the sleep from his eyes.

"Merry Christmas, Mom," was all he had time to say.

Adrienne pulled him over to the stockings. Then she said, "Candy canes," and at the same time ripped the wrapping off of the teddy bear. "A teddy bear! My own teddy!"

"I told you, Mommy. A tree, a teddy bear, a candy cane, and pumpkin pie. It's Christmas. The angels told me we'd have Christmas, and they were right."

Vincent came over and gave me a kiss and thanked me for the car. Adrienne heard and corrected him saying, "The angels brought it, silly."

So, we have a new tradition—the angels brought Christmas joy instead of Santa. *Nice tradition,* I thought.

Just then the doorbell rang. It was Louis and Ivonne. There were "Merry Christmases" all around and hugs and kisses. When things settled down a bit, Louis whispered that Ivonne had been feeling pretty low. He thought she needed to be with people—kids.

Turning to Adrienne, he said, "By the way I'd swear I saw some kind of white thing outside your door when we pulled up."

"That's snow, Louis. Christmas snow!"

"No, it wasn't the snow."

"What was it then?" she said, curious now.

"It was hard to tell because of all the snow around it, but I could have sworn it had wings."

I flashed him a look, but he ignored me, and Adrienne was already headed for the door. "An angel, an angel!" She opened the door and there sat a huge, white sack. "Mommy, Mommy, look!" Adrienne said as she and Vincent dragged the sack in the house, and then they started pulling gaily wrapped packages out. "Vincent, there's one with my name on it. Is there one with Mommy's name on it, too?"

"There sure is, Adrienne." While she started ripping off the brightly colored paper, Vincent passed me a box and started opening his.

I could feel the tears starting just as Louis stood up and bellowed, "Okay, ladies, get that oven going. I've got a huge turkey in the car that's going to take hours to cook."

Ivonne and I laughed and headed for the kitchen.

"Mommy, look." It was a huge, fluffy teddy bear. "It's a daddy bear for my little baby bear."

But there's no daddy for my little girl, I thought. The tears came now, rolling silently down my cheeks. I turned my head quickly and brushed them

125

away. Ivonne put her arm around my shoulder and comforted me. Tears were in her eyes, too.

Vincent was excitedly showing me a remote control car that he had just opened. There were other toys for the kids, too.

Then Louis was coming in, loaded with not only a turkey, but also fresh vegetables: broccoli, carrots, yams, canned corn, and peas. He also brought fresh rolls, butter, milk, eggs, and an enormous bag of marshmallows, which Adrienne saw immediately.

"Now we can have cocoa with marshmallows for Christmas breakfast."

"I'll get the cocoa," Vincent said.

"And I'll get the milk," Ivonne said.

"And I'll fry the eggs, while you stuff the turkey. But first. . . ." Louis handed me the big fancy box that I hadn't opened. Naturally, I cried some more.

"Stop your blubbering. That's good paper you're crying on."

I tore away the paper and lifted the lid. When I parted the layers of tissue inside, I found a warm, bright red, winter coat.

"Mommy, the angels did it. They remembered everything," Adrienne said.

"They certainly did." I looked from Louis to Ivonne, then back to Adrienne. "And we can never thank them enough."

"I will tonight when I say my prayers, Mommy."

"While you're thanking the angels, add one more item to the list, because they're really looking out for you," Louis said.

"What do you mean?" I asked.

"After all this time, Ellen's husband got a terrific job. Now she plans to stay home and take care of the kids."

My heart started pounding as I listened. Louis continued, "He told her to finish out the week since we're so busy, but starting the twenty-ninth, I need a new waitress on the day shift." He smiled. "Ellen told me to be sure you grab it, and Naomi said you better take it because she's not training another one."

I had begun to feel warm inside, thinking now we could make it. Suddenly, I remembered. "Louis, I still don't have a baby-sitter for Adrienne. I can't work during the day."

"What about the day-care center at the church?" he asked.

I didn't want anything more from these wonderful friends, so I ignored the question rather than tell him I had no money to pay for day-care.

Ivonne gave me a hug. "It's a day for miracles Beth. Maybe your Christmas angel will come up with one more. Now let's get that turkey in the oven."

A few minutes later, Adrienne came running into the kitchen again waving an envelope. "You forgot Father Ramsey's present."

"It's probably a Christmas card, honey." I tore it open and inside were ten fifty-dollar bills and a white card with a outline of a golden angel on it. It read:

Dear Mrs. Cahner,

A little angel whispered in God's ear that you might need help with the January rent. He put the word out and some good angels came up with money for the rent. The angels have also asked our day-care mothers to take care of Adrienne from

"MOMMY, I TALKED TO THE ANGELS"

January 2 to 31, for absolutely no charge, so her mom can go job hunting. Tell Adrienne her faith in prayer and her angels has not gone unnoticed.

Merry Christmas and God Bless,

Father Ramsey and his angels

"My goodness," Louis said, "whatever's in that card has got her crying again." Vincent came over, took the card from my hand, and read it aloud.

Vincent looked at me for a minute, but didn't say anything.

"What's wrong, Vincent?" I asked.

"It doesn't start until January second."

"Well, aren't you off from school till then?" Louis asked.

"I was saving it until after dinner, for a surprise," Vincent said, actually blushing. "I got a job starting tomorrow until school starts. Mr. Lincoln, the auto parts dealer, needs help stocking new merchandise at the store." He smiled at me.

"I'm so proud of you, Vincent." I hugged my grown-up little boy tightly. "Hey, Louis," I asked. "How about holding that job open for me for a few days?"

Ivonne had been quietly standing by Louis, but now she spoke out firmly. "No way, Beth. Then he'll expect me to fill in for you, and I'm too old to be on my feet all day."

"But—" I began to say.

She interrupted. "No buts. You go to work on the twenty-ninth, and I'll be here before seven A.M. to take care of this little sweetheart." She had Adrienne in her arms then, and I knew finally, that everything was going to be all right.

The angels had taken care of everything.

"MOMMY, I TALKED TO THE ANGELS"

That magical Christmas is in the past now, and we are already enjoying an early spring.

The café is doing great. Louis hired a business manager to run the place. He introduced him to me one day and then said, "I'm getting too old to do it all, Beth. Carl's going to save me a lot of work."

It wasn't love at first sight, but I certainly did notice him that first day. All the waitresses did, too. We started going to the movies or dancing on the weekends. Sometimes he would come over, and we'd watch TV and make popcorn.

I felt good when I walked beside him, and I felt warm inside when he held my hand. His kisses have melted that cold spot in my heart. There's still a lot of leftover hurt from Kenny, but I think Carl might be the one to finally take all the hurt away.

It might be out of my hands, anyway. The first time I took Carl home to meet the kids, Adrienne got terribly excited. "I knew it! I knew it!" she said with happiness in her voice.

Carl and I looked at each other, puzzled. He stooped down and took her tiny hands in his, and asked, "What did you know, sweetie?"

She leaned over and said, "I prayed that the angels would send me a new daddy, and here you are."

"Adrienne," I said.

He had stood there, grinning and enjoying my embarrassment. Suddenly, still holding one of Adrienne's hands, he took mine with the other and said very seriously, "I could never figure out why I answered Louis's ad. I was passing through this little town on my way to a big-time office job." He paused to see if he had our attention, then continued, saying, "I stopped for coffee, and when I glanced through the newspaper, the ad practically jumped off the page at me. Suddenly, managing a café appealed to me, and, suddenly, I found myself walking around town.

"I fell in love with the lovely old houses and the quietness of the town. It became totally irresistible, and I called Louis. He hired me on the spot."

He looked into my eyes, once again stirring feelings that I thought I'd never have again.

"You know, Adrienne, a young man handed me that newspaper when I walked into the coffee shop that day. Now that I think about it, he looked very much like an angel."

Carl, Adrienne, Vincent, and I get along very well. Vincent told me that he'll keep his part-time job, even if Carl and I decide to get married. He says he likes being responsible. And Adrienne keeps praying and hoping that she'll have a new daddy.

I love being in love with a man who won't run away when difficult times come. And I thank God daily for Adrienne's faith and for leading Carl to me.

Of course, miracles still occur. I know because God sent me a miracle. He gave me kids that will love me and a man who wants to share in that love. I thank God every day for His miracle.   THE END

MY BABY CALLS ME FROM HEAVEN

My miracle happened a year ago tonight, although it seems like just yesterday. It took place on Christmas Eve, and like that first Christmas centuries ago, replaced bitterness with peace and love.

Tonight as I write, snow is filtering softly past my window. It was like that on the night I talk of, and I'm carried back to its memory. Tonight, I feel I want to share my miracle with you.

But to understand it, you have to go back more than a year. You have to go back three years with me.

Darlene and I had been married only a short time then, and one day she told me we were going to have a child. We talked far into the night, happy with the knowledge that soon we would be three. And we were excited—like children ourselves.

Later on I began to know something of what Darlene was to face. She became sick too frequently, it seemed to me, even though she laughed it off. I began marking time as the months passed, began dreading the ordeal that was facing the woman I loved.

I don't think Darlene even noticed my fear. She was so happy, too happy to complain or be afraid.

There was a new sweetness about her, and her eyes took on a soft glow. Darlene was eager to be a mother and was thrilled over what was happening to her. I tried to gain some assurance from watching her, but the fear never quite left me.

I'll never forget the night she tugged at my arm. "Damien . . . Damien." I awoke fast, knowing what it was. "Damien," she whispered, "it's time. Call the doctor."

Her voice was tiny, her breath short. But still she smiled at me.

We rode to the hospital close in spirit and mind—and in body, too. I could almost feel the pain that tormented her. Here it was . . . then she relaxed. Then the pain came again. After one particularly tough one, she squeezed my arm.

"I think it's worse for you than for me, Damien," she said. "But it isn't really bad for me, darling. It's our child."

They rushed Darlene into bed at the hospital, but they let me see her for a minute. I kissed her gently, and she smiled at me again.

"Don't be frightened, Damien. We're so lucky, you and I. We're going to have a baby. God doesn't let people down, not when they want something as much as we do."

I didn't want my wife to see my face then, since tears were filling my eyes. I felt so helpless, so awkward. There was nothing I could do, and there was so much I wanted to do. I wanted to share Darlene's pain, to lessen in some way the strain that showed in her eyes, but I was helpless.

For a moment, I sat on the edge of her bed, my face buried in her hair, and we were closer than we ever had been. Then they took Darlene away.

When she returned, she came back alone. Literally alone.

The baby lived only a few brief hours. Something had happened—his life was over before it had had a chance to begin.

Something else happened, too. Darlene almost didn't make it. The doctors kept her in the delivery room for hours and were with her for hours more when they brought her back to her room. And I knew a greater terror than any I had ever felt—fear for the life of the woman I loved.

I forgot the baby. I hadn't known him. It was Darlene, her life a matter of a weak heartbeat and a muffled pulse—Darlene, near death for hours, fighting for her life.

For two days and two nights, I lived a nightmare. I neither slept nor ate except for an occasional cup of coffee the nurse insisted that I drink. Finally, they let me be with her. She was sobbing fitfully, calling my name now and then. I held her hand and prayed as I had never prayed before.

God heard my prayer.

Her very first words stabbed my heart. "The baby . . . how's our baby, Damien?"

I had to tell her. I had to crush the little-girl sweetness of that drawn face. I had to watch her dimpled smile fade.

"A heart condition?" Her voice was low.

"Yes, darling."

"Did you see him, Damien?"

I told her that I hadn't. I didn't tell her he meant nothing to me. But I did whisper all the love that flooded through my heart. In a moment she was asleep again, her face tight with tears that didn't come.

I had thought she would take away the baby's things in the nursery and convert the room back into a den, but she didn't. She was more quiet now, more thoughtful than before. But in her serenity was a beauty that motherhood—however brief and tragic—had placed there.

Darlene's new sweetness grew and enveloped me. She knew that life had to go on in spite of misfortune, and it was her way to make it happy for both of us.

I never did quite forget that night of fear, though, that night I had prayed so desperately to God to let Darlene live. That's why I was so glad and relieved when the doctor told Darlene, after a routine checkup, that she shouldn't try to have a baby again, that it would be too dangerous for her.

A year passed, then another six months. Darlene was pregnant again, and I became frightened, remembering the doctor's words.

I tried, of course, to be as sweet to Darlene as possible, tried to understand why she wanted children, why she wanted to risk her life. But there was bitterness in my heart.

I was always remembering the doctor's warning—when I looked at Darlene, when I heard her singing, when I held her close at night. I thought of being without her and I knew I could never bear such a life. And so I began to hate and resent the child that was growing within her.

It was on Christmas Eve, almost a year ago tonight, that we were sitting in front of our open fireplace while the flames danced gaily before our eyes. The only other light in the room was from our Christmas tree. There was warmth and comfort and I should've been happy, as I had been happy with Darlene on other Christmas Eves. But I felt an intruder in our midst, a third party who was risking Darlene's life.

The labor pains began about eight. We should have been opening Christmas gifts, but it was not to be that way. By ten I had called the doctor, and a few minutes later we were driving toward the hospital, cautiously because of the snow. It was a different drive this time. Fear rode with us.

Darlene had never said whether she knew how I felt. Right then she looked just as she had before.

But fear was in me—and hate. I hated that child.

By eleven, I was sitting alone in the hospital corridor. Lights on a small Christmas tree blinked off and on. Life . . . and death. They seemed to have a grim rhythm. I was numb with fear.

I didn't want the baby, only Darlene. I would never love this child if anything happened to my wife.

It was almost midnight when a nurse came hurrying down the hall.

"Nurse. My wife?"

The nurse smiled in sudden compassion and walked toward me. "She's all right, Mr. Anderson. And she said something you ought to know. She was praying to God to make Him help you to understand why she wanted this child."

"Then she'll pull through?"

MY BABY CALLS ME FROM HEAVEN

"Mrs. Anderson will be fine. Don't you worry. But there's trouble with the child—a little girl. We won't know for a while whether we can save her."

Tears were in my eyes. Darlene was all right. Darlene was fine. She was going to live.

And then it hit me—something I'd been too selfish to realize in the past nine months. Darlene must've known my thoughts, even though I had been silent. She must have known the hatred I felt—and known that it was hatred born of fear. Yet she had known something more, something only a woman can know—that life would be complete for us only if we had a son or a daughter.

So she'd taken the risk—and I had been a coward.

Oh, how I loved her.

And—strangely, suddenly—I loved the baby. I wanted our little girl to live.

I wandered out of the hospital without my coat. I passed a man I didn't know, but he smiled at me. "Merry Christmas," he said. I couldn't answer, for I knew my voice would be choked. But I smiled back as best as I could, for now I knew the real meaning of Christmas. It was love. I looked upward, and I stopped walking, for I saw a star. A star that held hope and promise for me, as it held hope and promise for men before.

I saw the curved doorway of a church, and I walked slowly over to the door and opened it. Close to the altar, I knelt and prayed for our daughter. She had to live.

Then suddenly, a little boy appeared in the room. He looked really familiar to me. He walked over to me and said, "I've come from heaven to tell you everything will be all right. I wish I had a chance to know you, but I'll know you when you come to our Father's kingdom. Now I have to go. I'll call you from heaven whenever I need to tell you something."

Before I could respond to him, he left. I couldn't believe what had just happened to me. Then I realized why he looked so familiar. He was my son—my son that had died and gone to heaven. And he had come to let me know that everything was going to be all right.

It's Christmas again, and my heart is full of gratitude because I am remembering my Christmas miracle. You see, our daughter did live. She's asleep in her room. I thank God every day for allowing my little boy to come to me. My little boy helped me to replace the bitterness in my heart with love. And I'm glad to know that he's in God's care.   THE END

MY VISIT FROM BEYOND

A MESSAGE FROM BEYOND

At eighty-one years of age, I realize that my parents could not possibly be living anymore. It is not so much their loss that I, a survivor of the Holocaust, am still mourning, but the ignominious way in which they died at the hands of the Nazis.

One night not long ago, after a particularly sadness-filled day, I woke up to see my parents standing at the foot of my bed. Dad wore his pepper-and-salt coat, and Mom, her ankle-length, gray velvet dress. Dad had his arm around Mom's shoulder, and both lifted a threatening finger at me.

"Please stop crying for us!" Mom said. "We can't be at peace until you are."

As I sat up and tried to touch them, they retreated and disappeared. Their message from beyond comforted me, and I have been feeling better ever since.   THE END

MY VISIT FROM BEYOND

VISIT FROM AN ANGEL

Dreams of my precious little nephew lying in his tiny casket had been haunting me for over a week. This night was no exception, so I quietly climbed out of bed and slipped out of the bedroom so as not to wake my sister. My brothers were both asleep, and my parents had gone out for the evening with friends and had not yet returned.

My thoughts drifted back to the day, only eighteen short months ago, that my nephew was born. I'd never realized then how ill he was. I knew he had cerebral palsy, but I really didn't know what that meant at the time. He had to have physical therapy daily because he had no control over his motor nerves, and he never smiled, talked, or walked because of his illness. When he was born, we were told by his doctors that he would probably die within the first six months of his life. But when we celebrated his first birthday, I knew that the doctors had been wrong.

Then, one night my brother-in-law called to tell us that my nephew had died. Although I was fifteen years old, I really didn't understand death. I did know, however, that death was final. It was at that moment that the idea to commit suicide came to mind. It seemed like the perfect solution. I would be with my nephew forever, and never again feel the pain his death was causing me.

I cradled my head on my arms as I cried. But then I felt something brush against my leg and I raised my head. When I looked down, I couldn't believe my eyes. My precious little nephew was smiling up at me!

"Don't cry for me. I'm okay!" was all he said, and then he walked toward the hallway and out the door. Just then, my parents walked in.

I turned for a brief moment, and when I looked back my nephew was gone.

I told my parents that my nephew had just been there, and that he said he didn't want us to be sad because he was okay. We went and sat down at the table so I could explain to them everything that had happened. When I finished, my father suggested that maybe I had fallen asleep and dreamed the whole thing. But I knew, in my heart, that my nephew had been there to visit me.

Suddenly, my mother stood up with her back to us. When she turned back around she had tears streaming down her face. She pointed to the carpet, and there, imprinted in the carpet, were tiny footprints. They led away from the table, and they disappeared at the entrance to the hallway. She believed, then, that my nephew had really been there.

I will always be grateful to my nephew for taking away the terrible ache in my heart. And I will never forget my visit from my precious little angel.   THE END

DEAR DADDY

My father died suddenly when I was just barely sixteen years old. I had never really felt close to him and regretted that as I was on the verge of adulthood, he was taken from me. I always felt our relationship wasn't complete. Although he loved me, he could never express his feelings.

Years later, I married. After several years of marriage, we decided to have children. A year later, we were thrilled when I found out I was pregnant. Tragedy struck, however, and in the sixth month I miscarried. It took another nine months to get pregnant again, and the doctor assured us that there was no reason to believe this baby wouldn't survive.

But our little boy was stillborn, and our hearts were crushed. I didn't know if I could ever even think about getting pregnant again. We had lost two children already. I told my husband I'd need some time to think over whether or not I wanted to try again. Maybe, I thought, the pain just isn't worth it.

On a bright day, I was drawn to the cemetery where my children were buried. I parked my car and walked over the acres of green velvet to the small markers where my two little angels rested. I stood there in the sunlight, staring at the markers, when I felt a presence. I looked up and saw a man standing about ten feet ahead of me. He was motionless, smiling, and watching me. I should have been afraid of this stranger, but I wasn't at all. I asked him if I could help him. He said, no, but he could help me.

When he was standing just a step away from me, I knew who he was. He was my father! "Daddy?" I cried. He answered, yes, he'd come to tell me that he loved me. I told him I loved him, too, and reached out my hand, wanting with all my heart to embrace him. His smile faded, and he told me to have hope. Looking down at the graves, he said to keep trying to have babies and to not give up hope.

MY VISIT FROM BEYOND

I held out my arms, tears of joy flooding my eyes and flowing down my cheeks. Daddy smiled again. When I'd blinked away my tears he was gone, but my heart was full of love and I knew that old wound had been healed.

I took his advice and kept trying to have children. Today we have a beautiful son and daughter. My visit from beyond not only healed the empty feeling with my father, but gave me the faith to try again. Today I have children in my life because of the visit from Daddy!

THE END

A CHRISTMAS VISIT

It was December and my grandmother was very ill. Granny's faith always amazed me. She could handle every family crisis. I'd see her lift her chin, straighten her back, then fold her hands in prayer.

She'd been growing weaker for over a year, but as winter progressed she rapidly went downhill. She was in and out of the hospital and we knew her time with us was growing short.

Finally, the doctors told us they had done all they could for her, and that it was simply a matter of days until she died. The week before Christmas Granny was still in the hospital. A tiny Christmas tree adorned her bedside table. Relatives were milling about, wanting to have one last visit with the lovely woman who had touched each of their lives. At lunchtime they all went out for something to eat, but I wanted a quiet moment with my grandmother. I asked her what she wanted for Christmas. She told me she'd like to have Christmas dinner with the Lord. Her words made my heart ache, but I knew it was really what she wanted. She was tired and her poor body was a painful prison for her. I nodded that I understood.

Granny asked if I had a Christmas wish. Yes! My heart screamed, I want you with me always! Just two years earlier, I had moved back home from sunny Southern California. I said I wished it would snow for Christmas. I hadn't seen a white Christmas in a long time.

Granny smiled weakly. I squeezed her hand. I knew I was tiring her out.

I went home and prayed for my grandma. The next day the doctors sent her home for Christmas. She went to stay with my aunt in the next town.

Granny grew weaker each day, and finally, the day before Christmas Eve, she slipped quietly away. I managed to cope that day and Christmas Eve. I stayed busy cooking and cleaning. My kids helped me take my mind off Granny's passing, too. They were too young to really understand the concept of death, and of course they were excited about Santa.

After the kids were in bed and I was huddled in mine, I cried endless tears for my tremendous loss. I didn't cry for my grandma; I knew her Christmas wish would be realized, she'd dine with the Lord. Hours later, I finally fell into a fitful sleep, but woke early Christmas morning. For that time of year, the weather was colder than usual. Dressed in long pants and a sweater, I poured my coffee with a heavy heart. I was mourning Christmas without Grandma.

MY VISIT FROM BEYOND

Opening the blinds, I stared in wonder out the window. White movement suddenly caught my eye. Snow! With each flake, my heart felt lighter. I knew that Granny remembered my Christmas wish.

Now, each time it snows, I smile and remember my Christmas gift from Granny, and I realize that she will always be with me.   THE END

❦

MY MYSTERIOUS GARDEN GUEST

My husband and I had just moved in to a new house and didn't know anyone in the neighborhood. A few days after we moved in, I noticed that an elderly lady would always walk down our street, and occasionally she would stop and look up at my house.

One day, I happened to be in my yard, working in my garden, when I looked up and saw the mysterious woman. I started to speak to her, but she was gone before I had a chance. I was a bit startled, so I went back into the house, and my husband told me that I looked a bit frightened. He asked me what was wrong. It took me awhile, but I explained what happened and asked him if he'd ever seen the old woman. But he hadn't.

I forgot about the strange woman for a few weeks, but then one day, while I was planting flowers in my front yard, a young lady approached me. She introduced herself as my new neighbor.

"Mrs. Taylor would adore those flowers you're planting," she said to me.

145

MY VISIT FROM BEYOND

I asked her who Mrs. Taylor was, and she told me she was the elderly woman that had lived in my house before we'd moved in. Her children had placed her in a nursing home, and she had died about a year ago.

I was about to tell my neighbor about the woman I'd seen walking around my house, but I decided that she might think I was crazy. But I knew that what I had seen was real. I knew that the mysterious woman was Mrs. Taylor, and that she was checking up to be sure that her garden was being cared for.

I've never seen Mrs. Taylor again, but I think of her every year when I work in my garden. I have a feeling she likes the pretty flowers I've been planting in "her" yard. THE END

MY GRANDMOTHER'S LOVE

I was the youngest in my adopted family and at times I felt unwanted by everyone but my grandmother. I always loved being with her and doing things for her. She would stick up for me when I had arguments with my adopted parents or my adopted sister. She was not only my grandmother, she was my best friend! There were even times when I could feel that I could read her mind. She was in her nineties and spoke mostly Italian.

One night when I was seventeen years old, I had awakened with a strange sensation that my grandmother needed me. I was heading out the door when a call came from my aunt, that my grandmother had fallen and gotten hurt. I drove straight to the hospital so I could be there when she arrived. She was in a great deal of pain so they took her straight into surgery to place a pin in her hip.

A few days later when she able to speak, she said that she had a dream that I was ten years old and was spending the night in her apartment. She said it was cold and she got up to get me another blanket when she had fallen. I told my grandmother that I loved her.

Shortly after my eighteenth birthday, I was watching TV when I felt my grandmother in the room. I turned toward her favorite chair, and there she sat! She looked at me and said good-bye. I thought I was imagining things. Then the phone rang and it was my adopted mother to say that my grandmother had just passed away, and she wanted to make sure that she said good-bye to me. I was so disappointed that I was not at the hospital, but I was told to go home earlier that day because I was exhausted. I tried to be strong, but as soon as I hung up I cried.

That night I had a hard time sleeping. I was very sad over the death of my grandmother. I felt so empty and when I did sleep it was fitful. Later on I was awakened to find my grandmother standing at the end of my bed watching me. I told her that I didn't want her to go and that I felt responsible for her death. She just shook her head and wanted me to rest. She tucked me in and kissed my forehead. I fell into a deep sleep thinking of her.

I woke up the next morning to find her favorite rosary under my pillow along with the broach that she wore on her Sunday dress. To this day, I don't know how they got there, but I cherish the gift.

I only wish that she was alive to see my two children. I think she has seen them, because my oldest told me he saw a strange woman standing at the foot of his bed. At first he thought it was me, but when he reached out, the woman faded away. My grandmother is always in my thoughts and when I feel lonely, I can feel her with me and I become stronger.

THE END

❦

MY LOYAL SNOWFLAKE

When I was five years old, my parents gave me a female puppy. Even though she was pitch black in color, I named her Snowflake. My parents laughed, saying that she was a St. Louis snowflake, dirty from smog. We called her Flaky.

Over the years, Flaky proved to be a very loyal pet. One day she was giving birth to a litter of puppies, and she knew when my school bus arrived. She stopped having pups long enough to walk the quarter of a mile to the bus stop to walk me home. She was my best friend, and as an only child, she was all I needed. When I was sixteen and busy with my teenage escapades, my loyal best friend became sick. Flaky had never been sick before, and I felt guilty for pushing her aside. I came home from school one afternoon and was worried when she didn't greet me at the drive. I went searching for her and found her lying in the grass in the backyard. When she saw me, she started wagging her tail.

Flaky tried to stand up, but she was too weak. Then I realized just how serious her illness was. With tears rolling down my face, I carried her into the house and laid her on my bed. When my dad came in from work, I begged him to let me stay home from school to be with her. We all knew she was dying. I think my dad knew watching her go would be too painful for me, so he sent me to school.

That next morning before leaving for school, I went back to my room one last time to see Flaky. Crying like a baby, I told her I loved her and kissed her good-bye. Even as I write this eleven years later, the tears are as fresh as they were then. She wagged her tail as best she could and licked a tear from my cheek.

During second period, in my food service class, I was busy with assembling ingredients for pancakes when I felt a rubbing against my leg. I jumped back to see what it was and saw nothing. Just then I heard Flaky's bark and I felt like my heart fell to the floor.

I ran from the classroom, down two flights to the secretary's office and quickly called home. When my mother answered the phone she sounded upset.

"She's gone, isn't she?" I asked. Mom told me it had just happened and she wanted to know how I knew. I never told her that Flaky had come to say good-bye.

As loyal as Flaky was in all the years we spent together, I have no doubt in my mind that even upon her death, she felt she had to let me know she was okay. I have family pets now, but none of them could hold a candle to Flaky. THE END

BURIED TREASURE

My grandfather was a wonderful man. It was horrible to watch him simply waste away after the doctors diagnosed him with terminal cancer. Always an assiduous saver, Grandpa had hinted at a hidden cache of money stashed somewhere within the confines of his messy basement. Even though he was weakening, Grandpa still stubbornly refused to divulge the whereabouts of what he referred to as, "the stash."

Unfortunately for us all, after a few months of relative quietude, my beloved grandpa went downhill quickly. He was hospitalized, so weak that even sitting up in bed was an impossibility. He tried valiantly to convey information about the hidden money to my mother and grandmother during the next months, as he lingered on in constant pain. After some three months in the hospital, Grandpa's suffering finally came to an end.

Fortunately, my grandparents' insurance paid for most of the medical bills, but there were still the funeral expenses to contend with. Grandma needed "the stash" more than ever. Mom, Grandma, and I had made a thorough search through Grandpa's belongings, but to no avail. We thought that perhaps Grandpa's fervent yet mostly indecipherable attempts to communicate toward the end had been to tell us that he had spent the money, or put it with some emergency cash he had saved in a safety deposit box. We gave up all hope of ever locating "the stash."

Several months passed, and as I was playing one day in the basement with my dog, I wandered into the cluttered room which housed my grandfather's tools. Also present was a large amount of craft supplies belonging to my grandmother, and a huge assortment of junk. My mind was on finding a craft project with which to while away the rest of the rainy afternoon; the missing money hadn't passed through my thoughts for weeks.

Suddenly, I had a prickly sort of sensation that someone was nearby, watching. Puzzled, I looked around, but no one was there. Even the dog had retreated to cleaner pastures. My glance was drawn inexplicably to a large tray laden with smooth rocks that we had gathered on a vacation years earlier, intending to take advantage of the pet rock craze. I felt the prickling sensation intensify as I moved toward the rocks, and the room seemed to fairly hum with an electric sort of energy. I lifted a toy ukulele from atop the smooth stones, revealing the corner of something metallic. My hands trembled as I removed the rocks to discover two tiny metal trays, tied together by a piece of string so that a slim cavity existed between them. Shakily, I untied the twine to reveal the hidden contents within, a half-inch stack of twenty-dollar bills.

As soon as I discovered the money, the atmosphere of the room changed from one of charged tension to that of great peace. I could hardly believe that I had uncovered Grandpa's "stash." My grandmother wept when I presented her with the $2500 that I had found in the basement. That amount went a lot further sixteen years ago.

I'm thirty-three now, and in all of the ensuing years, I've never found an explanation for what happened that day, other than that it was my grandfather's presence which led me to an overlooked pile of rocks in Grandpa's basement.　　　THE END

❧

THE ROSARY

My mother passed away suddenly at home in the early morning hours. My sister lived far from home, but flew in the very same day.

Our mom had a sweet habit of coming up behind us, squeezing our shoulders and leaning her head against ours. This was always her little extra touch of affection that she showed us.

My aunt was a nun and had given my mother a most unusual-looking, but beautiful rosary with smoky-colored green beads. I had never seen one like it before or since. My aunt had the rosary blessed by the Pope while she was on a visit to Rome, along with a flask of water. When she gave this gift to my mom, she had a pouch in which she placed both the flask of water and the rosary. Mon carried them with her, from that time on, in her purse.

When my sister woke the following morning as I came out of the bedroom, she said, "You know, I was sitting here in Mom's favorite chair, and I felt her come up behind me, give me a squeeze, and lay her head next to mine. It was the weirdest feeling."

At that time, Mom's purse was still where she had

always kept it, jus a few feet from her chair in the living room.

The next day, when people began to come to the house to pay their respects, I put my mother's purse in her bedroom for safekeeping.

After the funeral, when my sister was preparing to leave to go home, she asked me if she could have Mom's rosary. I told her yes and went to her purse to get it, but, to my dismay, the rosary was gone. Only the flask of water remained. I found this to be strange—Mom never removed the rosary from her purse—but thought maybe she had for some reason put the rosary in her room. I told my sister that when I went through Mom's things and came across the rosary, I would mail it to her. In going through her things, I never found the rosary.

Mom passed away two weeks before her birthday. On the morning of her birthday, my sister phoned me almost in hysterics. The first place my sister always headed upon waking up was to the kitchen to turn on her coffeepot. She said when she got to the kitchen, laying right there next to her coffeepot was our mom's missing rosary. My sister was scared to death. As I calmed her down, I told her there was no reason to be frightened—this was just Mom's way of letting us know that she was okay.

To this day, it is beyond me how that rosary traveled from where I lived to my sister's town. It made me a believer that there is more to death than we can know or explain. I believe that moving the rosary was our mom's way of telling us that everything was fine, and that she was in a divine place.   THE END

MY SISTER'S LAST WISH

I was only seven when my little sister died at the age of five in a car accident. She had told us several weeks before of a dream that she'd had. She told my mother and I that angels had come to see her and told her that they needed her to go with them. She also said that my oldest sister was coming home on Mother's Day to bring her a doll, and that she was not going anywhere until she got her doll.

We really didn't think anything of this, especially since my oldest sister lived nearly a thousand miles away and has never indicated to anyone that she was coming. Then, to our amazement, a few days before Mother's Day, she called and said that we were going to have a family reunion on Mother's Day, and she had made all the arrangements. By that time, though, we had forgotten all about my little sister's dream.

We had beautiful weather on the day of the reunion, with lots of friends and family gathered around us. Our fathers and uncles were fishing, the women were preparing a wonderful picnic lunch, and all of us kids were playing. My oldest sister had brought many gifts for my little sister and I, and the last present we opened turned out to be a matching set of dolls. My doll had a red dress and my sister's wore blue—her favorite color. She had this big grin on her face when she told me, "See, I told you she was bringing me a doll!"

It all happened so fast, that none of us ever had time to react. My little sister had crossed the road to see if Daddy was going to eat, and when she crossed back,

154

she was hit by a drunk driver and killed instantly.

I was devastated. My best friend, playmate, and sister was gone forever. All of a sudden, I felt like an only child, since all of my other sisters were married and lived so far away. I didn't really realize that my grief was so substantial, but I began to lose weight. I was unresponsive in school, and the teachers even called my mother to express their concern.

My mother tried to talk to me, but it didn't help. I just did not think I could face the rest of my life without my dear little sister. Then one afternoon, I was in the school cafeteria, not eating as usual, when I saw a bright light appear, and through that light walked my little sister. She was so beautiful and she looked so happy, I started to cry. She told me then that it was time for her to go, but that I was still needed here on earth to take care of our mother—that she was grieving, too, as much for me as she was for her. I tried to tell her that I wanted to go with her, but she said I was to live my life to the fullest and be happy. Then as quickly as she'd appeared, she was gone.

I soon began to eat and enjoy life again, thanks to my wonderful sister's visit from beyond. I grew up to become a happy adult with a wonderful husband, and I'm still taking care of our mother, just as my dear sister had said I would.   THE END

PLAYING WITH GRANDPA

When I was seven months pregnant, my father was very sick and in the hospital. I asked him to hang on until his granddaughter was born in two months. The strange thing was, I had no idea I was having a girl, or what made me say the word granddaughter.

Sadly, my father passed away before I gave birth, and he couldn't meet his granddaughter.

One night, two years later, I was watching TV and my daughter was in the hall. She was laughing so loudly she scared me, because she was alone. I walked over to see what was going on, but no one was there except my daughter.

I asked her what she was laughing at, and she said Grandpa was being funny and playing with her. I truly believed she saw him.

A few days later, I showed my daughter pictures of different people with my father. She picked him out in each picture and knew that he was her grandpa.

Another time, she was listening to the radio and she started crying. When I asked her why she was crying, she said the song reminded her of Grandpa.

In my heart, I know my father and daughter have a special bond, and he will always look after her. In a spiritual way, my father and daughter have met.

THE END

❧

MY SON'S GUARDIAN ANGEL

When our first child was diagnosed as severely brain damaged, we wept; it was the most tragic crisis we ever would face. He was a beautiful child with bright blue eyes and a happy smile, but the doctors had diagnosed that he would never walk nor sit by himself.

When I learned I was pregnant, my son was three years old. I continued to care for him until it became impossible to lift and carry him due to my condition, and we appealed to the state to place him in a controlled environment where he would have a trained staff to meet his needs.

He was ten years old when the state closed the facility where he resided. We were given the option of bringing him home or placing him in foster care. My husband said no child of his ever would go into a foster home, so we brought him home.

On the day my son arrived home, a care-giver arrived with him in a van and discussed his special needs with me. He was still eating pureed foods and taking a bottle. He wore adult diapers and was subject to seizures, she said.

I wanted to cry when I saw how thin he was, his little arms and legs looked like sticks. I vowed to take the best care of him and to see that he put on some weight. We converted the family room off the kitchen into his bedroom and set up his hospital bed where I could be near him.

Shortly after that, I was drying dishes in the kitchen when I heard the clear summons of a bell. I thought my son had found something to play with near his bed and continued wiping the dishes. The bell sounded again. I stopped to listen. It was so pure and sweet, and it rang exactly three rings each time.

Suddenly, my heart lurched as I raced to his bedside. It was impossible for my son to grasp and hold anything in his hands, and he certainly could not repeat the motion three times in succession.

MY VISIT FROM BEYOND

I was astounded to find his slim body had slid beneath the bars of the bed and he was hanging with his head caught between the steel rails and the mattress. I pushed and shoved until he was safely back in bed, then I searched the room looking for some object that might have made the clear sound of the bell that summoned me.

As I went from object to object in the room, lifting, shaking, rocking the bed, the rails, the dresser—anything and everything—it became evident to me that I had been summoned by my son's guardian angel who remained at his side, unseen, but quite aware of my son's dangerous predicament.   THE END

❧

CHIMES FROM HEAVEN

My husband's sister was only twenty-five years old when she was diagnosed with terminal cancer and given only two months to live. But because of her sheer determination and powerful strength, she proved the doctors wrong.

Her mother had always wanted a grandfather clock for her dining room. So for Christmas, unable to afford a full-size clock, she gave her mother a beautiful wall version of a grandfather clock.

My mother-in-law proudly hung the clock on her dining-room wall, but there was one problem: the hours came and went, but not one chime was heard from the little clock. My sister-in-law was upset and wanted to return it, but her mother refused and insisted the clock stay on the wall—chime or no chime!

MY VISIT FROM BEYOND

My sister-in-law's cancer got progressively worse. By the summer she was bedridden, and by Thanksgiving it was nearly impossible for her to even sit up. A couple of weeks before Christmas she was telling everyone that she'd be "going home" for the holidays.

We all thought it was her medication making her delirious—causing her to think that she was in the hospital and would be going home to be with her family at Christmas. But she knew exactly what she was talking about. On Christmas morning, at about ten minutes to twelve, my sister-in-law said good-bye.

At twelve noon, ten minutes later, the clock, still hanging on my mother-in-law's wall, chimed loudly twelve times. It has been chiming every hour on the hour ever since that day.

We believe that my sister-in-law was, and still is, sending a message to her family, telling them that she is happy and pain-free. Every time that clock chimes we think of her and know that she is watching over us.   THE END

PENNIES FROM HEAVEN

Things have been difficult for me in my adult life. I was raising both of my children without child support and sometimes I worked so hard I didn't know if I was coming or going.

One day I was walking into a gas station to pay for my gas when I noticed something glimmering in the sunlight. I bent down and saw it was a penny. I smiled and thought of my grandmother. She had been dead for almost twenty years, but I still remember the game we played when I was a child. "See a penny pick it up and all day long you'll have good luck," she would say. Of course, she always made sure that I was the one who found it. I picked it up and put it in my pocket without another thought.

Several months later, I was still finding at least two or three pennies a week that I'd save. I began to wonder about this game, but then an extraordinary thing happened. My ex-husband had been found and I started getting the child support that I so desperately needed. After that, things started going in a different direction for me. I was elated.

Today, two years later, I still find at least one penny a week. I started putting them in a jar because my life is still moving in a positive direction. I raised my children, I have a new car, a good job, and I found a wonderful man. I thank my grandmother for smiling down on me.   THE END

※

ENCOURAGING WORDS

I was always one to snicker at the idea of life beyond death. When my daughters were teenagers, I was very depressed, since I was having a problem communicating with one of them. She was spreading her wings too quickly, and way too fast as far as I was concerned.

I didn't believe in drinking or premarital sex, so in my daughter's eyes, I was a square. She had begun staying out all night and I promised her a new coat if she'd stop. Even that didn't work. I knew I was taking the wrong approach by trying to bribe her, but I didn't know what else to do. It seemed that no matter what I said or did, she still came and went as she pleased. Some said I should just let her do what she wanted at home because I'd at least know where she was, but I couldn't let her break my moral code in front of me.

I was so upset during those awful years. Finally, after a big argument, I ordered her out of the house. She moved in with her boyfriend, got pregnant, and they married. The marriage lasted until the baby was a month old.

Then my daughter and granddaughter moved back in with me. But she was still unhappy at home. She married again when her daughter was two years old. Soon after, they moved to Texas. I missed my daughter and granddaughter so much, my heart felt like it would break. I was so upset and disappointed with life.

One morning, I was lying in bed when a strong, but gentle, voice said, "There is hope."

I looked around the room, but there was no one around. I never saw anybody that day, but I know a spirit of some kind had said those encouraging words.

Now, whenever I get upset, I stop, relax, and remember those encouraging words—"There is hope."

THE END

❧

THE IMAGE OF MY MOTHER

My mother died while giving birth to me—a sad

fact which has always haunted me. In fact, it's colored every aspect of my life, up to and including my career choice as a funeral director. The void left by growing up motherless has been deep and painful. As a child, I felt so different and alienated from the other children who proudly bragged about their moms and all the special things they did together. The images of mothers and daughters seemed to be ever present, especially on holidays like Mother's Day and Christmas, always reinforcing the emptiness.

My birthday was especially painful because each year it was a reminder of the day my mother had been taken from me. My only wish was to see the reassuring image of my mother just one more time.

In August of 1993, that prayer was answered. Because of my work as a funeral director, I spend a lot of my time in cemeteries. But the draw to cemeteries and the beyond transcended my work. I found a strange comfort there; the serenity and peace I felt could be found nowhere else.

On a beautiful, sunny August day, I went to a cemetery in Queens, New York with a photographer. We were working on a unique calendar of cemetery photos. In addition to my regular job, I had also been a model and this was my current project. It wasn't the first time we had taken pictures in a cemetery, but this time certainly was different. The sun shone a brilliant golden color over the photographer's shoulder as he snapped frame after frame of me posing among the tombstones. As he focused in on me, he began to squint.

"I'm seeing the oddest bright light reflected in my lens, but I'm not shooting into the sun," he explained. He continued to take pictures under these adverse conditions.

It wasn't until the film was developed that we realized

something extraordinary had occurred. I received the happiest surprise of my life when one of the photos clearly showed the image of a young woman who looked startlingly like me. I knew it was my mother who had died at the tender age of twenty.

I'd finally been given the thing I'd hoped for and never believed I'd see. This photo brought me the peace I've always yearned for and confirmed my belief in Heaven.

I know my mother is in a better place, as are the spirits of all the people whose burials have been entrusted to me over the years. My professional experiences have given me more of an understanding of death than the average person, and it makes perfect sense for spirits to hover around the cemetery. Next to a church, the cemetery is the most spiritual place you can be. It's very comforting and you get a sense of eternity.

A newspaper article documented my encounter, and I've gone on to speak about it on talk shows. I hope others who have lost loved ones can gain comfort from my experience. I want them to know they haven't really lost anyone. Their loved ones are in a better place.

I continue to visit the cemetery and although my mother has never appeared to me again, it is the place I most strongly feel her presence. I know she's watching over her child and keeping me safe.   THE END

A SYMBOL OF FRIENDSHIP AND LOVE

My best friend and I were soul mates. We could finish each other's thoughts and sentences—something only a ten-year friendship and love could accomplish. We spent many days and nights at the beach, feeding the sea gulls. It was a daily routine we enjoyed for years. Watching the sun rise or set with the hundreds of sea gulls flying in the sky was breathtaking.

When he was killed it was a shock! My best friend was gone forever. I cried nonstop for days. I couldn't get over the fact that he was no longer in my life.

The morning of his funeral, it was only fitting to be at the beach at sunrise to say good-bye to him. There wasn't a sea gull in sight. That was strange, because I'd never seen the beach without sea gulls. I'd brought three carnations with me, tossing them into the water as a symbol of love, friendship, and forever. As I threw the flowers into the air, I saw through my tears that a sea gull had flown out of nowhere and caught one of the carnations in his beak. As the bird flew into the air, so graceful and free, it swooped down and dropped the carnation next to the other two flowers. I can't explain the feeling of peace and love that I felt at that moment. I knew that he was still with me and our love and friendship would last forever.

It's now fifteen years later and I can still feel his love and guidance in my life.   THE END

HELPFUL GHOST

In the early 1980s, work was hard to find in my part of the country. It was one of those summers that my two cousins and I decided to travel down the coast to look for work. We'd been traveling for over an hour on the interstate in the pouring rain when we saw a man walking along the road carrying a gas can.

We decided to stop and give him a ride. When he got into the car, we noticed the strangest thing—he didn't seem to be wet and there were no smelly fumes from the gas can. We told him we were looking for work and we started talking about the economy. Then he asked us to stop before the next exit to let him out of the car.

He told us to get off at the exit and go to the church in town. Then he said the minister there would give us food, shelter, a full tank of gas, and three days of work.

We thanked him for the information and he thanked us for the ride. We got off the exit and he continued walking. My cousin turned around to see him, but he had suddenly vanished from the road.

We drove to the nearest gas station and called the church. The minister said yes that he would do all the things the man had told us. He came to the gas station and then we followed him back to the church for a hot meal and a warm bed.

As we passed through the living room, there was a picture of the man we had picked up hitchhiking on the fireplace mantle.

We told the minister that the man in the picture was the one who'd sent us to him.

"Are you positive?" the minister asked.

"Yes, I'm positive," I answered.

"Is he someone you know?" one of my cousins asked.

The minister said it was his son who had been killed in Vietnam thirty years earlier.

MY VISIT FROM BEYOND

He must be thinking that I'm lying, I thought to myself.

I insisted I was telling the truth, and my cousins agreed. The minister said he believed me.

He told us that over the years, about thirty people had been led to the church by his deceased son.   THE END

❧

THEY'RE PLAYING HIS SONG

My grandfather was the dearest person in the world to me. He often made up silly rhymes or sayings to make me laugh as I sat on his lap in the living room. He was always trying to cheer me up when I was down.

My grandfather died of cancer when I was fourteen and I missed him so much. I visited my grandmother at her country house as soon as I got my own car and was able to drive. I knew she was lonely and enjoyed having company around.

One particular night, I was driving my grandmother home from church and I turned on the radio to listen to on the long ride home. There on the radio, a song was playing that sent my grandmother and I into tears, so much so that I had to pull over to the side of the road. It was a song my grandfather used to sing to me, something he'd made up especially for me—or so I thought.

I quickly wrote down the name of the radio station and the announcer's name, as I'd missed the title of the song. I rushed to a pay phone, called the announcer, and described the song I'd heard in detail so he could tell me the name of it.

To my surprise, the announcer didn't know what I was talking about. He'd never heard of the song, and definitely hadn't played anything like it while he was on the air.

I hung up the phone slowly and looked at my grandmother. She had a strange look on her face, and I believe she knew what had happened before I even had a chance to tell her. We both knew that my grandfather had given us a special message to let us know that somewhere, he was thinking of us.   THE END

A CALL FROM HEAVEN

Because I was the only granddaughter out of many grandsons, my grandmother and I were very close. She was there when I finished high school and when I got married. She even came to the hospital when my first child was born, and waited patiently with my husband.

Soon after I became pregnant with my second child, my grandfather died. It seemed as though my grandmother had just given up on life. She always had her children and grandchildren around her, but to her, life was nothing without her husband.

One day, I was sitting beside her bed waiting for her to wake up from her nap. I noticed she was holding out her hand. She woke up and said to me, "Go and get my Bible." I brought her the Bible and she just pointed to a picture of Heaven and said,

"I'm going there soon."

She also told me she'd sewn the outfit that she wanted to be buried in and told me where she'd placed it. I began to cry. My grandmother looked up at me and said, "Don't cry for me. I want to go." She also said if there was any way possible, she'd come back and tell me what Heaven was like. She fell back to sleep, but this time, she never woke up from her slumber.

Somehow, we all made it through her funeral. It was so hard to picture my life without my grandmother.

A few nights after the funeral, I was awakened by the telephone ringing. I sat up and turned the light on and was startled to see that it was two o'clock in the morning. When I answered the phone, I nearly passed out. It was my grandmother.

I got up out of bed to make sure I wasn't dreaming. She said, "Honey, no one can even comprehend what Heaven is like. It's so beautiful. There's no pain or suffering. I'm with your grandfather now, and I'm very content. We love you."

The line went dead. My husband kept saying, "Who was that?" I just smiled and said, "That was Granny. She just wanted to tell me what Heaven is like."

My husband just looked at me in amazement and said, "Honey, it's late. I think Granny would want you to get some sleep."

I know my husband didn't believe me, but I also know my grandmother is happy and is exactly where she wants to be. It's been twenty years since that day, but every time the phone rings, I think about my grandmother.   THE END

BLESSED BUTTERFLY

Our town has had a very touching and sad experience this year. A very fine young man in our community was diagnosed earlier this year with cancer. He was a star baseball player, college student, and avid hunter. His father is a deacon in our church, his mom a hairdresser, and his little brother an all-around typical young boy.

This young man and his struggle with cancer did things that never had been accomplished in our community. He brought all the churches in the community together as one, the way God had planned it to be. He brought young people and families into church that otherwise would never come to know God and his love. He showed everyone around him what courage truly was, and how to keep the faith up no matter how bad things got. He was a perfect example of what faith can do. But the pain got worse and it was evident that he was about to lose his battle.

The young man's mother spent endless hours with him. They discussed the arrangements for his funeral, and he explicitly planned his own final service. But his mom wanted some kind of a sign from him to assure her that once he was past this life, she'd know that he was okay. It was decided that a butterfly would be her sign from him.

On the day he passed away, the mother and father were taking a walk and talking. Suddenly, a beautiful butterfly flew around them and then landed at their feet. At that moment, the father said, "Well, Mom, there's your sign." When the mother saw the sight, she instantly knew her son was okay. At that moment, the butterfly flew away.

No one will ever know how that butterfly found those two people on that day. But everyone rests assured that God had a part in letting them know that their son was okay. Their son was safe in the arms of our heavenly Father who shared that precious boy with that earthly family.   THE END

THE RESCUE

When I was growing up, my mother was always there when I needed her. Even after I got married and had kids of my own, Mom was there to help me out, offer advice, or just listen to my troubles.

When she became terminally ill, I wanted more than anything to be by her side. But I was in a hospital five hundred miles away, with a compound leg fracture. Not only did I miss my mother's last moments in this world, but her funeral as well. I felt awfully guilty. She had done so much for me, and it seemed I had done so little for her. I didn't even get to tell her good-bye.

Two years later, my office sent me out of town on business. The company put me up in a second-rate hotel, and it was so uncomfortable that I had to take a sleeping pill to get any rest.

I woke up to a roomful of smoke and heat. The hotel was on fire! Somehow I made it to the hallway, where I collapsed, coughing and confused. The smoke was just too much for me.

"For heaven's sake, get up," someone said, and I looked up to see my mother, looking as young as she did when I was a child. "You'll have to be there for the people who need you," she said, and then she showed me the way out of the burning building.

The firemen said it was a miracle that I made it out. I know that's true. And I also know that, just as I need my mother, my children need me. It's a big tradition I have to uphold, and I try to live up to it every day.   THE END

MY SPECIAL ROSEBUSH

My husband had just passed away a few months ago. Feeling lonely, I walked outside and sat on the back patio remembering happier Father's Days.

Today I had helped my neighbor celebrate his one-hundredth birthday. The excitement was over now and I was alone.

After a while, I got up, and walked over to the flower bed next to the house. Something caught my eye. Looking closer, I saw a tiny bright-red rosebud.

Now, a bud on a rosebush may not seem unusual, but this one was. This rosebush hadn't blossomed in years. After the death of my twenty-two-year-old daughter fourteen years ago, one of my daughters bought me the rosebush for Mother's Day. This bush, which was in memory of my daughter, was small, but for the first few years had red roses almost as big as the bush, lasting all summer long. Then one year the bush stopped blooming. Not another rose blossomed year after year.

My husband and I talked about replacing the bush, but for some reason we didn't.

This year that rosebush grew so well the trellis in back was green with foliage. Still, not another blossom until now.

I felt comforted. A red rosebud on Father's Day on my daughter's bush. I felt it was a message from above telling me the two of them were happy together in heaven with Jesus.   THE END

AN EVIL SPIRIT
HAUNTS OUR HOME

It began the first night we were in our new house. It didn't seem like much at the time, but when I think of it now, it's like the first tiny crack in the dam.

Kendall and I were sprawled at opposite ends of the couch. We were exhausted from unpacking boxes and moving furniture. Five-year-old Andrew was finally tucked into bed. After the dishes were done, even fifteen-year-old Dexter had gone to bed. Now ten minutes later, he was back.

"Aunt Nadine, my room is cold. Where did you pack the blankets?" Dexter asked.

"Your room is cold? It can't be."

He shrugged. "Come and see for yourself if you don't believe me. It's really cold."

If you don't believe me. The words summed up his whole attitude toward Kendall and me. He'd never wanted to live with us, and he let us know it every time he had the chance.

I thought about the long walk to the end of the hall. It doesn't sound like much, but I was really beat. And

I still had to finish unpacking the kitchen boxes.

"I'll take your word for it." I groaned. "The blankets are in that detergent carton in Andrew's room. Try not to wake him."

Dexter didn't move at first, as if he wanted to say something more. Then he shook his head and walked away.

"Funny kid," Kendall murmured.

"Like Henry, I guess. Kimberly was a chatterbox," I said.

Darn! My eyes were stinging. I forced myself to get up and go back to work in the kitchen—anything to keep busy, to shut out the memories that still hurt. Kimberly and Henry had been dead four months, and I still couldn't accept it. Kimberly and I had been closer than most sisters. She'd practically raised me after Mama got sick. Now she was gone, and I wondered if anyone could ever fill the empty place she left in my heart.

Work eases that kind of pain, and my new kitchen was full of work. You never know how much junk you have until you have to pack up and move. The first box I opened held the things for the hard-to-reach cupboard over the refrigerator.

"Hey, aren't you ready to quit?" Kendall came from the kitchen door. "This stuff can wait till tomorrow."

I dragged out a kitchen chair and climbed up to reach over the refrigerator. "I was looking for the coffeepot and skillet. As long as I've got these other things out, I may as well put them where they belong."

"I thought you packed a special box with the kitchen stuff we'd need right away," he said.

"I thought I did, too, but I can't find it."

Suddenly, a wave of dizziness came over me, and I

had to grab the refrigerator for support.

"Come on, Nadine! Now that's enough! Get down from there. If we can't find that box in the morning, we'll go out for breakfast."

He held out his arms to steady me. When I was down, he almost crushed me with a bear hug. "Take care of the woman I love," he growled. "If you don't, I'll have to beat you or something."

I laughed. "Make it 'something,' okay?"

He raised his eyebrows. "Tonight? What are you, some kind of sex fiend?"

I looked up at him. I felt happy and warm with love. Then I suddenly remembered my sister, and all that happiness was swept away. It could happen that fast with Kendall, too. I might say good-bye to him one morning and never see him alive again.

"Honey, hold me!" I moaned.

"Come on, kitten. Let's go to bed right now," he ordered.

That scary feeling didn't go away even when Kendall pulled the sheet over me. Mama's death had been hard to take—caring for her for months, knowing it would happen. Kimberly's death I couldn't accept at all. One minute, she was alive; the next, she was gone—thanks to a drunk driver and a blind curve. I'd reacted badly. I'd clung to Kendall and Andrew and to all the familiar things of my life—our apartment, our neighbors, the old-fashioned grocery where I did my shopping twice a week.

I'd still be clinging to those familiar things if it hadn't been for Dexter. He had nowhere else to go. My father was in Florida, and Dexter had never known him very well. Henry's father was closer, but he lived on a pension and his health was poor. So Dexter had to live with us—and it became obvious that our apartment just wasn't big enough for four people. I'd hated leaving. Hated it even more because, for all our sacrifices, Dexter acted as if he was doing us a favor.

For Kimberly's sake, I tried to love him, but it wasn't easy. I couldn't see anything of Kimberly in him except in his physical appearance, and that was only now and then—when he forgot himself and smiled. His actions and the way he spoke, those were all his father's.

I'd never liked Henry. He seemed to make Kimberly happy, but I'd always found him cold and—well, hostile. I felt he could see right through me and didn't like what he saw.

Dexter was just like that. He never criticized me. In fact, he didn't talk much at all. But he seemed to be waiting for me to do something stupid so he could laugh at me—to himself, of course. In the apartment, he used to sit for hours, staring at newspapers or his crime magazines. Most boys his age would've been thinking about sports or cars or girls, but I could never figure out what was in Dexter's head.

I found myself trying to fake the emotion I couldn't feel. I talked to him, cooked the foods he liked, and bought him the magazines he wanted. But it was an act.

I wished I could be like Kendall. Sometimes, I thought he loved the whole world. The few times that love wasn't returned, he didn't seem to notice, either. He liked having Dexter around. He'd accepted him as a son, which was more than I could do, in spite of my love for Kimberly.

The next morning, I found the box I'd been looking for in the living room. For some reason, it had been stacked with the boxes containing Dexter's crime magazines and scrapbooks of crime stories clipped from the papers.

Dexter got up with a temper as bad as mine had been. He complained about a big dog barking right outside his window all night. But sunshine poured in at the kitchen window and infected all of us with its cheerfulness. Dexter's mood improved, and he started joking with Andrew, making him laugh.

While the coffee perked and the eggs cooked, Kendall made a shopping list for the hardware store. Our new house had been empty for several years, and there were a lot of repairs to be made. Dexter offered to clean out the garage while Kendall was gone.

"Oh, as long as I have to be downtown anyway, I thought I'd stop at the bank and open a savings account for you," Kendall said. "You'll have college to think of in a couple of years. I hope you'll budget part of your paper-route money for savings."

Dexter nodded. "Are you going to die?"

Kendall and I stared at each other across the table.

"There's no insurance money left," Kendall said slowly. "We needed it to make the down payment on this house. Don't you remember? We had to arrange it with your father's lawyer. I'm sure we talked about it."

Dexter's eyes widened. "No, we didn't talk. I couldn't have agreed to anything like that. Dad said that money was for my education. How could you spend all of it? It was a big policy. You stole it! You stole my money and spent it on yourselves. That money was mine!"

"Stop that!" I said sharply. "No one stole anything from you. The money was for you, yes. But what about all your expenses until you go to college? Kendall will be paying those, too. He can't do that and buy a house, too. And we couldn't let you go on sleeping on the sofa and sharing a closet with Andrew."

He was shaking his head, getting up from the table. "You didn't have to make me live with you. You just did it so you could get your hands on that money! I could live with Grandpa Humphrey."

He turned and ran out of the kitchen. Kendall got to his feet.

"Let him go," I said. "He won't listen to reason now. Give him time to calm down."

"I guess you're right," he said. "It's crazy! He has everything just a little wrong, and it makes us sound like a couple of cruel monsters."

I did feel sorry for Dexter. I blamed Henry for the misunderstanding. His policy had been a small one and had to cover funeral expenses. For a man who gave the impression of being cautious, he had been just the opposite when it came to savings and insurance. With what was left of the insurance and our savings, we were able to make the down payment on a house—but only because we found a bargain, a house no one else wanted.

As for Dexter living with Grandpa Humphrey, Henry's father, that wasn't a possibility. Grandpa Humphrey hadn't thought it was a good idea. He was afraid he might have another heart attack and die right in front of the boy.

"That would be a terrible experience for a kid who has already been through too much," he'd said to me.

As Kendall said, Dexter had things just a little wrong. Kendall looked worried when he left the house. If Dexter didn't believe us, I knew Kendall would worry that my nephew would think we were thieves.

It took a couple of hours to get the kitchen in some sort of order. I could have finished sooner, but Andrew was "helping." Just as I was finishing, there was a knock on the back door.

My visitor was a tall blonde, about forty years old. "Hi!" she said. "You must be my new neighbor. I'm Natalie."

I introduced myself and Andrew and invited her to come in.

"No, I know how it is when you're moving. I just frosted a cake, and you and your boys are probably starving. Come over and have some," she said.

It was a welcome invitation. I called Dexter from the garage. He almost forgot himself and smiled when he heard about the cake.

Natalie was full of information about the neighbors and shopping and schools. Dexter and Andrew were stuffing their faces, so we talked without interruption. Finally, though, I began to notice Andrew's danger signals. He was bored and restless.

"Aunt Nadine, I'll get out Andrew's bathing suit and let him play in the hose while I finish the garage. Is that all right?" Dexter asked.

I smiled at him gratefully.

"Nice to see a teenager who's so considerate," Natalie said. "What do the boys think of the house?"

"I'm not sure," I said. "Andrew would be happy any-where but it's harder for an older boy. Dexter didn't sleep well last night. He said a big dog was barking outside his window." I looked around her neat house. "I guess it must belong to one of the other neighbors.

It doesn't look like you have a dog."

"A big dog?" Natalie said. "The Straytons have a terrier, but they never let him outside. No, the only big dog we ever had around here was the Borensteins's German shepherd."

"The Borensteins?" I asked.

She looked from me to her empty cake plate, flustered, as if she'd said too much. "Yes, the original owners of your house. The Nettlesons bought the place from them."

"Maybe the dog ran away," I said. "And it came back last night."

She shook her head, and I could see embarrassment in her eyes. "Well, it sounds as if you don't know what happened in the house."

Her story surprised me. I knew there must've been a reason why our house was empty for so long, but the truth was worse than my wildest guess.

The original owners, the Borensteins, had had one child, a son, Patrick. Patrick had apparently been emotionally disturbed. Natalie told stories of his torturing animals and scaring younger children. But his parents didn't believe he was sick.

"He had this dog, a big German shepherd," Natalie said. "It was a vicious animal, trained to be mean, a guard dog, really. Everyone was afraid of it but Patrick.

"Well, one day, it snapped at him, and, in a fit of anger, he—he put a rope around its neck and hanged it."

I was sick to my stomach and sorry I'd asked, but I couldn't let her stop.

Patrick's father had found the dog and punished the boy. Natalie didn't know the details, but apparently, the father had been frightened to find out his neighbors were right. His punishment had been harsh. That night, Patrick shot and killed his parents as they slept. Then, out of fear or remorse, he hanged himself.

"I've been in the room that used to be his," she said. "At times, it gets so cold—as if the walls were made of ice. There's a feeling of hate in the room. I could almost believe Patrick is still there."

Cold. Dexter had said something about his room being cold. I shivered.

"Oh, I've upset you! I am sorry. But I thought you should know," she said.

"I'm not upset," I told her.

She didn't look convinced. "Don't pay much attention to all the stories that are going around. Okay, the Borensteins died and the Nettlesons got a divorce shortly after they left, but that's just coincidence. People who love each other—well, you don't have to worry about a bad-luck or haunted house."

I'd told her I wasn't upset, but I found myself feeling frightened. I tried not to think about it, but it was almost as if I was afraid to go inside. I walked around the yard, enjoying the sun. Finally, I went to the garage to talk to Dexter.

Andrew played in the house while Dexter loaded Andrew's wagon with stacks of newspapers. There was already a big pile of them by the curb, waiting for the trash pickup.

Dexter pointed to the open garage door as I walked up. "What do you think?" he asked.

"Much better," I said. "A little more, and we may be able to get the car in."

"Yeah. There's a pile of tools and wood and jars of nails. I thought Kendall ought to look through it before

I started throwing anything away."

"Dexter, about this morning—" I said.

"Sorry I lost my temper," he interrupted. His words were short as if he was still angry. But it was a hopeful sign, it seemed to me.

"If you thought we stole that money, I don't blame you for being angry," I said. "I want you to understand. I'll be glad to go over the figures with you. You could even talk to the lawyer. We needed a house—for you as well as the rest of us. Even with the insurance, we were lucky. If we hadn't found this place—"

Dexter pulled a pack of chewing gum out of his jeans. He offered me a stick. "Aunt Nadine, have you noticed anything funny about the house?"

"Funny?" I asked. "You mean because the price was so low? I understand someone died here, and that's why no one wanted it. Is that what you mean?"

He shook his head. "Not exactly. But if someone died here, that might explain it. Do you ever hear noises? Or see things?"

I felt a little impatient. Dexter was the last person to believe in superstitious nonsense.

"Old houses are always noisy. As for seeing things, you're not trying to tell me you've seen pale, floaty things in dark corners, are you?"

I tried to keep the scorn from my voice, but he must've guessed. He muttered something under his breath and went back to work. I felt frustrated and angry. Nothing was settled. He'd just brushed off my explanation of the insurance problem with questions about ghosts. It was as if he wanted to go on thinking the worst.

Kendall got back about one. The house was starting to look livable, and I could find things like spoons and fabric softener and screwdrivers when I needed them. That afternoon, I ignored the two or three boxes that were still to be unpacked and gave Kendall a hand with the repairs. Almost every door in the house was sticking, and we had to take them off their hinges and turn them over so Kendall could plane the bottoms.

While we worked outside in the shade, I told Kendall about meeting our neighbor.

"She seems nice. She told me about the school and where to shop," I said.

I debated with myself whether to bring up what I'd found out about the former owners. I finally decided not to. Kendall kept up with the news. He probably knew about the Borensteins. Maybe he hadn't mentioned it because he was trying not to worry me.

"How did you manage to keep Andrew quiet long enough to talk?" he asked.

"Oh, Dexter noticed Andrew was getting squirmy. He brought him over here to play in the hose."

Kendall looked thoughtful. "He does that a lot, doesn't he? Helps out without being asked, I mean."

I nodded.

"Did you thank him for it?"

I jerked and almost dropped the door I was steadying. "You make me sound like a little girl who has to be reminded of her manners," I snapped.

"Well, did you?" he repeated softly.

"I forgot."

Kendall put down the plane and came over to put his arm around me. "Nadine, what is it with you and Dexter? You keep him at arm's length—like you're afraid of him. Why? It's not like you. Don't you love him?"

AN EVIL SPIRIT HAUNTS OUR HOME

I was fighting to hold back tears. I didn't want to admit the truth—not to Kendall. But I'd never lied to him.

"No," I said, my voice harsh and ugly. "I've tried but I can't. He's too much like his father. And you know what I thought of Henry."

"That's not true," Kendall said. "Oh, he doesn't chatter like Kimberly did. He's thoughtful and more sensitive. But no one who knew Kimberly could doubt that Dexter was her son. Do you remember how she used to catch her breath just before she started to talk. He does, too."

My hands were sweating and my head pounding. Why did he have to keep talking about her, reminding me.

"Are we going to finish this job tonight?" I asked.

His arm dropped from me. "Yes, of course," he said.

He didn't bring up the subject again in the weeks that followed and I certainly didn't. As for Dexter, well, it seemed to me he was sulkier than ever, complaining about how cold his room was and how sounds of barking and other weird noises kept him awake at night.

As sulky as Dexter was, though, I have to admit that he did help a lot. And there was certainly plenty to do in that old house. Every weekend, Kendall and Dexter and I worked like crazy, painting and making repairs.

We put in a particularly long, hard day the fourth Saturday we were there. That evening, Kendall decided we deserved a treat and took us all out for supper. We were all tired—that was why Kendall suggested it—and that was why I finally lost my temper with Dexter.

AN EVIL SPIRIT HAUNTS OUR HOME

We had ordered our meal, and I was trying to interest Andrew in counting the cars that passed the window so he wouldn't get impatient and start jumping around. But the food hadn't arrived by the time Andrew ran out of numbers and lost interest. Kendall got up to talk to the waitress about rushing our food. Andrew climbed up on the bench he shared with Dexter to see where his father was going. He was bouncing up and down like a frog getting ready to jump.

Dexter snapped at him—something unimportant about Andrew getting dirt on his pants.

"Don't you talk to Andrew like that!" I said, my voice more harsh than I intended. "He's only a baby."

"I guess I know where I stand in this family." His words hissed back at me. "Nowhere!"

It went downhill from there, Andrew looking on in shocked silence.

"Why don't you just come out and say it?" Dexter demanded. "You can't stand me, and you don't want me around."

"That's not true. Kimberly was my sister and—"

"Don't lie to me!" he shouted, causing heads to turn in the restaurant. "I can take anything if you'd just stop lying."

He walked out while I sat there with my face burning. Kendall followed him out and managed to calm him down. Somehow, we all choked down some food. But even Kendall couldn't smooth over what had happened between Dexter and me. It was too final, too painful.

With that blowup on my mind, it was no wonder I didn't sleep well. I finally dozed off, only to be awakened a long time later by a noise. I couldn't see the clock, but there was moonlight at the window. I heard the noise again and sat down.

Dexter was standing outside our open bedroom door. The light was weak. I could see he was holding something long and dark, but I couldn't see what it was.

"Dexter, is that you? What's wrong?" I asked.

He didn't answer. Panic turned my skin icy. Our fight, his anger about the insurance, Natalie's story, my own feelings about him—it all added up to a living nightmare, and I was too scared even to scream. That thing in his hands looked like a gun. But that was crazy! We didn't own a gun.

"What are you doing?" I gasped.

Why didn't Kendall hear me? His soft snores made the whole thing even more unreal. I turned to shake him awake.

"What—what is it?"

"It's Dexter!" I said. "Kendall, go see." I looked across the room. The moonlight showed an empty doorway.

We went to check Dexter's room. He was asleep or pretending to be. There was nothing in his room that looked like a gun.

"He must've been sleepwalking," Kendall whispered. "Or maybe you dreamed the whole thing."

Dreamed it? Oh, no! I had been wide awake. And I was awake for the rest of the night—facing the truth about my nephew.

Dexter had resented having to come and live with us. He knew a sick grandfather would be more lenient with him than a healthy aunt and uncle. He resented it even more when he found out about the insurance. With his interest in crime, he probably heard about the Borenstein murders when they happened. Or maybe he read it later in his crime magazines. Whichever it was, he used that story, planned his actions as coldly as Patrick Borenstein planned the murder of his parents.

All his talk about seeing things and hearing things— the complaints about the cold and the big dog, and, worst of all, his actions that night, were calculated to get us to send him away.

My nephew was sick! He wanted to terrify us. How far would he go? Was he a danger to Kendall and me? Was he a danger to Andrew?

That was the thought that sent cold chills through me, Kendall and I could take care of ourselves. Dexter wasn't crazy enough to shoot us. But even words could hurt Andrew. Dexter's thoughtless hints about ghosts could give Andrew fears that would frighten and haunt him the rest of his life.

"Don't say anything about his sleepwalking last night," Kendall warned as we were getting dressed. "With what he's been through, it's perfectly natural, and we're not even sure—"

The anger in my eyes stopped him before he finished. That was the worst part about having Dexter come to live with us. Kendall and I had never had a serious disagreement, never doubted each other. Dexter had changed that.

I did agree that we shouldn't mention the night before. I was going to talk to Dexter's grandfather later that day. I would give Dexter what he wanted, but I wouldn't give him the satisfaction of knowing he'd scared me into it.

Kendall got ready for work. I fixed his breakfast and went into Andrew's bedroom to help him get dressed. When I came out again, I could hear angry words coming from the kitchen. Kendall came down the hall, his lips set tight.

"Dexter began to move in with Andrew," he said shortly. "He says there's a ghost in his room. I told him he could do it but to leave the furniture till tonight so I can help."

"Ghosts!" I muttered disgustedly. I kept my voice down, knowing that Andrew was all ears behind me. Why make a fuss about it? If I could be persuasive enough with Dexter's grandfather and later with Kendall, Dexter might be out of the house by that night. Then maybe my family would know peace again.

After Kendall left, I started on the breakfast dishes. Dexter was in his room, and Andrew was playing somewhere in the house.

Suddenly, I heard Andrew screaming. I ran into the hall. Dexter had his arms full of his clothes and was crossing the hall to Andrew's bedroom. Andrew, yelling at the top of his lungs, had both arms around Dexter's leg, trying to stop him. Neither of them saw me.

"Andrew, stop it! Your dad said I could do this."

"No! Don't want to share my room."

"Stop it!" All of a sudden, Dexter dropped the bundle of clothes and raised his hand.

"Don't you dare hit him!" I screamed.

His hand came down slowly, but he didn't look ashamed. He just transferred his anger to me.

"Uncle Kendall said I could move in with Andrew. He promised."

"He didn't know it was going to upset him so much. You're not going to force Andrew to do this if he doesn't want to," I said.

"What about me? You forced me to come and live with you. You forced me to give up the insurance money so you could buy this house. And now you're forcing me to live in the same room with a ghost. When do I get to count around here?"

"Ghosts," I snapped. "Don't bring up that nonsense!"

"Yes, a ghost!" Dexter yelled. "Look, I don't expect you to love me. You're so wrapped up in Kendall and Andrew and yourself that you don't have any time to spare for me. Okay, I'll learn to live with it. But you could at least consider my feelings once in awhile. There's a ghost in that room, and I won't stay there!"

Andrew, scared by the argument and the talk of ghosts, began to cry.

"Dexter, go to your room. We'll talk about this later, after Andrew calms down."

"I'll go to my room all right. I'm going to pack. I'm not wanted around here now that you have my money. I'm going to live with Grandpa." He looked at me as if daring me to argue.

I put my hand on Andrew's shoulder and nudged him toward the living room.

"Maybe that would be best," I said. "We were a happy family before you came along. I'd give up this house and a lot more to have that back again."

He opened the door to his bedroom, walked inside, and slammed the door in my face.

I started to go after Andrew to talk to him and get his mind off ghosts. Then I noticed it was icy cold in the hall. The frigid air had come pouring out of Dexter's room when he opened the door. It was a hot day. Where could that cold air be coming from?

I knocked. He didn't answer.

"Please open this door. I want to check something," I said.

I knocked again, but there was still no answer. I tried the knob. Cold air rolled out of Dexter's room like a cloud. The shades were drawn, and I couldn't see Dexter. I stepped inside and called his name again.

He was crouched at the far end of the bed, huddled there like an animal. He was staring at a shadowy corner, his lips moving soundlessly. I gasped. There was something in the room, in that far corner. It was a feeling of hate, almost real enough to touch. It was evil! And it wasn't coming from Dexter. He didn't know I was there. He crouched, staring, scared out of his mind.

His face, I couldn't take my eyes from his face. Why had I never noticed before the strange look in his eyes that made him look so much like Kimberly? Not the Kimberly who was always getting me out of scrapes. This was the one who couldn't talk for over a week when Papa told us Mama was sick and would never get well. This was the face of a lost child.

Suddenly, I realized that Dexter hadn't been lying. He hadn't cooked up some crazy scheme. He really believed there was a ghost in his room.

My legs began moving without directions from my head. Maybe the directions came from my heart. I knelt beside Dexter and put my arm around his shoulder.

"It's Aunt Nadine. Please answer me. What's wrong?"

He licked his lips. "Can't you see? He's there. He wants me to get something out of that corner. Oh, God! He wants me to do something, and I don't know what. Aunt Nadine, it scares me." His voice rose. "It scares me!"

I felt his fear and the hate. They were cold, shuddering feelings that came in waves and made me sick.

I put both arms around Dexter and forced him to turn to me. "There's no one in this room but you and me. Listen!" I ordered. "I love you. You were wrong when you said I didn't. And so was I. I couldn't accept your mother's death, and you're just like her. I wanted to forget. I tried to pretend I didn't love you so it wouldn't hurt so much."

What was I fighting? I didn't know. But it was a fight. I was struggling to win Dexter's soul. The thing fought with me, sending out waves of hate, sick and disgusting.

"I know I've made mistakes. But I love you. I won't shut you out again. I won't let you run away. We need each other. Please, Dexter, give me another chance."

I knew I had won when he put his arms around me and began to cry.

"I'm sorry, Aunt Nadine. I've been so scared. Mom and Dad went away. And Grandpa didn't want me. That thing—the ghost—he said you didn't want me, either. He wanted—wanted me to get something from that corner, and he—he said I should make you pay for hurting me, too."

"There is no ghost. There's no one here but you and me," I said.

He raised his head to look in the corner. "No, not anymore," he said. "But there was. What was it?"

What was it? I didn't know then, and I still haven't found the answer.

When I think of that morning now, I get cold chills. I almost lost Dexter, my only link with Kimberly. I almost killed the love we had for each other.

AN EVIL SPIRIT HAUNTS OUR HOME

Just in time, we pulled back from the brink. Since then, six months ago, I've never let him doubt that he is a member of our family, a brother for Andrew, a son for Kendall and me. Only once have we talked about what happened. Once the four of us were watching a horror movie on TV. When it was over, Kendall took Andrew to bed. When they were out of the room, Dexter turned to me.

"It seemed so real at the time," he said.

I knew what he was talking about, and I had to hold back a shudder. Then he reached across to take my hand, and I was all right again. He loved me enough to forgive me.

There's something I've never told anyone. That morning, after Dexter calmed down, I sent him outside with Andrew. I raised the blinds on his windows. I wanted to let the light and the warmth of the sun take away the last of that hateful chill in his room.

The brighter light showed how loose the linoleum was in one corner. I don't know what made me pull it up and lift the floorboard, but I did. I found the gun there, the one the police had never been able to find after Patrick Borenstein shot his parents, the same gun Dexter must have carried the night he walked in his sleep. I turned it over to the police, never mentioning it to Kendall or Dexter.

Ghosts? No, I don't believe in them. I just believe in love. When people don't have love, they imagine strange things. That has to be the answer. Doesn't it?   **THE END**

THEY TRIED TO BREAK UP OUR MARRIAGE

My family was outraged when I told them Bob Bennett and I wanted to get married the summer after we both graduated from high school.

"You're too young, Ann," Mom wailed. "Why, you're nothing but a child."

And Dad was furious. "I never heard of such nonsense. What'll you use for money?"

Bob already had a job at the milk plant, and he had saved several hundred dollars working the summer before. But Dad practically hooted when I said that. "How far do you think a few hundred dollars and Bob's paycheck will go toward buying furniture and all the things you'll need to set up housekeeping? Ann, don't be a little simpleton. Let Bob work and save his money for a year or so. Then we'll see."

"Please, honey," Mom pleaded. "Wait. There's no hurry. You and Bob need to know a lot more about each other before you take on a serious thing like marriage."

THEY TRIED TO BREAK UP OUR MARRIAGE

That's ridiculous, I thought angrily. Bob and I had grown up together in Ferrisville, we'd known each other all our lives. The mere thought that there was anything left to learn about each other was just plain silly. We'd been going out for almost a year now, and were so crazy about each other that every minute spent apart was just wasted time as far as we were concerned.

But if my folks were opposed to the idea, Bob's folks were even more violently set against it. Especially his father—and his father ran the show at their house.

"He wants me to go to business school," Bob said gloomily. "That's the whole trouble. But I just can't see myself doing that when I've got a good job at the milk plant, with a chance for advancement. Besides, even if we get married, I could go to night school, couldn't I?"

"Of course," I said. "To hear them talk, you'd think getting married was the end of everything."

Bob drew me close. "They're not going to keep us apart, Ann. We don't have to have their consent. If we went away someplace to get married, you could say you were eighteen. And once the knot was tied, they couldn't do anything about it."

"You mean just run away and get married?" I asked a little doubtfully.

"Why not? Don't we love each other?"

It was tempting, and even more exciting to think of doing it that way. Who wanted a big wedding and all that fuss? Not me, I was sure. I just wanted Bob—to love and to hold forever. Yet, the thought of my own parents held me back. I loved them, too, and I hated to shock and hurt them that way.

THEY TRIED TO BREAK UP OUR MARRIAGE

"I—I don't know, honey," I said fearfully. "Let's—well, let's try harder to get their consent first. Then, if they just won't be reasonable, we'll have to do it our way."

But they weren't going to be reasonable, we soon saw that. Every time Bob tried to talk to his father about it, they had a big fight. Finally, one night soon after graduation, Mr. and Mrs. Bennett came over to confer with Dad and Mom. Mr. Bennett was really raging. Bob was their only child, he said. They had plans for his future, and those plans didn't include a ridiculous teenage marriage. He even had the nerve to hint that it was all my fault, that I was trying to rush Bob into a marriage he didn't want.

Dad blew up at that. "We're no more anxious to see Ann marry your son than you are to have him marry her," he snapped. "You just keep your boy at home, and you won't have to worry about Ann."

"A good idea," Mr. Bennett lashed back. "There's only one way to handle a thing like this and that's to stop it." He wheeled and pointed his finger at Bob. "You heard him, young man. He doesn't want you hanging around here any more, and neither do I."

Bob jumped up, his face white with anger. "I'm no child," he shouted. "You can't treat me like that." It was sickening. By the time the Bennetts left, everybody was mad at everybody else. Mr. Bennett marched Bob off as if he were a naughty four-year-old.

I burst into tears the minute the door closed. "I—I hope you're all happy." I sobbed. "Making a great big fuss like this out of a simple little thing like Bob and me wanting to get married. You'd think we wanted to rob a bank."

"I'd be happier if you did," Dad said coldly. "Now let's have no more nonsense, young lady. After the way Roy Bennett talked tonight, I wouldn't let you marry that young fellow if he were the last male left in the world."

So the whole thing had gone from bad to worse. Bob and I were desperate. He called me the next morning. "If Dad thinks he's going to keep me away from you, he's crazy," he fumed. "I'll pick you up at seven tonight, and we'll talk, honey."

We drove out into the country to our favorite parking spot that night. Bob held me close as he poured out his anger and resentment. "I'm sick of being pushed around," he said. "Dad can't get it through his head that I'm just not going to give in to him the way Mom always has."

"He made my father awfully mad," I said. "Oh, Bob, what can we do?"

"We can run away and get married. We're not asking them for anything, and it's none of their business. What if you aren't eighteen? You're no child and neither am I."

Maybe if our folks hadn't got into that row over us, we wouldn't have done it. But I was pretty mad at Mom and Dad by then, too. Sure, they'd take it hard. But they'd get over it, once it was done. And what right did anybody have to keep Bob and me apart?

So, in a fever of excitement, we made up our minds. We'd slip out of town the next Friday night and drive down to Winfield, just over the state line. We could get the license there in the morning, and be married immediately.

Everything worked out for us those next few days. I sneaked downtown Thursday afternoon with my suitcase and put it in a locker in the bus depot. Bob and I picked it up there Thursday night, and he stowed it in the trunk of his car.

"Just one more night, sweetheart," he whispered, hugging me close before he let me off at the house. "I don't know how I can wait even that long."

"Me, either," I said tremulously.

I couldn't sleep that night. It made me sick to think of what I was doing to my folks. But it's their own fault, I kept telling myself defiantly. They're practically forcing us to do it this way.

Late the next day, alone in my room for the last time, I wrote the note I was going to leave for my parents. "Dear Mom and Dad," I wrote. "I love you and hate to do this to you. But I love Bob, too, and we just can't wait. We're going to be married tomorrow and we'll be back Sunday night. Please, please try to understand and forgive me."

It made me feel weepy, sitting there in the pretty room where I'd slept practically every night of my life, writing words like that to my mother and father. Yet, as I looked around at all the things that had been so precious to me through the years—my CD player and CDs, the pennants and Polaroids tacked up on the wall, even the collection of stuffed dogs I'd started when I was ten—I didn't really regret leaving them. They were childhood things, and already they belonged to the past.

Right after dinner, I showered and dressed and slipped the note halfway under the hand mirror on my dressing table. My heart was in my throat when I hurried downstairs. Bonnie, my kid sister, was in the living room watching TV, and Dad was out in the sun parlor reading the paper. He looked up casually as I hesitated in the doorway.

"Where are you going, Ann?" he asked.

"Down to the diner with some friends. Where's Mom?"

"She went down to the basement for something."

I wanted desperately to see Mom just once more, but I knew it would look funny if I went plowing down there just to say good-bye to her. As casually as I could, I said, "Tell her bye for me, Dad. See you later."

Bob was waiting impatiently in the parking lot behind the diner. We drove straight down to Winfield and got there at about eleven that night. "We'll go to separate hotels," Bob said. "I don't want anyone to think we rushed things that way, honey."

I squeezed his hand. Somehow, the fear and guilt were gone now that I was with Bob. He was so good and wonderful, and I loved him so much.

"Don't sign your own name on the hotel register," he said just before he left me. "Our folks might make a good guess about where we've gone and have the police after us by morning."

We had no trouble getting a license the next morning. I gave my age as eighteen, Bob said he was twenty-one. At two o'clock that afternoon, we were married by a justice of the peace. When Bob slipped the gold band on my finger and later bent to kiss me, it didn't matter that we were standing there in the presence of complete strangers. The solemn thrill of the moment was just as deep, just as true, as it would have been if we'd been married at home.

We went to a small motel that night, registering as Mr. and Mrs. Paul Chandler. Our wedding night was everything we ever dreamed it could be. When I woke in the morning, sunlight was pouring into the room, and Bob was leaning over me, smiling tenderly. "Good morning, Mrs. Bennett," he said softly. "Are you as happy as I am?"

"Oh, yes, yes—" I cried, hugging him. "Happier than I can ever tell you, honey."

We cooked our own breakfast in the little kitchenette, and lingered over it until almost noon. "I wish we didn't have to go back at all," I said. "I wish we could stay here forever." I looked around the room. "I love this place, darling. It's ours, and I'll never forget it."

"Me, either," Bob said. Then he reached over to press my hand gently. "Worried about facing them, honey?"

"Well—a little," I admitted.

"I'm not," he said. "Nothing they say or do can ever spoil things for us, Ann."

Brave words! But even Bob looked pretty gloomy as we pulled back into Ferrisville early that evening. "There's Dad's car," he said as we drew up in front of my house. "They—they're waiting for us, Ann."

I'll say they were—both Mom and Mrs. Bennett all red eyed and weepy, Dad sitting there staring glumly at the floor, and Mr. Bennett pacing angrily up and down. Tears crowded to my own eyes as I saw Mom—then I rushed to her arms.

"Oh, honey," she wailed. "Why did you do it?

How could you treat us this way?"

"I'm sorry I had to hurt you, Mom," I said. "But, oh, I'm so happy. Don't be sad about it, please."

Cold eyed with rage, Mr. Bennett cornered Bob. "So you defied me, deliberately ran off and got yourself into this mess!"

"It's not a mess, Dad," Bob said. "And I don't regret it."

"You will," his father raged. "You'll spend the rest of your life regretting it, you young fool."

"Roy, it's done," Mrs. Bennett said, trying to soothe him. "Can't we just—just make the best of things?"

"No," he snapped. "This is the end of everything I had planned for Bob. I'm washing my hands of the whole business right now." He turned to glare at Bob. "If you think you'll ever get one cent of help out of me, you can think again. You're on your own. Is that clear? I don't want to see you or even hear from you."

"Roy!" Mrs. Bennett cried. She ran to Bob and put her arms around him. "He doesn't mean that, honey."

"You'll find I mean every word of it," Mr. Bennett said coldly. "Bob took matters into his own hands, now let him pay for it."

"That's all right with me," Bob said defiantly. "We don't need your help, and we don't want it."

Mr. Bennett grabbed his hat. "Come on, Libby," he said. "There's nothing more to say."

"But . . ."

"You heard me. We're going home!"

He stalked out, and, with one last tearful look at Bob, Mrs. Bennett followed.

Dad got up heavily when the door closed. He looked so old and gray that remorse really hit me. I had been mean to my parents, and they didn't deserve it.

"Well, you kids asked for it," Dad said grimly. "I should tell you what Bob's father just told you—you've certainly got it coming. But you're my daughter, Ann, and I don't have the heart to do it." He looked at Bob. "I don't suppose you even know where you're going to sleep tonight."

"We—we'll go to a hotel," Bob said. "And we'll start looking for an apartment tomorrow."

Dad's laugh was bleak and bitter. "I thought so. Rush off and get married without even knowing where you're going to live. That shows what a couple of children you are."

Bob flushed. "We'll manage," he said.

"You'd better stay here until you can find an apartment," Mom said wearily. "You can't waste money on hotels with all that's ahead of you." Tears filled her eyes again. "Oh, honey, if you'd just waited—"

It was a week before we found an apartment. It wasn't much of a place, but we were anxious to move in. Although they were trying hard to make the best of things, the folks felt pretty bitter toward us. I guess you couldn't blame them. But living at home with long faces and reproaches wasn't much fun for us, and we grabbed the first halfway decent place we could find.

It was three rooms over an electric appliance shop, furnished shabbily and badly in need of redecorating. The faucets dripped, the doorknobs fell off in our hands, and when it rained, we had to set a kettle under a leak in the corner of the bedroom.

We didn't care. "We'll paint it ourselves as soon as we get settled," Bob said. "At least it's ours." He drew me close. "I'm not sorry," he said. "I don't care how Dad acts. I've got you, and that's all that matters."

Those first weeks of our marriage were wonderful. Everything was so new and exciting. We were busy as beavers, fixing up our shabby little apartment. More than half of Bob's savings were gone by then, but we didn't let that worry us. Pat Rogers, my best friend, threw a shower for me, and I got a lot of things we really needed. Mom ransacked the attic for odds and ends we could use, and Bonnie came over to help me paint and fix curtains. Bonnie was practically the only one who thought Bob and I had been smart to get married.

"Gee, Ann," she'd say wistfully, looking around the apartment, "it must be fun to have your own place and be your own boss."

And it was fun. I loved keeping house and having something good on the stove when Bob came home at night. It was such a thrill to have him burst in and throw his arms around me. And if my cooking turned out to be a flop, neither of us really minded. We'd laugh and go out to a drive-in for hamburgers. Then, after a movie or a session at the diner, it was wonderful to go home together to our own place. Yes, I was happy—wildly happy those first few months.

We threw a big party for our high-school group of friends, and all summer, we had a stream of company. We went out a lot, too—with Pat and Larry

THEY TRIED TO BREAK UP OUR MARRIAGE

Welter, especially. They were as much in love as we'd been, and envious of the happiness we'd found.

"Wish I had the nerve to run off and get married the way you did," Pat said to me more than once. "But you know my parents. They'd never get over it."

Bob's parents hadn't gotten over it, either. At least his father hadn't. His mother phoned him and came to see us a couple of times. But all she did was cry and tell us how Mr. Bennett just couldn't forgive Bob. We'd feel so guilty and unhappy after she'd been there that we almost wished she'd stay away.

Even when my parents came over, they never looked happy. Mom would look around our little place, and, even though she wouldn't come right out and say, "Oh, Ann, this is terrible," I knew that was what she was thinking.

By October, I was pregnant. Bob was so proud and excited that he was ready to burst. As for me, the thought of a little boy with Bob's wavy hair, deep-set eyes, and quick smile was thrilling. But, at the same time, I was a little scared. Bob's paychecks never seemed to stretch as far as they should, and now we had to save toward hospital and baby expenses. With all the good intentions in the world, our savings didn't mount very fast.

Bob worried about our finances all the time. "Honey," he said finally, "I think I'll try to pick up some extra work. Red Benson asked me if I'd help out at the garage evenings and weekends. What do you think?"

I hated the thought of Bob being gone so much.

Still, we needed the extra money. So I agreed, and all of a sudden, the ball was over. I sat home alone evenings. Of course, I couldn't run around with the kids while Bob worked. Even the nights he was home we didn't go out. We just couldn't afford to.

Life got pretty dull during those long months while we were waiting for the baby. I tried not to mind, but sometimes I couldn't help feeling sorry for myself. Pat, or one of the other girls, dropped by occasionally, but they were busy with more exciting things. Besides, it wasn't much fun listening to their chatter about dances and parties and clothes.

"Everybody seems to be having fun but us," I said to Bob. "We just sit home and worry about money."

"Well," he said gloomily, "it's no more fun for me than it is for you. But we've got responsibilities."

Mom wasn't very sympathetic, either. "It's childish for you to be fussing about fun, when Bob's working so hard to make ends meet," she said. "You should be thankful he's taking his responsibilities as seriously as he is."

I felt a little ashamed then, because it was true.

Our Stevie was born the following June. He was a darling—the picture of Bob as I'd known he would be—and so good. Life took on new meaning, with Stevie to keep me busy and interested. But Mr. Bennett still wouldn't forgive us. Mrs. Bennett came to the hospital once and visited us after I got home.

"Roy won't even let me talk about the baby," she told Bob. "He said I wasn't to see Stevie at all, and if he knew I was here, he'd have a fit."

Bob flushed angrily. "Dad has no right to act that

way," he said. "Someday he'll regret it."

By November, I was pregnant again.

"Oh, Ann," Mom wailed when I told her. "How will you ever manage with two?"

"Other people do, I guess we can," I said. It hurt and angered me that my mother should make such a fuss about me having a family. But in my heart, I wasn't much happier than she was. Babies cost money, I'd found that out.

"Well, you simply can't stay there in that small apartment," Mom said. "It's an awful place anyway. It's time you found something better."

That was true enough. With all the things we had to have for Stevie, the place was bursting at the seams. I could pick up and pick up and it still looked cluttered and untidy. The leaking roof and the warped doors weren't big jokes any more— they were irritating and inconvenient.

"Well, I don't know," I said doubtfully. "Bob says we can't afford anything better."

"I'd rather help you with a little money every month than have you stay in that apartment," Mom said. "You talk to Bob about it."

When I did, Bob sighed gloomily, the way I knew he would. "Honey, we're just able to make ends meet now. It's foolish to talk about a more expensive apartment."

"But it's awful here," I protested. "I can't stand it. My parents would help us with the extra rent, Bob. Mom said so."

Bob's mouth tightened. "I don't want their help. We can manage by ourselves."

"That's not fair to me," I cried. "I'm the one who has to put up with this place."

THEY TRIED TO BREAK UP OUR MARRIAGE

In the end, we did find four rooms over on Western Avenue, for a hundred dollars more a month. "I guess we can manage it," Bob said. "We'll have to, because I'm not going to take any help from your parents."

In one way, I was proud of Bob for being so independent. But it was hard being tied down the way we were with his working nights. Once in a blue moon, we had Pat and Larry over, or went bowling or dancing with them. But entertaining cost money, and so did bowling and dancing. More and more we just stayed home, watched TV until ten, and went to bed. And the nights Bob worked, I watched TV alone.

In January, Bob and about a dozen other men were laid off at the milk plant. He looked sick when he got home that night and told me. Of course, he could draw unemployment compensation for some months, but it wasn't nearly enough to get along on.

"Don't worry, honey," I pleaded. "We'll manage. You'll find another job, maybe even a better one."

It was two months, though, before he did find a job, driving a truck for a roofing firm. And it didn't pay as well as his old job. Meanwhile, we had an awful struggle. The bills piled up, careful as we tried to be, and we were forced to borrow money from my family.

I knew how much Bob hated that, and it didn't do our marriage any good. For one thing, it gave my folks an excuse to butt into our affairs. They were always criticizing or handing out advice.

Bob got mad at me one day when I went downtown and bought a new dress. He blew up right in front of Mom. Then she got mad at him. "What do you want Ann to do?" she demanded. "Go around looking like a ragamuffin?"

"It isn't that bad," Bob said. "And Ann knew we couldn't afford it this month."

"I'll pay for it then," Mom snapped. "She's still my daughter."

"I don't want you paying for Ann's clothes," Bob shouted. "I'm her husband, and I'll take care of her myself."

Mom didn't come right out and say that he was doing a poor job of taking care of me, but the expression on her face said it plainly enough. Bob and I had a terrible fight after that. It got to the point that practically every time I wanted to buy something or do something, he'd look at me suspiciously. "I suppose your mother gave you that idea," he'd say.

Sometimes it was true, but I resented Bob's attitude. "I don't know where we'd be if it weren't for my parents," I said. "Yours would let us starve to death."

That hit him on a sore spot, and, the next thing I knew, we were arguing bitterly. I ended up in tears, and then Bob relented and took me in his arms. "Oh, honey, why should we be fighting like this?" he said.

"I don't know!" I sobbed. "Everything seems to go wrong, and you're so mean about my family."

"I'm sorry, honey. But I wish they'd remember you're my wife," he said. "I hate taking their help. Remember how we swore we'd get along on our own?"

"Yes, but life isn't that simple," I said wearily. "I

guess I never thought about babies and bills when we were planning to get married."

There was a lot I hadn't thought about when we rushed so impulsively into marriage—I knew that now. Not that I regretted it. I still loved Bob with all my heart. And, as hard as things were, I kept telling myself I didn't mind, as long as I had Bob.

Mom took Stevie when I went to the hospital late in July. I was so weak after Todd was born that she wouldn't hear of me going home to the apartment.

"Ann needs somebody to look after her," she insisted. "Home with us is the best place for her for a couple of weeks."

It was easier at home, with Mom and Bonnie to wait on me. But it made it even harder to go back to a crowded, messy apartment and the endless round of chores that went with two babies. Bob helped all he could, but I was so tired and cross most of the time that I guess I wasn't too pleasant to live with.

Maybe that's why Bob started staying out nights—not very often, but often enough to make it plain that the honeymoon was definitely over. A couple of times, he went bowling with Bud Farmer and Johnny Pedersen. Bud and Johnny were old friends of his, but I didn't like the idea of Bob running around with them. They weren't married and they had freedom and money that Bob didn't have. When Bob started coming home later and later, I really got mad.

"For Pete's sake," he said irritably. "I can't very well tell people my wife says I have to be home by ten-thirty, can I?"

"Why can't you? Just because Bud and Johnny

are free to stay out till all hours doesn't mean you are." Bob scowled.

"Well, I'm not playing the henpecked husband just to suit you. Besides, with all the worries I've got, I need a little outside relaxation."

"I need a little, too," I said. "But I'm certainly not getting it. If you think it's any fun being cooped up here month after month with two babies—"

Bob jumped up so violently that his chair tipped over with a crash. "If you ask me, it's marriage that's no fun," he said. "I was a darned fool to ever get myself into it."

It was the first time Bob had said such a thing, and, for the rest of the morning, tears came to my eyes every time I thought of it. When Mom stopped by after lunch, I was weeping and complaining as usual.

"Well," she said, "you were both too young, that's the whole trouble. But nobody could tell you."

"I didn't know it would be like this," I wailed. "We're always arguing. It's just work, work, work— never any fun."

"I know, honey—but there's no use complaining about it," Mom said. "You'll just have to make the best of it."

After Mom had gone, I pulled myself together. *Maybe,* I thought, *part of it is my own fault. Maybe I'm not trying hard enough to hold up my end of things.*

I looked around. The apartment was a mess. I hadn't even done the breakfast dishes, let alone the lunch dishes or cleaned the carpet. No wonder Bob preferred going out with Bud and Johnny to staying home in such a sloppy place with a cross, nagging wife. I had been getting pretty careless.

I jumped up and got to work. I vacuumed the entire apartment and washed the dishes. I even made spaghetti and meatballs—Bob's favorite.

The place really looked nice when Bob came in, and he noticed it, too. "Hey, what've you been doing? Geting ready for company?"

"Nope," I said casually. "I just felt ambitious. Guess what's for dinner?"

He grinned. "I can smell it. And, boy, I'm hungry." We ate dinner in peace, for a change, and Bob even offered to help with the dishes—the first time in weeks. By the time I had Stevie and Todd tucked in for the night, he'd finished reading the paper, and we watched TV for a while.

"Let's stay up for the late movie," I suggested. "I'll make coffee and we'll have a snack."

Bob yawned and stretched. "Oh, gosh, honey, I have to get up so darned early. Some other night, huh?" At ten o'clock, we went to bed as usual. I'd worked so hard to make the apartment nice, and I'd cooked his favorite dinner, and the only thing you could say for the evening was that we hadn't argued. He could stay out all night with Bud and Johnny, but he couldn't sit up past ten with me.

The next day, I was really in the dumps. Nothing seemed worth bothering about. I even resented the things I had to do for Stevie and Todd—the baths, the feedings, the nap Stevie didn't want to take. Finally, when he just wouldn't go to sleep, I got them both up, dressed them, and took them over to Mom's.

Mom was cutting a pattern on the dining-room

table. "It's a formal for Bonnie," she said. "Bill Bordson asked her to the school dance."

When Bonnie came in from school, she was glowing all over. "Mom tell you the news, Ann? Just think! Bill Bordson—that hunk! Gosh, I'm so excited I'm ready to flip."

I knew just how she felt. Two years ago I'd been the same way—young and happy, looking forward to dances and parties. Now that had all changed. I could have cried when I thought of how drab and dull life had become.

It was five by the time I got home—barely time to make dinner. I wasn't in the mood for fussing with it anyway. The apartment was a mess again, too. *Well, to heck with it,* I thought. I opened a can of stew and fried some potatoes. Todd was cross as a result of having missed his nap. He was crying when Bob walked in. Bob had the annoyed look that he always got when he heard one of the babies wailing.

"What's the matter with him?" he demanded.

"He's just cross," I said.

"Maybe he needs changing."

"I changed him ten minutes ago," I flared.

"Well, you don't have to be so nasty about it," Bob lashed back.

We were fighting again. I was too miserable to even care. Bob didn't say anything when he sat down to the canned stew, but his face was expressive.

"Well, you don't need to sulk," I said. "I was too busy to fuss with anything."

"Busy doing what?" he asked. "The way this place looks, I'd think you spent the day in bed."

THEY TRIED TO BREAK UP OUR MARRIAGE

I jumped up, so mad I couldn't see straight. I ran into the bedroom, threw myself down across the bed, and wept. Then I heard a crash and a slam from the kitchen. Stevie began to howl. I sprang up and ran back into the kitchen. Bob was gone. Before he'd left, he'd hurled the plate of stew into the sink.

That's the last straw, I thought as I tried to calm Stevie. I'm through with this miserable marriage. I can't stand another day of it.

I dressed the children, packed a few of their things and my own, and called a cab. But when I got home, Mom and Dad were too upset to be very sympathetic.

"You can stay tonight if you want to," Dad said grimly. "But in the morning you'll have to patch things up with Bob."

"I'm through with Bob," I said. "I'll never go back there as long as I live."

"Don't be foolish, Ann," Dad said. "You're a grown woman now. You took on a job. You can't quit just because you're tired of the job."

I looked at Mom. She shook her head disapprovingly. "Dad's right, Ann. It would be an awful hardship for us to take in you and two babies. It just isn't fair to us, or to Bonnie."

"I'll work," I pleaded. "I'll go out and get a job tomorrow—if you'll just take care of the kids for me during the day, Mom. Please, please—you've got to help me."

They wouldn't give in to me, and in a way, I couldn't blame them. In the morning Bob came, looking upset and ashamed. He admitted the fight had been his fault and told me he was sorry. But more than just that fight was wrong with our marriage, and I knew it. Maybe Bob and I still did love each other, but that love was slowly wearing away.

"I can't face any more of it," I said bleakly. "If my parents won't let me stay here, I'm not going back. I'll get a job and take care of the kids myself."

"You can't do that, honey," Bob said. "Stay here a few days and get rested up. You're all tired out." I shook my head. "I'm tired all right—tired of marriage. And so are you."

Bob didn't look at me. "That might be true, Ann," he said. "But we can't afford to admit it. We've got responsibilities and obligations."

"I don't care," I said stubbornly. "I've had all I can take."

Bob got up, his face tight. "Well, if that's the way you feel about it, I'm willing. It's no picnic for me either, believe me. But you'd better think it over and be sure."

I spent the next few days begging my family to let me stay. Dad held out, but Mom began to weaken. One night, I overheard her say to Dad, "Maybe we'd better face up to it, Dick. If she goes back, it'll mean more babies. In the end, they'll probably break up anyway. Then there'll be three or four youngsters to worry about instead of two. Oh, Dick—I don't know what's best. Ann looks terrible, and I worry about her."

"We've raised our kids," Dad said. "It isn't fair that we have to start all over again with Ann's children."

"I know, but she's our daughter. We can't let her down, can we?"

"No, I guess not," Dad said.

It made me feel awful to hear them talking about me like that. When Bob and I eloped, I felt like such an adult, so sure of myself. Now, I felt like a naughty little girl who'd bitten off more than she could chew. I was so ashamed of having to ask my parents to take me in. Yet I knew that if they let me, I'd stay. I just couldn't go back.

The next morning, I got up feeling so sick that I couldn't eat breakfast. Mom shot me an apprehensive look. "Are you pregnant?" she demanded sharply.

"Of course not. It's just—nerves over all this mess." But I was pregnant. The next few mornings were the same. When I went to the doctor, he confirmed my suspicions. I came home and wept bitterly.

Mom was a wreck, too. "You'll have to go back to Bob, Ann," she said. "You can't break up your marriage at a time like this."

"Why did it have to happen?" I sobbed. "It isn't fair! It just isn't fair!"

It was two days before I could pull myself together enough to call Bob. He came over for me. As we drove out into the country, I told him. "Well," he said slowly, "I guess we're stuck."

"You don't look very pleased," I said.

"Well, you aren't. Why should I be? Besides, Dad said—" He stopped.

I stared at him. "You've seen your father?"

He nodded. "I thought we were washed up, Ann. I told my mother. Then Dad called and wanted to have a talk with me. He said he'd still pay for a year of business school and give me a chance to make something of myself. That is, if I broke up with you."

"And what about the kids?" I asked.

"Dad said he'd help support them until I could get on my feet again. Of course, he didn't know about this." Bob paused. "I guess the only right thing is for us to go back together. Maybe we could still make a go of it, Ann. I—I hate to let the kids down. And I guess I hate to admit that I made a mistake."

Tears came to my eyes. "If that's all you feel about it—that it was a mistake—"

Bob reached for me. "I didn't mean that the way it sounded, honey. Maybe if everybody else wasn't so sure we made a mistake, we wouldn't be talking and feeling that way ourselves. Honey, I've missed you—"

His arms went around me, and his lips searched for mine. And, unexpectedly, all the old feelings flowed back over me. I realized that I'd missed him, too. Despite everything, I did love him.

"I'm willing to try it again," I whispered. "And I'll try hard, I really will. We'll show them we aren't beaten yet."

So we got back together, and we tried. But it wasn't easy. I had a miserable pregnancy and was half-sick most of the time. The only bright side was that Mr. Bennett had relented a little. He never came to see us, but Bob was free to go home and visit, and Mrs. Bennett occasionally took Stevie and Todd for a day, which was a big help to me. It gave me some time for myself.

"Roy's really crazy about the children," she confided to me. "But he hates to show it."

Well, maybe he was crazy about the kids—but he certainly wasn't crazy about me. He still blamed me for ruining his plans for Bob.

My parents resented that even more than I did, and Mom hinted that Bob had no business being friendly with his father as long as his father refused to be friendly with me. "Bob's first loyalty should be to his wife," she said.

I didn't want to make a big issue out of it, even if it did hurt me to have Mr. Bennett act that way. But it wasn't any fun when Bob would go off with the kids to visit his folks and not take me.

When I said so, Bob tried to smooth it over. "Dad'll come around if we just give him time, honey," he said. "Let's not push it too hard for the moment. After all, he's made a big concession already."

"Big concession!" Dad snorted when he heard that. "A big lot of nerve, I call it."

My parents couldn't help showing Bob their resentment of Mr. Bennett's attitude, and Bob couldn't help feeling it wasn't fair to blame him. "The trouble with us is we have too darned many in-laws," he said.

But in-laws were only half the trouble. Slowly but surely, we were drifting back into the old pattern—me feeling sorry for myself, Bob staying out nights again with the fellows, and both of us flaring up over the littlest thing.

In the spring, Dad started talking about our buying a small home. "You might as well be making payments on a house instead of throwing money away in rent," he said. "Why don't you suggest it to Bob?"

"And use what for a down payment?" Bob demanded when I did mention it to him.

THEY TRIED TO BREAK UP OUR MARRIAGE

"I think my parents would lend us the money," I said.

"No, thanks. I'd rather live in a tent."

"You don't have to be that way about it," I said. "At least my folks are willing to help. That's more than yours would do." There was a pause. "Well, ask your father then," I said.

"I already have, as a matter of fact," Bob admitted. "He said our marriage would have to be a lot more stable than it is before he'd want to risk any money on it."

"I like that one!" I said sarcastically.

"Well, you can't blame him. After all, you did walk out once."

"Sure, everything's always my fault," I said. "I don't know why I don't walk out again. I'm fed up."

"So am I," Bob snapped. "If anybody walks out, it'll be me."

It was childish to squabble the way we did over such things, but once we got started, we just couldn't seem to stop. "You should complain," I cried. "Try living my life sometime and see how you like it."

"If you didn't spend so much time pitying yourself, things might be better around here," Bob said.

I was so mad I snatched up a clothes basket and started down the rickety outside stairs to get the rest of the washing. Maybe there were tears in my eyes, maybe I was just so upset by our quarrel that I wasn't paying attention to what I was doing. Whatever it was, my foot suddenly caught on something, my ankle turned, and I fell. I screamed for Bob as I went tumbling all the way down the steps to the concrete walk. My head hit something, and pain seemed to be tearing through my whole body. I tried to scream again. Then everything went black.

I came to my senses in a hospital bed, with Mom and Dad standing there on one side, and Bob and his mother on the other side. They didn't have to tell me I'd lost the baby. I knew it.

"It's my fault, honey," Bob said. "I made you mad, and then you—you went tearing down those steps too fast and—"

"Yes, it's your fault all right!" I heard Mom say angrily. "Ann never should have been living in a place with such a dangerous outside stairway. She could have killed herself."

Their voices went on and on. I closed my eyes and wished I really had killed myself.

The Bennetts kept Stevie, and Todd stayed with my family while I was in the hospital. Bob came to see me every night, but I didn't seem to care whether he did or not. I found myself thinking that I never really loved Bob at all. It had been a teenage infatuation, and now it was over.

When I left the hospital, my parents took me home with them. The night after I got home, Mom said to me, "The Bennetts were here the other night, Ann. We tried to talk this thing over as sensibly as possible. We all agree you and Bob can't go on like this and that it's better for you to part while there are just two children. They'll keep Stevie and we'll keep Todd."

"It's all right with me," I said listlessly. "I can't face going back, and I guess Bob feels the same way."

"It's a blessing you lost that baby," Mom said.

THEY TRIED TO BREAK UP OUR MARRIAGE

I looked away. I didn't really feel that way about the baby. It had been a girl, and, in spite of everything, the thought that I'd never hold her in my arms haunted me. The next day was Sunday. When Bob came, he and I tried to talk calmly. "Our parents are right, Ann," he said. "We were too young for marriage. I'm sorry—but I guess we tried as hard as ' could. I'll go to business school the way D wants, and—and just chalk these three years up t experience."

His face was so glum and strained that something clutched at my heart. Did I love him, after all? But if I did, why had we made such a mess of things? People who loved each other managed to get along. And we hadn't.

I cried a little after he'd gone. We'd agreed that a divorce was the best thing—yet that sounded so horribly final. In my heart, I knew that if Bob had really begged me to, I might have gone back. But he hadn't. It might as well be final, I thought gloomily.

It was bitter and hard, though, the last time I saw Bob in the attorney's office. I was full of doubts and misgivings. Maybe it was the wrong thing to do, maybe we were making a terrible mistake. But I couldn't afford to let myself have any doubts. Everything was settled.

Bob left town two weeks later to go to business school in Montfort, and I went to work in a supermarket. That wasn't very glamorous or exciting, but, for a few months, it kept me going. And after the drudgery of keeping house and caring for babies, it didn't seem like very hard work.

But living at home was no picnic. Todd made

extra work for Mom, and she'd get tired and moody. After the novelty of helping wore off, Bonnie sulked if she was asked to even lift a hand.

When I wanted to go bowling or to a movie with some of the girls at the store, the folks were grumpy about it. They seemed to feel that if Mom looked after Todd all day, it was my duty to look after him at night.

"We didn't let you come home so you could run around and have a good time," Dad said. "Todd is your responsibility."

On top of that, I resented the way everyone was giving me advice. After all, I wasn't a child any more. I was working and paying my way. To have people telling me what to do and how to do it made me mad.

After three months of polishing up my high-school computer skills, I found a better job with a big paint firm. Things were getting so strained and uncomfortable at home that I moved into a tiny apartment nearby. My mother looked after Todd during the day, and I picked him up after work. I soon found a woman in the apartment house who would keep him on the nights that I wanted to go out. I felt it was a much better arrangement. At least I didn't have my parents watching every move I made.

Yet, I was terribly lonely after I moved into the apartment. For the first time, I found myself really missing Bob. If it hadn't been for Todd, I'd have gone crazy. He was company for me and helped to fill the long evenings.

But after his bedtime, I'd sit alone and wonder if I was really better off divorced. I no longer saw much of the old crowd. Pat and Larry, along with half a dozen other kids who graduated with me, had just gotten married and were busy with their new life. I was just as left out as I had been before.

Bob and I timed it all wrong, I thought bitterly. *We got married too young, and now we're divorced too young. We ruined a lot of things for ourselves by refusing to wait.*

Twice a week, I went over to the Bennetts' to get Stevie. Now that Bob and I were no longer married, Mr. Bennett was at least polite to me, if not friendly. But there were many things I didn't like about the way they handled Stevie, and if I said a word about what they were doing, I was practically told to mind my own business. That made me furious.

"They act as if Stevie were theirs, not mine," I said to Mom. "I don't like it one little bit. Believe me, if I can get a good raise and afford it, I'm going to take Stevie back with me."

"Well, we'll see," Mom said. "Be thankful they look after him for the time being anyway, and don't be fussing over every little thing."

About three months after I'd gone to work for the paint firm, we got a new accountant, Vic Wilson. Vic was one of the few young, attractive men in the office, and when he asked me for a date, I accepted. To tell the truth, I hadn't thought much about dating, but I found myself looking forward to an evening out with Vic. I was even a little flattered that he had picked me instead of one of the other girls in the office.

We dined and danced until midnight at a nice place on the edge of town. Vic asked me all about myself and listened sympathetically.

"You poor kid," he said. "Hardly more than twenty, and you've been through all that. No wonder you wanted out."

Then he told me he'd been married, too, and divorced after four years of it. "Luckily we didn't have a family," he said. "That complicates things. I think we were both glad to call it quits. I know I've never regretted that."

"Neither have I," I said, although that wasn't quite true.

It seemed so strange to be with another man—strange, and even a little wrong. That was silly, of course. Bob and I were divorced, the decree had been handed down last month. No, the only thing wrong was that it wasn't Bob who was smiling at me across the table, it wasn't Bob who held me in his arms when we got up to dance.

And it wasn't Bob who walked up the apartment stairs with me later and kissed me good night. Almost involuntarily, I found myself pulling away from Vic. He smiled, a quick smile that flashed across his lean, dark face.

"Did I hurry that a little, Ann?" he asked gently. "I'm sorry. But we had fun, and I thought you wouldn't mind."

"I didn't mind," I said. "It's just that you—"

"That I'm someone else—that's what you mean, isn't it? I know the feeling, honey. But after a while it goes away, believe me. When do I see you again? What about Saturday night?"

"I'll see if I can get a baby-sitter," I said.

I knew Mrs. Carlson would keep Todd with her any night, but it cost money. And I really had to count the pennies. If I'd thought that single life was going to relieve me of financial worries, I'd been wrong.

The next date with Vic wasn't quite as nice as the first one had been. We went to a bar for some drinks, and then took a drive. Vic parked and wanted to start some heavy making out. When I pushed him away, he got angry.

"Don't give me that, Ann. You've been married and know the score," he said.

"I'm not dating just to be taken out on some country road and mauled," I told him bluntly. "If you don't like it, take me home."

He took me home all right, and he still wasn't speaking when he let me out in front of the apartment.

But on Monday morning, he cornered me during our coffee break. "I'm sorry about Saturday night, Ann," he said. "I guess I had the wrong idea about you. Would you be willing to sort of overlook it and take in a movie with me tonight?"

"I don't know," I said. "I'm afraid you're pretty fast for me, Vic."

"I promise I'll behave," he said meekly.

I had to smile. "All right," I said. Then I remembered about the baby-sitter, and that I had just a few more dollars to last until payday. But maybe Mom would take Todd. At least I could phone her and see.

She wasn't very enthusiastic about it. "Dad and I were going to a movie tonight. But I suppose if it's important, we can," she said. "What were you planning to do?"

I told her, and there was a disapproving silence. "I don't know that you should be dating, Ann," she said finally.

"For heaven's sake, why not, Mom? I'm divorced."

"I know, but—" Her voice trailed away. "What kind of a fellow is he?"

"He's very nice, Mom," I said, but I resented the question. After all, I wasn't a little girl at home any more.

"All right, I'll keep Todd," she said. "But there's not much point in picking him up after your date, we'll probably be in bed. Leave him here until tomorrow night after work."

Vic kept his promise, only claiming a long good-night kiss at the end of the evening. But when he asked me to go dancing Thursday night, I told him I couldn't. "I can't afford a baby-sitter until the end of the week," I said. "And I can't ask Mom to keep Todd so soon again."

He grimaced. "Families are a complication. Well, suppose I come up and help you baby-sit?"

I shook my head. I didn't want to start that. Dating and having a man in my apartment were two different things.

"Okay," he said. "But we're going to live it up Saturday night then. Promise?"

Thursday night, as I stood ironing blouses, I wondered if I had been a little foolish refusing to let Vic come to the apartment. It was lonely at night, after I'd put Todd to bed. And when I couldn't afford a baby-sitter very often, was there really anything wrong in letting Vic come up? After all, I liked him, and he'd been behaving himself.

A couple of weeks later, I had to refuse a date with Vic again. When he urged me to let him come to the apartment, I finally agreed. He brought beer and a pizza, and we sat around until almost eleven, just talking and laughing and watching TV.

When Vic finally did draw me close, it was in a gentle way. "You aren't afraid of me any more, are you, honey?" he asked.

"If I were, I wouldn't have let you come here," I said. Maybe it was the beer, maybe it was just an overwhelming longing for closeness with someone, but Vic's arms suddenly seemed warm and familiar. I let him kiss me—until I realized we were both trembling. Then I drew away guiltily.

"Who are you afraid of now, sweetheart?" he whispered. "Me—or yourself?"

"You—you'd better go, Vic," I said.

He kissed me again, lightly and quickly this time. "All right, honey. I don't know why I let you get away with things like this. I guess I'm just too crazy about you to put up much of a fight."

I couldn't sleep that night. I lay there, thinking of Bob and feeling perfectly miserable. Was it loneliness that made me respond to Vic the way I had? Or was I falling in love with Vic? After all, there was no reason why I shouldn't fall in love with someone else. But Vic didn't strike me as the marrying kind. He often said that he'd made that mistake once and didn't intend to make it again.

I did a lot of thinking during the next few days. Mom kept asking me about Vic. She knew I was seeing him pretty often, and I could tell she was uneasy about it.

"Are you serious about this fellow, Ann?" she asked me one day.

"Oh, heavens, Mom," I said irritably. "I don't

know." Maybe Mom hoped I would get married again and take Todd off her hands. Or maybe it worried her to see me interested in a man for fear I'd make another mistake. I couldn't tell for sure.

As for me, I didn't know what I wanted. It was fun to be dating again, to be courted and taken dancing and dining. Fun to see that special look in Vic's eyes when we saw each other at work. But aside from that, it wasn't any fun to be living the way I was. I was still horribly lonely, and as worried about money as I'd ever been. Even my work at the office was getting to be pretty monotonous.

At Christmas, Bob was home for several days. He came over to see Todd and brought Stevie with him. We didn't know what to say to each other and just sat there, watching the kids play together. Stevie was starting to talk, and he called Mrs. Bennett "Mommy." That didn't make me very happy, especially when I heard him call Bob "Daddy." Evidently, as far as the Bennetts were concerned, Stevie was still Bob's child, but not mine.

"I hear you're dating," Bob said finally.

I nodded. "A little. Who told you?"

"My parents mentioned it."

Trust them to know, I thought resentfully.

"I hope he's a nice guy," Bob said. "I mean—I'd like you to be happy, Ann."

I looked away. I didn't even want to talk about Vic. "What have you been doing?" I asked.

"Working hard. I've got three more months to go, and then I should be able to get a good job."

"Coming back here?"

He shook his head. "Never. I like Montfort. I'm going to try to find something there."

When he got up to go, I walked to the door with him. He was carrying Stevie. The sight of them together twisted my heart. Bob stared at me for a moment before saying, "Any regrets, Ann?"

I swallowed. "You mean about—about getting divorced?"

"Yes."

"I—I don't know, Bob. I guess I've missed you. But—well, we just couldn't seem to make it work out."

It was his turn to look away. "That's for sure," he said grimly. "Well, maybe I'll see you again before I leave."

When he was gone, I went into the bedroom and cried. I didn't even know why. I just knew I felt miserable. I talked to him once more before he went back to Montfort. I told him that as soon as he started working and could send support money for Stevie, I wanted to take Stevie with me.

"Why?" he asked.

"Because that's where he belongs. And taking care of Todd is hard on Mom. If I have the money, I can hire a woman to look after Todd and Stevie while I work. Besides, I don't like some of the things your parents do, and they aren't very cooperative when I suggest anything."

"They're good to Stevie," he said. "And I'm afraid they'd miss him terribly if you took him."

"I can't help that," I said. "I'm sorry we had to make the arrangement we did, but we only did it so you could go to school."

"Well, we'll see," he said. "I'll be home again at the end of this semester."

I had the blues again after that talk. But my next

date with Vic cheered me up a little. Vic was getting to be a habit—a nice habit, even if he was a little hard to handle at times. Worries never seemed very real when you discussed them with Vic. He could shrug off anything with a happy-go-lucky smile.

I knew I was getting to depend on Vic almost too much. He had moved right into my life, and I'd passed the point where I could lightly push him out. On the nights we didn't have a date, he'd often call and ask to come up. I'd say "no" at first—then let him persuade me.

I knew I was playing with fire. Even if I didn't love Vic, he had the power to stir me. I'd been able to hold him off so far, but he was getting more and more insistent. Sooner or later there'd be a showdown, and that would be the end of Vic and me. I was determined not to get myself into an affair. Marriage, maybe, if I found the right man, but nothing else.

Late in February, I got a bad shock one day at work. During the coffee break, I was talking to Doris Andrews, one of the single girls. I knew that Doris thought Vic was quite attractive, and she'd been a little less friendly to me since Vic and I started dating.

"How are you and Vic doing these days, Ann?" she asked casually.

I shrugged. "Same as usual. We went dancing out at Garden Park last night."

She looked at me, a sudden nasty glint in her eyes. "Vic better hurry up. He's only got about three weeks left to win that bet."

"Bet?" I stared at her. "What bet?"

She laughed. "Well, I suppose you wouldn't

know, would you? The first week Vic was here, he made a bet with a couple of the fellows that he'd be moving into your place in less than four months."

A feeling of sick shock went through me. "I don't believe that!" I said.

She shrugged. "Kid yourself if you want to. But Vic's the kind of wolf who likes to play the divorcees. Safer, he claims."

I don't know why it left me so shocked and sick. I'd never had any illusions about Vic's intentions. But that he could have put the whole thing on the basis of a bet with some of the men at the office. . . . Or had he? Doris was jealous, she could have been lying to me.

"I don't believe it," I repeated numbly to myself. But in my heart, I did believe it.

Vic came up to my desk just as it was time to leave. "How would it be if I dropped around at eight with a pizza, Ann?" he asked.

I stared at him, loathing him. "No, thanks," I said coldly.

His jaw sagged. "What's the matter?"

"Nothing," I said evenly. "Just keep away from me."

"Are you crazy?" he asked in complete bewilderment. "Ann—what's wrong?"

"Forget it," I snapped. "Just don't bother me any more."

He was still staring at me when I walked past him and out of the office. I barely had Todd in bed that night when he phoned. I hung up as soon as I heard his voice. I went to bed and lay there, swallowing back tears. He wasn't worth tears. But it was a shock to my pride to realize that all I meant to him was a safe, easy date.

The next day Vic cornered me and demanded an explanation.

"I don't owe you any explanation," I said.

"I think you do," he said in a low voice. "I've been pretty decent to you, haven't I, Ann? Why should you treat me like this?"

For the first time, the thought really went through my mind: *What if it isn't true? If it wasn't, I wasn't being fair to Vic*. That made me weaken. "I—I can't talk about it here," I said.

"Then meet me at the Alpine tonight, Ann. Please. Give me a chance to defend myself, if somebody said something about me that you don't like."

"All right," I said. "I'll see you around eight."

Over drinks at the Alpine, I blurted it out. Vic flushed angrily. "It's a dirty lie, Ann. How could you believe a thing like that?"

I stared down at the glass in front of me. "I couldn't think of any reason why Doris should tell me a lie."

"I can. She's jealous. She'd like to make trouble." He reached for my hand. "Ann, the whole thing makes me sick. You've got to believe that it's not true."

"I wish I could, Vic."

I suppose I wanted to be convinced. I'd come to depend on Vic's companionship and attention. Anyway, before the evening was over, Vic had convinced me.

"I don't know why I believed it," I said finally. "I guess I owe you an apology, Vic."

"I don't care about that, honey," he said huskily.

THEY TRIED TO BREAK UP OUR MARRIAGE

"Just as long as you don't throw me out of your life." It was late when we got out to the car, and about ten degrees below zero. The car heater wasn't working. By the time we reached the apartment, we were half frozen. Vic pleaded with me to let him come up for a few minutes, just long enough to warm up. I couldn't very well refuse, as late as it was.

"I'll get Todd from Mrs. Carlson while you unlock the door," I said, handing him the key.

"No, wait—" He pulled me close. "Todd's all right for a few more minutes."

We went into the apartment. Without even turning on the light, Vic shut the door behind us and drew me to him in a tight embrace. His kiss was long and ardent. "You could show me you're really sorry for believing that story, honey," he whispered against my lips. "Let me stay with you tonight."

My heart sank. "Vic, please—don't talk that way. I'm not looking for an affair. I couldn't do a thing like that."

"That's not what your kisses have been telling me, Ann. Can't you see I'm crazy about you? And I'll make you happy. You'd never regret it. Trust me, honey."

I tried to draw away, but his arms wouldn't let me go. "I can't take 'no' for an answer, honey—not any longer. I've been patient, haven't I? But I'm human—"

His lips, his voice, the strength of his arms were overwhelming. I wanted to yield, but something wouldn't let me. "No, Vic," I whispered desperately. "I—I just can't."

At that moment there was a rap at the door. We

jerked apart. "Damn!" Vic said.

"Who's that?"

"Turn on the light," I whispered. "It must be Mrs. Carlson."

It was. She stood there, blinking against the glare of the light. "Thank heaven you're back, Mrs. Bennett," she said. "I was so afraid I'd done the wrong thing when I let Mr. Bennett take Todd. But you did know about it, didn't you?"

I stared at her. "What do you mean? Know about what? Where's Todd?"

"This man came. He said he was Todd's grandfather, and you'd asked him to pick up Todd. He did act sort of funny. It worried me afterward, but I—" Her eyes were on Vic, and suddenly I saw the big smear of lipstick along his jaw. *Oh, Lord!* I thought.

But I couldn't worry about what Mrs. Carlson was thinking. Something was wrong, terribly wrong.

I swallowed hard. "It's—it's perfectly all right, Mrs. Carlson. You go back and get to bed. I'll pay you in the morning if that's all right."

She turned away and I closed the door. My heart was pounding as I stared at Vic. "Why should Bob's father have come here and—and practically kidnapped Todd? He hates me, Vic. He's up to something."

"Oh, nonsense." Vic shrugged irritably. "Forget the kid, Ann. He's perfectly safe with his grandfather." He reached for me. "Where were we when that fool woman blundered in?"

I jerked away. "Vic, leave me alone!" I said. "Can't you see I'm scared?"

He pressed me hard against him. "Don't worry, it's all right, honey. If they want Todd, let them have him. We could have a lot more fun if you weren't stuck with the kid. Forget it and kiss me—"

His lips were searching for mine again. A wave of revulsion went through me. How could I stand there letting Vic kiss me when I didn't know what had happened to Todd? I pushed him away again. "Let me go!" I cried. "Can't you see how I feel? I've got to find out about Todd."

"Oh, to hell with Todd!" he snarled.

He tried to grab me again, but I fought him. I couldn't believe this was the same man I'd known for so many months. "I'll scream if you don't get out of here!" I cried. "I swear I will."

He gave up in disgust, hurling me halfway across the room. "All right, you lousy little cheat," he snarled. He grabbed his coat and hat and stalked to the door. Then he turned to give me one more coldly furious stare. "So I lose the bet! That's okay with me. I've wasted enough time on you—and I mean wasted."

I sank onto the couch, half-sobbing with shock and exhaustion. Whatever I'd believed of Vic, I'd never dreamed he could be so cruelly insulting. Not that it mattered. He was the least of my worries.

I choked back my sobs and hurried to the phone. My fingers trembling, I dialed the Bennetts' number. It rang and rang, and there was no answer. *Oh, God,* I thought wildly, *what can I do?* I hung up for a moment, and then called a cab. "Hurry, please," I begged.   Then I thought of my parents. I reached for the phone again. It was Dad who finally answered. Fighting tears, I told him what had happened. "You know how he hates me, Dad," I cried. "He's trying to take Todd away from me—I know he is. There's no other explanation. I'm going over there. Please come and help me."

"Ann, wait—listen, we'd better find out—"

"No, I can't wait. I've called a cab and I'm going straight over there."

I was downstairs and waiting when the cab pulled up. I hurled myself in and gave the driver the Bennetts' address. Huddled in the seat as the cab seemed to crawl across town, I felt as if the whole world had crashed in on me. All I could think of was Todd—his smile, his baby softness, his arms around my neck.

Mr. Bennett can't do it! I kept thinking wildly. *He can't take my baby away from me!*

The cab pulled up in front of the Bennetts' house. I paid the driver and hurried up the porch steps. There was a light on upstairs. I rang the bell again and again. When no one came, I started pounding on the door.

They finally came—both of them. "What are you doing here?" Mr. Bennett demanded harshly.

"I want Todd," I cried. "Who do you think you are, coming to my apartment and stealing my baby?"

"Listen, you little fool—"

"Roy!" Mrs. Bennett cried. "Stop it. Let the child in. We've—we've got to discuss this."

I'd never heard Mrs. Bennett speak so firmly to her husband. I guess her sharp tone surprised him. He stepped aside and let me come in.

"Where's Todd?" I cried.

Mrs. Bennett touched my arm. "He's upstairs and perfectly all right, Ann. Now please, you must calm down, and we'll explain."

A car pulled up in front. My parents came running up the porch steps. *Oh, thank God,* I thought. I threw myself into Mom's arms as she came in. Dad was right behind her.

"What's the meaning of this?" he demanded. "Why did you take Todd?"

"Because this daughter of yours isn't fit to have him," Mr. Bennett said. "The way she's been running around is shameful."

"Running around!" I cried. "That's not true. I've dated one man a couple of times a week. That's no crime. And I've never left Todd alone. I've always had a woman to look after him."

"I'm not charging you with neglect," Mr. Bennett said. "I'm charging you with immorality. Night after night that man has gone to your apartment. I've got the proof. You'll have a hard time denying it."

"But there's nothing wrong with that," I said. "I mean—" I stopped, struck with the realization of how very wrong it could look.

Dad turned to me. "Is that true, Ann? Were you letting Vic come to your apartment?"

"Yes, I was. But it was perfectly innocent, Dad. Nothing wrong ever happened."

"You'll have a chance to prove that in court," Mr. Bennett said. "If you can."

"Court!" Mom exclaimed. "What do you mean by that?"

"I mean I intend to sue for custody of these children. I'm not going to allow my son's children to be brought up by a woman who is morally unfit."

Dad's face was hard and grim. "All right, Bennett," he barked. "Go ahead and ruin my daughter's reputation, if that's what you're determined to do. Meanwhile, get both of those kids down here. Until you win your suit, Ann has custody, and neither one of them will spend another night in this house."

"They're here and they'll stay here," Mr. Bennett shouted. "Don't try to intimidate me."

"Call the police, Dick," Mom said. "We'll just see about that."

Dad started for the phone. Panicky as I was, I had just enough sense to realize that if the police came the story might end up in the newspapers—especially if Mr. Bennett put up a fight. And who'd be hurt the worst? Todd and Stevie—and Bob, too. It wasn't fair to them. I stumbled to my feet.

"No, Dad—wait. I'd rather—rather let him keep them here than fight over them. If I've done wrong, I'll just have to take the consequences, until we can see a lawyer and find out what's right." I turned to Mr. Bennett. "If you really cared about the children or about Bob, you wouldn't have done this, Mr. Bennett. But you don't care who gets hurt, as long as you can spite me. Well, I'm not going to have my children pulled back and forth, just because you're out to make trouble for me."

Nobody said a word for a moment. Mrs. Bennett had started to cry and Mom's eyes were bright with tears.

"Very well," Mr. Bennett said gruffly. "At least you're being sensible about it."

"And it's more than you deserve," Dad flashed at him. "Come on," he said, turning to Mom and me. "Let's get out of here."

Once in the car, I burst into hysterical sobs again.

Mom held me close. "Don't worry, honey. We'll do something."

"I'll see an attorney in the morning," Dad said furiously. "We'll get a court order to have the children returned to you until Roy Bennett can prove his charges in court."

But what if he could prove his charges, at least to the satisfaction of the court? Appearances were against me. Would any court believe me when I said that Vic and I had done nothing wrong? How could I prove that?

I tossed through what was left of that hideous night. My parents had taken me home with them, and I don't think they got any more sleep than I did. In the morning, they looked awful. Mom's face was gray with worry and exhaustion, and Dad's so haggard and lined that he seemed to have aged ten years. It made me feel terrible to realize what this ugly mess was going to mean to them.

After a hurried breakfast, Dad and I went downtown to see the same lawyer who'd handled my divorce. He listened to the whole story, and then looked at me gravely. "You did let this man come to your apartment, Mrs. Bennett? He was a frequent visitor, I take it."

"Yes," I said. "And I realize now how it looks. But I swear it was innocent."

He nodded. "Unfortunately, there will be little for the court to go on but appearances. You may be able to convince them you were guilty of nothing more than indiscretion—you may not. A great deal will depend on which judge is sitting. It's apt to be Judge Connolly, and he's usually pretty severe on the mother in this type of case."

"Do we have to leave the kids with the Bennetts until this comes to court?" Dad demanded.

"No, your daughter still has custody, and we can get a court order compelling Mr. Bennett to return the children. Possibly, the mere threat of such action will make him reconsider. Why don't you talk to him again and see? If he refuses to cooperate, we can resort to the court order."

Armed with this information, Dad and I drove over to the Bennetts' just before noon. With the long strain, I was ready to burst into tears at any moment, but I was determined to control myself. Then, as we drove up, I saw Bob's car standing in the driveway. It was almost the last straw. To have to face him too, with these ugly accusations hanging over me . . . .

We rang, and Mrs. Bennett came to the door with Todd in her arms. Instinctively, I reached for him, and he stretched out his chubby little hands. "Oh, darling, darling," I whispered, hugging him close to me. "Mommy's missed you."

We went into the living room where Mr. Bennett and Bob sat. "We've been to see an attorney," Dad said. "The children are to stay with Ann until this thing is settled. If you won't give them up, Roy, we'll be back with a court order that will force you to."

I couldn't look at Bob. He was holding Stevie, and he got slowly to his feet. "Nobody's going to make any fuss," he said evenly. "That's all over. Ann and I are the only ones who have any right to decide anything about these kids. Nobody here has shown they have more real sense of responsibility toward Stevie and Todd than we have."

He turned to his father and his face was bitter. "You had no right to do what you did, Dad. If you believed Ann was misbehaving, you should have come to me about it, not taken matters into your own hands."

Mr. Bennett sprang to his feet. "Are you such a fool that you'd stand by and see her practically living with another man, and still think she's fit to bring up your children?"

Bob walked over to where I stood. "Ann, look at me. Was there anything between you and him, Ann?" he asked in a low, strained voice. "Were you—was it like Dad says?"

I shook my head. "No, Bob, it wasn't. I was a fool to ever allow him to come to my apartment, but I only did it because I was so lonely and lost. I was a fool—but that was all. I swear it."

"That's good enough for me," Bob said. He turned to look at all of them. "Ann was my girlfriend for a year, and my wife for three years. Never, in all that time, did she give me any reason to think she was an immoral person. Nobody's going to tell me she's suddenly turned into one, because I won't believe it." His eyes went resentfully to his father. "Maybe, if you'd ever taken the trouble to get to know her, Dad, you'd have realized how ridiculous your accusations sound."

My heart was beating so violently with love and gratitude for Bob that I thought it would burst. I sank into a chair, covering my face with my hands.

"You can go ahead with your plans, if you insist," Bob went on to his father. "But I'm warning you that if you do, I'll go into court and defend Ann. And I'll never set foot inside this house again. I mean it,

Dad. You were unfair to her from the start, and I was too much of a kid to stand up for her. I let you push me around, the way you always had. I even let you pressure me into breaking up our marriage. But I'm not a kid any longer. I'm a man, and I'm going to rely on my own judgment."

Mr. Bennett just sat there, staring sullenly at Bob.

"Get the kids' things, Mom," Bob said. "Ann and I are going to take our children for a ride—if nobody minds too much."

The whole thing was like a dream—terror and misery suddenly melting into joy and relief. Half dazed with the miracle of it, still clutching Todd, I followed Bob and Stevie out to the car.

"I guess it's too cold to drive around with the kids," Bob said. "But I wanted to get away from the folks, so we could talk. Let's go over to your apartment. I could do with a cup of coffee."

He told me then that his mother had called him early in the morning before his father was up. He hadn't even waited to eat breakfast before leaving for home. "Mom didn't approve of what Dad was doing. She felt sorry for you, Ann."

We put Todd to bed and settled Stevie on the floor with some toys. Then, we sat down to coffee in the tiny living room of my apartment. Bob flashed me a smile as he tasted the coffee. "With all your faults, you always did make a good cup of coffee," he said.

"With all my faults," I said huskily, "I didn't deserve to have you come to my defense like that, Bob."

"Why not? I've been doing a lot of looking back these past few months, Ann. And I know one thing—you were a good wife and a good mother. There were plenty of nights you could have gone out while I had to work, and you never did. Maybe that was part of the trouble. You were tied down too much, and I was such a dumb kid I didn't realize how hard it was on you."

I swallowed thickly, without saying anything. I was thinking how good it was to have Bob sitting there, how natural and right.

"As for me," Bob said. "I got too serious too fast, again because I was a dumb kid who figured that was what you had to do. I took all the fun out of our marriage, because I was so intent on proving I was mature enough to live up to my responsibilities. Maybe if we hadn't always had to be proving ourselves to somebody—my folks or yours—we might have made our marriage work."

I nodded slowly. "I guess that was the price we paid for being married too young, Bob. But, oh, I wish—" I broke off and stared across the room.

"Wish what?" he asked after a moment.

"I wish we had waited and still had our chance."

There was a long silence before he said, "We still do have a chance, Ann—if we want it. I think we've both learned something by all this. Or didn't you mean what you said—that you'd felt lonely and lost?"

"I meant it, Bob. It was awful, really." I turned and looked at him. "You said something to your father that I didn't understand. You said he had pressured you into breaking up our marriage."

He nodded. "That was true. He really worked on me while you were in the hospital after the miscarriage. He convinced me we'd made a hopeless mess of things. Then, when you acted as if you'd just as soon call it quits—well, I couldn't see any point in begging you to come back." Bob paused. "If I had—"

"Oh, Bob, if you had, I'd have been willing. I wondered why you didn't."

He got up slowly and came toward me. Drawing me to my feet, he held both my hands in his and gazed straight into my eyes. "Ann," he said softly, "I get through school next month. I've already got a good job lined up with a wholesale grocery company in Montfort. Let's try again—down there, by ourselves. You and me and the kids."

My heart leaped.

"We never stopped loving each other, did we? Underneath everything—we didn't, did we, Ann?"

"No, Bob, we didn't." It was true. I'd never cared for Vic. I'd only turned to him out of loneliness.

"I dated other girls," Bob said. "They didn't mean a thing to me. I kept thinking about you and the kids. Maybe I was growing up—slowly. It's too bad we had to do our growing up while we were trying to cope with all the problems of marriage. But it's done now, and this time I think we're really ready for marriage."

The tears in my eyes—tears of joy and gratitude—said all that I could say. Bob kissed me, and, as our lips met again, I knew there could never have been any other man for me.

"We'll wait two months, until I get a paycheck and can find an apartment for us," Bob said happily when we drew apart at last. "Let Mom keep Stevie so she can gradually get used to having to make a break with him. And you stay at home, so Dad won't get any more crazy ideas. I told him this morning that, from now on, if he wanted to enjoy his grandchildren, he was going to have to treat their mother with respect. I told him that what he'd done had been an insult to me—inferring I didn't have the brains to pick a decent girl for my wife."

I wanted to laugh aloud with joy. "Well, I don't think I was so dumb," I said. "I managed to pick a decent boy. Oh, Bob, remember how we stayed apart that night before our marriage? Somehow I'd forgotten that, along with so many other good things about you."

Two months later, Bob came home for us. Our divorce had simply been vacated at our request, since it wouldn't have been final until a year had passed. We were man and wife again and starting a new life when we left Ferrisville that day.

"First stop, Winfield," Bob said.

I looked at him and he grinned. "I stopped and made reservations at our honeymoon motel on the way up. Same unit and everything—only they're putting in beds for the kids. We're going to do this right, honey. We're going to start over from the very beginning."

And it was right—right and wonderful to lie there that night, with Bob in my arms and our babies asleep, remembering the magic of that first night together almost four years before. And remembering this time to never, never forget!

And I haven't. Bob and I have been back together for over two years now. We have a little daughter, Sue, to take the place of the baby we lost. Never once have either of us regretted that we tried again. Older and wiser now, we know that nothing in the world is worth working for as much as a happy marriage. But that's something you have to learn with time. When you're young, you think that marriage will work all by itself. But it won't—you have to make it work.

The Bennetts come to visit us almost as often as my parents do. Dad Bennett has finally reconciled himself to our marriage. He knows now that Bob and I have a solid marriage, and he's shown me in a dozen little ways that he regrets all the trouble he made. As for me, I hope I'm mature enough at last to forgive and forget.

I realize now that Bob and I did it the hard way—the way that probably ends in disaster nine times out of ten. We're just one of the lucky couples who managed to survive, despite the odds. When our little Sue gets old enough to find a boy and start thinking of marriage, I know I'll say to her, just as Mom said to me, "Please wait."

But, if she won't wait, then I can only hope the boy will be as good and wonderful as Bob.   THE END

I WASN'T READY TO KISS HIM GOOD-BYE

My five-year-old came running in the house all excited. "Mommy I picked you a flower! Isn't it pretty?" I took the pink flower from my little boy and observed it. He waited impatiently for my reply.

"It's perfect, Timmy, just like you." He flashed me his gorgeous smile, and my heart filled with love. I gave him a hug and kiss. Then he ran back outside to play. My Timmy is a perfectly healthy five-year-old little boy thanks to modern medicine.

My story started when my husband, Pierre, and I had been happily married for over two years. We had a beautiful baby boy named Paul. Our son was about five months old when I suspected I was pregnant again. I went to the doctor, and my suspicions were confirmed.

I knew that I should have been happy, but I felt as though a bombshell had been dropped on my life. I had an infant, I had lost all my weight from my previous pregnancy, and I had just been promoted to manager at my company. Things were going so smoothly. . . .

For the first two months of my pregnancy, I made life miserable for my husband and myself. I was actually mad at Pierre because I was pregnant again so soon after giving birth to Paul.

In my third month, I began to accept the fact that in seven months, there would be another baby. I even began to think it would be nice to get the bottles, diapers, teething rings, and all the other things that went with infancy, over at the same time, rather than starting all over again when Paul was older. And the idea of my children being playmates appealed to me a great deal also.

My husband came home one night with a yellow rose in his hand. Yellow roses were my favorite.

"What's this for?" I asked.

He said, "Just because I love you. I know you were depressed for a while, but it's so good to see you happy again. Things will be terrific, you'll see."

But in the months that followed, things were not terrific. In my third month of pregnancy, I thought I was coming down with the flu. I took the day off from work and went to the doctor.

I took Paul over to my friend's house. Then I went to the naval hospital, since Pierre was in the Navy. When I got to the hospital, the doctor examined me and said I had the flu, but he couldn't prescribe anything because of my pregnancy. I went and picked up my son, feeling just as miserable as when I left.

I decided we should go grocery shopping since I was off work for the day. When we got home, I took Paul into the apartment. Then I went to take my groceries out of the car. When I went out to get my last bag, my pants suddenly felt wet. I looked down and saw I was standing in a small pool of blood. I ran back into the apartment. I was so hysterical, and I couldn't even begin to contemplate what I should do.

Just then, the phone began ringing. I was crying as I answered it. It was my mother, calling from Baltimore. My mother, the lifesaver. It seemed she always knows when I need her.

"Honey, what's wrong?" Mom asked.

"Mom, I think I'm having a miscarriage. I just started bleeding very badly. It's like my water broke, only it's blood and it won't stop."

"Kendra, hang up the phone and get in contact with Pierre at the base. Tell him to come and take you to the hospital. Don't try to drive yourself," Mom ordered.

I did as my mother instructed, and Pierre was home in half an hour. Then we had a twenty-minute drive to the hospital. The doctor examined me, thinking perhaps I was not pregnant after all, because of the way I was bleeding. I insisted that I was. He pulled out my medical file, then confirmed that I was, indeed, pregnant.

The doctor said, "Mrs. Peterkin, you are pregnant, but the chances of you carrying this baby are slim."

I asked the doctor what I could do to prevent having a miscarriage. He advised me to go about my regular routine and said that whatever happened was beyond my control.

I continued to work, knowing that I shouldn't, but we were dependent upon my income to help meet our financial obligations. When I went for my checkups, I tried to get the doctors to sign disability papers, so I could quit my job and receive compensation, but they refused. Finally, in my fifth month of pregnancy, after bleeding constantly for two months, it stopped.

When I went for my next checkup, the doctors said things seemed to be looking good. I felt so relieved; it was like a big weight had been lifted from my heart. During my fifth month of pregnancy, I felt terrific. I was pleased about the way things were going. I had never been much of a believer in God, but I began asking God to watch over my baby. I felt I was going through this ordeal as punishment because I hadn't wanted the pregnancy originally.

During my sixth month of pregnancy, I began to have problems again. I was very weak. My legs began to swell, and I had varicose veins erupting from my hips to my toes.

It was the procedure, in the navy hospital, to get a different doctor almost every time you had an appointment. The doctors I had seen had all been men, and I felt they had no compassion for a sick pregnant lady. At the beginning of my seventh month, I felt like I would die. I was having such a hard time. I was very worried about the baby. They only gave me a twenty-five percent chance of ever delivering it. I knew it must be a strong baby to survive that ordeal, but I had very strong fears that it would all end in tragedy.

Pierre went to the doctor with me for my next checkup. "This has gone too far, Kendra. You're quitting work whether or not the doctor signs those papers. Our baby's life is at risk," he said.

That time a female doctor examined me. She reviewed my record and was appalled at the fact that I was still working with all the complications.

"I'm surprised you ever carried this baby," she said honestly. "Bring me the necessary forms to fill out and sign for your compensation. Then go home for the next two months, kick your feet up, and take it easy."

I felt that God must be looking out for my baby and me.

But my planned two months of taking it easy turned into three days. On the third night, after I quit my job, Pierre worked his regular shift at the base and then worked another. When he finally came home and went to bed, he might as well have been comatose.

It was almost ten when I heard Paul wake up.

"Good morning, bear!" I said.

He smiled as I called him by his nickname. I lifted him out of his crib, and a very sharp pain shot through my stomach. I sat down on the floor, but it seemed to get worse so then I lay down, thinking it would only be for a few minutes. The pain kept getting worse, and I couldn't even sit up.

Our bedroom was right across the hall from the nursery. I kept calling for Pierre, but my voice was so weak, and he was in such a deep sleep he didn't hear me. I was worried about Paul. He needed to be fed and have his diaper changed, and I was unable to care for him. The bedrooms were upstairs, and I was afraid Paul might crawl out of the room and fall down the stairs.

He was a year old, but he wasn't walking yet. I always let him crawl up the steps, but I wouldn't let him go down by himself. I was afraid he would fall. My husband thought I was just overprotective. He felt we should just teach our son how to go down the steps so we didn't have to worry about it.

To my amazement, my little boy just stayed in the nursery and tore it to pieces. He was having a blast and was quite surprised that his mommy was letting him get away with it. Four hours later, when Pierre finally woke up, that was how he found us. Me in labor, and Paul going wild.

"What's wrong, babe?" my husband asked.

I had a stubborn streak, and by then I was very irritated with him for sleeping through all of it. "What's wrong?" I cried. "I've been stuck here in labor all morning. Paul is soaked and starving, and you just stay in there sleeping!"

"You can't be in labor! You're only seven months into the pregnancy."

I finally got him convinced it was not false labor, and he made arrangements for a sitter and packed me a bag. I was so angry at him, and I told him I wouldn't go to the hospital, but, of course, I did.

During the ride to the hospital, Pierre said, "Look on the bright side, babe, our baby will be born now, and we'll have it all over with." I wished I could've been convinced that easily. My thoughts kept telling me that if our baby came, it would never survive.

I was admitted into the hospital and went directly to the prep room. The nurse asked more questions, but when she found out I was only seven months pregnant, she took it upon herself to assume it was false labor and told me I didn't need to see a doctor right away.

When I felt I could stand it no longer, I cried, "Please have a doctor examine me! I had a baby just a year ago, and I know I'm not in false labor. My last baby was born only fifty-four minutes after I was admitted into the hospital. My total labor time was only two hours. With that baby they didn't examine me immediately, either. They said since it was my first pregnancy, I had plenty of time. When the doctor finally came to check on me, I was ready to give birth. The baby was born so quickly. I was never prepped or taken to the labor room. I just went straight to delivery, and my baby was born. If my labor patterns are similar, I know this baby will be born quickly. May I see a doctor now?" By that point, I was nearly hysterical.

I must have convinced her. The doctor finally came to see me. After the doctor examined me, he said, "Mrs. Peterkin, you are definitely in labor, but, since you're only seven months along and because of past complications, I am going to stop your labor for at least twenty-four hours. We are not sure what complications your baby may have. A birth at seven months can mean the baby could have severe lung problems. I feel if your baby were to be born now, the chance of survival would be very slim." I gave my consent to stop the labor.

The next thing I knew I could hardly breathe. Everything was blurry and spinning around. I kept fading in and out of consciousness. I could hear voices but nothing was making any sense. Someone kept asking me crazy questions like if I was addicted to any drugs or alcohol or if I had fallen recently. I learned later that those were questions they asked during premature labor, trying to determine a cause.

I heard someone say, "She and the baby are both in distress. I can't get a heartbeat from either one."

I think someone started shaking me.

I thought: *I must be dreaming. My baby and I might die!* I called out for Pierre, but he wasn't there.

"Mrs. Peterkin, we are going to induce your labor and try to save your baby," the doctor said.

Nothing was making any sense at all. I was so scared, and I knew something terribly wrong would happen if my husband was not in that delivery room with me. I needed his love and strength to help me be strong. If something were to happen to my baby or if I were to die, I didn't want to be alone. I needed my husband by my side.

I finally won because when I was wheeled into delivery, my husband was there in a surgical gown and mask. The baby had been conceived from our love, and I felt we should both be there to welcome it into the world—with our love. When Paul was born, I felt like Pierre and I became one. He was my strength, my coach, and my inspiration. He gave me the courage that no doctor possibly could have. With him by my side, I knew I could deliver that child.

The delivery was rough. I couldn't breathe properly, and they had to use forceps to deliver. Finally, my baby boy was born. They rushed him straight to the intensive care unit and placed him in an incubator. I could only think: *Thank God, we survived it! My baby and I are both alive.*

My husband woke me up in recovery. "Kendra, everything seems to be going fine. The baby has no birth defects, and his lungs seem to be strong. Right now it seems the main concern is that he's so small." Pierre smiled at me. "We have a little fighter on our hands. I think he looks a lot like Paul did, only smaller. The hospital wanted a name for the baby immediately, so I told them Timothy Lee, like we had decided."

"That's fine, sweetheart," I said.

Before Pierre left, we clung to each other for a few moments and both ended up crying, releasing all of our fear and anxiety. He told me to try and get some rest. Pierre was going home to be with Paul. The poor little guy had probably thought we had abandoned him.

Later in the evening, I was transferred to the maternity ward. It was depressing—all the mothers had their babies, and I hadn't even seen mine yet. He was on a different floor, and he couldn't be brought to me because the doctors were still concerned about my health. I wasn't even permitted out of bed.

I had a restless night. As soon as dawn broke, I rang for a nurse to get a wheelchair and take me down to see my baby. When I went into that unit, my heart broke. There were at least a dozen tiny babies hooked up to needles and machines, all looking so helpless—and perhaps hopeless.

When I reached my baby, I couldn't believe how tiny he was. He looked so sick and helpless that I feared he would never survive. The nurse offered to wrap him in blankets so I could hold him. His lungs were strong and he didn't need oxygen, so she said he could come out of the incubator for a few minutes.

I was afraid to hold him. He seemed so delicate. I thought I would hurt him, so I just caressed him from outside the incubator.

When I went back upstairs, I called my parents.

My dad asked if I thought my baby would survive. It really shook me, hearing my fears voiced out loud.

"I don't know, Daddy. He's so tiny. I'm afraid to even hold him," I admitted.

I got off the phone and went to lie down for a while. The nurse rang and told me I had a visitor. When I went to the waiting room, I was thrilled to see that Pierre had brought Paul with him.

But my son was fussy the whole visit. I guess he didn't understand why I wasn't at home. He never had been away from me, except when I worked. He cried when he left. I was so upset that I wanted to leave with them, but I knew I couldn't.

Usually, the hospital only kept new mothers overnight, two days at the most. But, the doctor kept me for a week because of my poor health. He didn't think I was strong enough to be back home with my active little boy.

The next day when I went down to see my baby, his skin was yellow. The doctor said he had jaundice but assured me this was very common in premature babies. Timmy had stopped eating and was losing weight, which he certainly couldn't afford to do.

And it was just the beginning for my baby, the first of many problems. They were constantly doing new tests and trying to provide treatment for him. Every hour of every day seemed like a touch-and-go situation for him. I still hadn't held him yet. With all the complications, I was trying to keep myself from getting too attached. He just seemed to keep getting worse, and the doctors weren't sure what was wrong with him or how to treat him.

My husband didn't understand my feelings; he

held our baby every day. He thought if something happened, the baby should have at least known love. But it was somehow different for me, a mother. Not that the pain was any greater, but that baby had actually been a part of me, and no other bond could compare with that. I just didn't think I could accept the pain of loving and losing a child.

The day I was released from the hospital I forced myself to forget my fears and hold my baby. The nurse wrapped him in three blankets, thinking he wouldn't seem so small. I kissed my precious little son, and told him I loved him, then I said good-bye. I walked out those doors crying, but I refused to look back. I felt such a loss at going home empty-handed. I was sure my baby would never come home to me.

Nearly a week went by without progress. My brother called me from Baltimore. He knew what I was experiencing, since he'd lost a baby a year earlier. He said Mom and Dad wanted to come and be with me. We decided, though, that since Mom was working she shouldn't come. In case the worst should happen, we knew she would need time off. Dad was retired, and I knew he would feel better being with me than sitting home worrying.

My brother said he would put Dad on a plane the next day. I felt better knowing my father would be there for emotional support and to take care of Paul when I went to the hospital.

The doctors called often, asking for my consent to run tests on the baby or to try another treatment. I was never really sure what I was consenting to, but I told them to do whatever was necessary.

On the day Dad was to arrive, the hospital called

and said it urgently needed to do a test on my baby. They couldn't wait for me to come and sign the papers. I couldn't remember what the test was called, but they were to insert needles into the baby's head. I was told it would be very painful.

We went to the airport to meet my father. We took him and Paul home before going to see Timmy. I decided to make a brief phone call to the hospital before we left to see if there were any results on the test. I was told they had canceled the test. I was very disturbed by this, since it had seemed to be so urgent. When we arrived at the hospital, the doctor was gone, and they seemed to have no explanation for the cancellation.

That night was very restless for me. I tried to turn in early, but I couldn't get to sleep. I got up and overheard Dad and Pierre talking. They were saying that I didn't realize the serious complications my baby was having. They were probably trying to protect me, but I felt like screaming.

I knew how sick the baby was, but they weren't willing to talk with me about it! Whenever I cried or got upset they tried to comfort me, telling me everything would be fine. They tried to be strong for me, but they didn't want to listen to my fears, even though I knew they shared them. I desperately needed a shoulder to cry on.

Once Pierre got angry and shouted at me, "Don't bury our baby before he's dead!" I knew we were both experiencing the same pain. I wished we could have been closer and tried to find comfort in each other.

The next morning, a new doctor called me, saying he had been assigned to my baby's case. He wanted Pierre and me to come in and sign papers for Timmy to have a complete blood transfusion. We were apprehensive about this. However, nothing else seemed to be working, so we decided to give it a try.

I went back home at the doctor's request. He said he would call when the transfusion had been completed. Hours passed, and I never received a call. I wanted to call the hospital, but Dad convinced me not to, saying I would get word as soon as possible. When Pierre came home from work, I was pacing the floor. Still no word. We kept trying to think no news was good news.

Eventually, I could take no more. I phoned the hospital and was informed that the transfusion had gone beautifully and my baby was doing fine. They had postponed calling us just to make sure things continued to go as well as expected. They were being considerate of our feelings. After all we had been through, they didn't want to give us false hope.

But I was still a little angry that they hadn't informed us of the progress sooner. I was excited by the news, though. For the first time, I felt real hope for my baby. I said a little prayer of thanks. We rushed over to the hospital immediately. Timmy was sleeping peacefully. He appeared to have lost some of the yellow tint to his skin.

The next day, when Pierre went to work, Dad and I took Paul and went to the hospital. Dad was very excited. He had only heard about my sick little baby but hadn't the chance to see him until that day. Dad stood outside the nursery looking in through the glass.

I WASN'T READY TO KISS HIM GOOD-BYE

When I went to Timmy's incubator, I couldn't believe the change. He didn't look at all like the same baby. The yellow tint to his skin was completely gone. He looked healthy, even though he was still very tiny. He was kicking and crying. My baby was three weeks old, and I never had heard him cry before. I knew in my heart that my little fighter was going to be fine. The nurse saw Dad standing outside and told him he could come in and hold Timmy. My father was thrilled, a real doting grandpa.

I practically had to drag Dad out of the nursery. He was so infatuated with this new baby, he couldn't seem to get enough.

Before leaving, Dad asked Timmy's nurse, "Do you think my grandson will survive?"

The nurse replied, "Sir, you would not believe the change in this baby in the last twenty hours—it's a miracle. After all he's been through and the progress he has made, there is no doubt in my mind. Your new grandson will be just fine."

Those words were music to my ears. I had never been happier in my life.

I was so convinced my baby would be home soon that I started making him baby clothes—newborn clothes were still too big. Two days after the transfusion, my baby started to gain back the weight he had lost. Every day he was getting bigger and stronger, and he was no longer in the incubator. That whole week my baby seemed to thrive.

At the beginning of the next week, Pierre was getting ready to leave for work when the phone rang. I wondered who could be calling so very early. I held my breath as I was informed it was the hospital, not knowing what to expect.

I got off the phone, crying, and ran to throw myself into my husband's arms. He was unsure of what I had to tell him. However, my tears were from overwhelming joy. The doctor had just informed me I could come and take my baby home. But I wasn't expecting it quite that soon. I thought he would have to be at least five pounds. Pierre and I rushed over to the hospital to bring home our baby boy.

At first, I was a nervous wreck. The doctor instructed me to wake Timmy and feed him every two hours. I was afraid I wouldn't hear the alarm go off. He would let out a little cry when he woke up on his own. It took all of his energy, so by the time I got the bottle ready, he would be asleep again.

My father was such a help to me in that first week while Pierre was working. Paul was very jealous of the baby. Dad would try to help in every way possible by feeding and changing the baby so I could comfort my oldest son and get him adjusted to his new brother. Then, during the night when the alarm would go off for me to feed the baby, Dad already would be up taking care of him. He'd tell me to go back to bed and get some rest.

When Pierre came home from work, he would take almost constant care of the kids until bedtime. He was a proud daddy and willing to help in any way he could to make things easier for me. He enjoyed giving them their baths and feedings. He never seemed to think of it as a chore.

Finally, Dad decided Pierre and I had things under control. I felt I had my strength back and that I could juggle the schedule of two babies, so my father went back home.

I WASN'T READY TO KISS HIM GOOD-BYE

I decided not to go back to work. I was still nervous about the baby, even though he was doing fine. I didn't trust anyone with him. I knew if I went back to work I would be too nervous. And Paul also needed me to help him get adjusted.

I worried for months, always afraid something would go wrong. I would get up three or four times during the night, just to make sure Timmy was still breathing. The doctors kept a close eye on him and saw him a few times a week to make sure he was doing fine.

Timmy was tested constantly for hearing and vision problems, just as a precaution. He had a problem with his neck—one of the muscles in his neck was shorter than the others, and it made his neck lean to one side. I was trained by a physical therapist to do exercises on his neck. The doctors felt by the time he was a teenager, the problem would no longer exist. However, after treatments, at the age of five the problem had been fixed.

During the first year of Timmy's life he seemed to be a little behind schedule in certain activities. He ate his first baby food at six months, crawled at nine, and walked at sixteen. The doctor assured me that was perfectly normal for a premature baby. Since he had been released from the hospital, Timmy has been a happy, healthy little boy. His only sickness has been an occasional cold or ear infection.

Now my son is a very active little boy, and he shows no signs of difficulty from his birth. Just by looking at him, you can tell how ornery he is. He likes to aggravate his brother, he enjoys driving me crazy at times, and he idolizes his father. He's a very independent little boy who wants to do things his way. If he thinks he's right, he'll stand up to anybody. He came into this world a little fighter, and he hasn't changed a bit.

He's in kindergarten, which is exciting for him. My son is a precious little boy and one of the greatest joys of my life. I look at the little guy and know everything we went through to have him was surely worth it. He knows I'm writing this story about him, and he is very excited.

I wanted to tell my story for a few different reasons. One is because of all the negative publicity around lately about giving and receiving blood. There is a special person out there in the world somewhere. I will never know who it was, but, because they were caring enough to donate blood—a gift of life—my son is alive today.

I would also like to offer some hope, strength, and encouragement to mothers. For any mother who has lost a baby, my heart goes out to you. I don't know the actual pain of losing a child, but I know what it feels like to come close.

For mothers of sick babies, no matter how slim the chances may seem, don't give up hope and faith. I will always feel guilty and regret the negative feelings I experienced during my first two months of pregnancy. I look at my little boy and wonder how I could ever have had such feelings.

I think perhaps I doubted the existence of God for too long. When I was able to pray and asked for help—even though it was a long, painful period— my prayers were answered. I was rewarded with my son's life. THE END

MY LAST LOVE

As soon as my best friend, Allison, and I were old enough to start daydreaming about boys and romance, we always saw our dreams coming true in exotic settings . . . like on a tropical beach with palm trees, white sand, exotic flowers, and trade winds caressing us.

Well, the first time we actually got to a beach was the year we graduated from high school. That's what you did when you graduated . . . went to the beach the next day. It was the only thing anybody thought about just before graduation: the Jersey Shore, three hundred miles away. We'd all heard stories about the exciting experiences people had the year before, and naturally we all expected something wonderful would happen to us, too.

The week before graduation, Allison and I spent every waking hour getting ready for the trip. We had new bikinis, and we would lay out in the sun as much as possible so we wouldn't burn when we got to the beach. We went shopping for crazy beach towels and sunglasses, and we tried to tune out our parents' nagging advice to be "careful" . . . to remember we were "good" girls.

On graduation night, everybody cried and hugged good-bye because school was over, even though most of us would be seeing each other the next day at the beach.

Allison and I started out the next morning with two other girlfriends, Jenny and Amy. As we drove along the highway we'd pass other cars loaded with classmates, and we'd all wave and holler. And of course we'd see cars filled with kids we didn't know from other schools and towns. Lots of the cars had signs hanging on them saying, "Jersey Shore or bust!"

"I hope I meet somebody who lives in a town near us," Allison said. "Remember that girl last year who met that boy? They just got married."

"Me, too," I said. "If he lives too far away, across the state, it would be a problem getting together."

"Well, I'll be glad just to find somebody to date at the beach," Jenny said. "You can't go to the beach and not have a boyfriend."

"Yeah, I guess you're right," I said. "Something is better than nothing."

We drove into town and saw the dark blue of the ocean at the ends of the streets.

"There it is, there it is!" we squealed. It was the first time any of us had ever seen the ocean.

We rode up and down, looking for the old house with the apartment we were renting for the week. The traffic was so slow, bumper to bumper. Everybody was like us . . . pretty girls with their heads out the car windows and handsome boys sitting in the backs of jeeps, hollering.

It was heaven, sheer heaven.

"Am I ever glad I saved my money for this," I said. "Now I don't care that I made ten million hamburgers last year, working to save this money."

We finally found the apartment and carried in our stuff in. The sun was still out, so we put on our new bathing suits and walked down to the beach. We stood there a minute, looking around to see what other people were doing. Only a few people were in the water. Most everybody else were in little groups sitting on towels, their radios turned up, laughing and talking to each other.

We spread out our towels and sat down, too.

"I know I'm going to get burned," Allison said, reaching into her beach bag for her suntan lotion. "Here, Dyanne," she said to me, "rub this on my back, will you?"

"Hey, I'll do that," a boy said. He was sitting on the next towel over.

"I'll help, too," his friend said.

We giggled, staring at them through our sunglasses.

The first boy sat down on Allison's towel. "I'm Jimmy," he said. "Where are you from?" He didn't try to help her with the suntan lotion. Boys can be just big talk. Then his friend joined us.

"We're from a small town north of Philly," I told them. "Where are you from?"

So we got to talking. The boys had just graduated, too. They were staying at a motel up the beach and were with two other guys, who eventually came and sat with us. One had a Frisbee, and we all got up and threw it back and forth. Nobody really paired off, but we all eyed each other.

"Where are you going tonight?" Jimmy asked us.

"We're not sure," Allison answered, pretending she knew where to go.

The boys looked at each other. "Why don't you meet us later?" one said. "Come over to the Shanty Shack at nine. They have a good band tonight."

"Okay," Allison said. "We'll be there."

"See you later," Jimmy said as he and his friends walked off down the beach toward their motel.

We sat there watching, waiting for them to get out of hearing distance.

"I kind of like the brown-haired one," I said then. "Who likes who? All four of them are great. We don't have to pair off, though. Just think . . . we already have somebody to dance with and we just got here."

"I guess we'd better eat and start getting ready," Allison said. "I get the shower first. This sand is already in my hair."

We got up, gathered our towels and beach bags, and walked back across the dunes to our apartment.

"I'll fix hot dogs," I said. We had brought as much food from home as we could to save money because someone had told us how expensive everything was at the beach.

We gobbled our food down so we would have plenty of time to get ready. And we had to find the Shanty Shack, which we now know was the hottest place to hang out. I was the last one to get into the shower; and by then all the hot water was gone. It was the quickest shower in my whole life. We were all glad we had brought our own hairdryers instead of just one. You would have thought we were models in Paris the way we worked on ourselves. It took Allison twenty minutes just to put on her eye shadow.

Finally we were ready. We got in the car and drove down the street to get gas and ask for directions to the Shanty Shack. Then we decided to ride up and down for a while like everybody else was doing.

"Look at the roller coaster!" I said. "Let's go there tomorrow." I could hear the screams of the people on it.

"Yeah, the rides throw you up against whoever you're sitting with," Allison said as she waved at a boy standing on the corner.

By then it was almost nine o'clock, time to meet the guys. The neon lights were blinking everywhere, and the crowds on the streets were even bigger than before. The sky over the sea was dark, but the streets were lit up like noon.

When we finally found the Shanty Shack, the parking lot was so full that we had to park two blocks away. It was the first time any of us had been in such a place. At home the bars were just beer joints and young people couldn't go to them. This was a nice place for kids our age to hang out.

We could hear the music before we even got inside. Little groups of guys and girls were standing around outside, talking to each other. We walked inside, and for a second it was like going into a dark movie . . . our eyes had to adjust.

"Where are the guys?" I asked, trying to look around into the crowd.

We stood there a minute, just looking, and then

saw an empty table over by the wall. We walked to it and sat down, pushing our chairs so that we could look around.

"May I take your order?" a waitress asked.

"I'd like a beer," Allison said, trying to act like a college student.

"Sorry," the waitress said. "We only serve soft drinks here."

We ordered sodas, and when the waitress walked away I said, "I'm kind of relieved. I don't think I would like beer anyway."

We looked at the band and then at the dance floor. Lights under it flickered pink and green and red. Our eyes searched the whole huge room for the boys.

"Maybe they're just late," I said.

We sat there a few minutes, looking through the smoke. Then we noticed four guys at the next table looking at us.

"Hey, do you want to dance?" one asked.

"No," I said, "we're waiting for somebody."

"Maybe we should dance," Jenny said. "It doesn't hurt to make new friends."

"But we have dates," I said. "If they come in and see us dancing, they'll think we don't want to be with them."

"I guess you're right," she said.

We kept watching everybody. Some people could really dance. We wanted to learn new steps, so we watched closely. One boy was really funny. He kept trying to dance, but then he would stumble and get his feet all twisted up.

"It's ten o'clock," Allison said. "I wonder where they are."

In a few minutes we saw where they were.

"Look," Allison said. "There they are." She paused. All four of us turned our heads to the door. "Oh, no."

"Maybe they're just walking in together," I said, staring at the four boys . . . with four girls.

We watched them walk across the room to a table. Then they pushed up another table so they could be close together, and all eight of them sat down. In a couple of minutes they all got up to dance.

"Who do they think they are?" Allison asked nobody in particular.

"Well, let's leave," I said. "There are plenty of other places to go. They're not the only fish in the sea."

We got up and tried to walk out by the tables near the wall so that the boys wouldn't see us. We didn't want them to know our pride was hurt and that we had been waiting for them. We walked past other guys standing outside the door.

"Leaving so early?" one asked.

We just walked on by without answering.

We walked down the street to our car. Two people in the car next to us were kissing. We got in and drove down the street to the amusement park, with its rides and roller coaster.

When we got to the line to buy tickets, we saw that it snaked around the side of the roller coaster. We waited a long time and we got to talking to some boys. Nobody stood in line at the beach without talking to everybody else.

"Let's ride together," the guys suggested. "We'll hold your hands when you scream."

MY LAST LOVE

We did ride with them. They were nice, though not as handsome as the ones who'd stood us up. Then we walked around with them and bought cotton candy. It was fun, but it just wasn't the same. We had had our minds set on the others, and getting stood up just threw a wet blanket on everything. These four said they would follow us home to our apartment, but we just weren't in the mood to bother so we told them that maybe we would see them tomorrow.

Then we walked up and down the boardwalk, looking in the shops at seashell necklaces and posters of good times at the beach. Finally, we decided to go back to the apartment.

"Let's walk on the beach," I suggested. "We can see how the beach looks when you get to kiss in the moonlight.

Back at the apartment, we took off our nice clothes and put on jeans to go walking along the beach. It was awfully nice. The wind was blowing, but it was not too strong, and the sand was still warm between our toes. Way off across the horizon we could see a ship with blinking lights.

We sat down. People were walking along the beach in the dark, mostly couples holding hands. Then we heard voices coming nearer, voices we recognized . . . the four guys who'd stood us up!

"Listen," I said. "Do you hear them?"

We didn't say a word. We strained our eyes in the dark, looking down the beach in the direction of the voices. As they got closer we could see that it was the four boys, still with the four girls. They were all paired off, holding hands. We didn't say a word as they passed by us.

"Well, it's not as though we really knew them," Allison said.

"But they were rats to stand us up," Amy insisted.

"That's true," I agreed. "But tomorrow is another day."

"But it still hurts your feelings to get stood up on your first night at the beach," Allison said.

We went inside and got ready to go to bed. It had been a pretty exciting day. We had two big beds in one bedroom.

"This bed feels like the mattress is made out of rocks," I said.

"And there is sand in it even though I took a shower," Allison said. "I wonder how people stand the sand all the time."

The next morning we headed right down to the beach. We didn't see the four guys again, but we talked to other ones. We talked to some girls, too, who were staying in the apartment next to ours and they invited us to a party at their place that night.

The party turned out to be lots of fun, everybody dancing and laughing. It was really funny when Allison was sitting on the porch railing and fell off backward onto the sand below. Thank goodness the porch was near the ground. We made lots of new friends, and from then on we were never alone on the beach or at night.

We went back to the Shanty Shack every night. We even got kissed a few times . . . not by anyone special, but at least we could tell ourselves we'd been kissed at the beach.

Sometimes we would talk to our other friends from school and we would ask each other, "Meet anybody special yet?" Then we would all lie and say, "You wouldn't believe how great he is, and he's going to visit me when I go home." Nobody was sure of what was real and what wasn't. Finally the week ended and it was time to go home. We hated leaving our new friends. Everybody cried and promised to meet again the next year, but we knew it would never be the same, not like this. We promised the boys we met that we would write to them, and they said they would write us.

It was sad as we packed up the car. We had more to take home than we came with . . . two teddy bears we had won throwing balls, and each of us had new T-shirts with "Jersey Shore" written on them.

As Allison drove out toward the highway, we looked back at the ocean against the blue sky. After a few miles we could no longer smell the ocean. It was sad, just sad, having to go back to another world from the merry-go-round world we had lived in for a week. There's a magic about the beach like nowhere else.

We told our families what a great time we had, and then we met other friends who were also at the beach and compared notes. For a couple of weeks we watched for the mailman to bring us letters from the guys we'd met. We did get one letter each, all four of us, and we wrote back, but then after a while the letters stopped, and we stopped writing, too.

Life went on. Allison and I went back to work at the fast-food place, and by fall we decided to move down to Philadelphia to get jobs. We wanted more out of life than living in a small town. Philadelphia was where everybody went to try to get a job. It was the biggest city in the state, and we heard from our friends who had already moved there that there was plenty of excitement going on. Allison and I were almost nineteen and we wanted to do something besides fry hamburgers and ride every night from one hangout to the next.

We had enough money saved for a month's rent, so we packed up the car with our clothes and went to Philadelphia. We spent the first night in a motel. It was pretty awful. Some man followed us from the lobby and asked if we wanted to go out with any guys that night. He was fat and had greasy hair and smoked a cigar. At least we had enough sense to know there was something strange about him.

"If you speak to us again," I said, "we're going to call the police."

We made sure the door to our room was locked. The next morning we looked for an apartment. We knew we couldn't afford a fancy one, but we found a one-bedroom apartment that was nice. It was unfurnished, but it had a pool. Even though it was too late in the year then to be able to sit around a pool, we knew it would be nice when spring came.

We moved in right away. All we had were two folding lawn chairs to sleep in, a pot and a frying pan, a couple of plates, and our clothes and blankets. We had big plans for what we would buy later.

We felt pretty good that night, even in our bare apartment.

"I just know something great is going to happen to us," I said.

"Yeah, and I hope the greatest thing is that we can buy beds," Allison said.

The next morning we went to the telephone company to get a number, while we were there, we went to the personnel office and filled out applications. Both of us had done well with shorthand and typing in high school so we thought we'd at least submit an application. We decided to drive around and fill out applications at other offices as well. But it was pretty discouraging because nobody even bothered to interview us. We just filled out the forms and left.

That night we made hamburgers for supper. We were afraid to spend our money too quickly. We wanted to go to a movie, too, our second night in the big city, but we didn't want to spend that extra money.

Every day we went looking for jobs. Allison went one day, and I went the next, taking turns staying in the apartment in case anybody called us for an interview. By the weekend we were really discouraged.

"What should we do? Should we go home?" Allison asked.

"Well, we still have three more weeks of paid rent," I said. "I just hate to give up so soon."

On Monday morning the call came for Allison. It was a furniture company looking for a secretary. She got dressed in her navy blue suit, the only one she had, and a white blouse. We had read magazines to see how business girls looked.

I stayed home to answer the phone in case I got a call, but none came. In a couple of hours Allison came back. I thought she would knock the door down getting in.

"I got it! I got it!" she cried. "I start work tomorrow. And guess what? I can buy furniture at a discount. We can get twin beds. No more sleeping on those chairs."

I was happy for her, but sad that nobody had called me.

The next morning Allison went to work. I stayed home in the morning in case a call came and then I went out in the afternoon. I had to ride the bus since Allison had taken the car.

A week went by and still no call.

"I guess I'll have to get a job frying hamburgers again," I told Allison. I felt embarrassed that she would be getting a paycheck and I was not able to pay for anything. She had even bought us a steak, the first one we had, and the furniture company she worked for was sending us twin beds, charged to her account.

I had just come in from filling out an application at a restaurant one day when the phone rang. It was the telephone company. They wanted to interview me for the job of a data processor.

I wanted to jump up and down and scream. I got out the iron and laid a towel on the kitchen counter to iron my one and only suit.

When Allison came home and heard the news, she was happy, too.

"Maybe now we can start going places," I said. "We can go to the singles' bars and movies and concerts and all kinds of things."

"Hey, wait," Allison said. "I don't want to rain on your parade, but don't count on the job. Of course you'd be perfect for it, but remember they are probably interviewing a lot of people."

I wished she hadn't said that, but she was right. And I couldn't sleep for worrying about it. I think I got up half a dozen times that night to walk the floor.

The next morning Allison caught the bus, and I

drove her car to the telephone company. I was there at ten-thirty even though my interview was at eleven.

My hands shook as I took the typing test. I had to type numbers, and I was sure I made a thousand mistakes.

"Could you come in to work next Monday?" the personnel manager asked me. "You scored higher than anyone else who has been interviewed."

Boy, life was great then. I had a job and Allison had a job, and we had money. Oh, not much money, but enough to get by. We could eat something besides hamburgers now and then, and we each bought a new skirt and blouse, and we put our money together and got a couch. That was a step up, not having to sit in the lawn chairs. We put them out on our little patio.

And best of all, we could go places. At first we just went to the movies. But as we made new friends at our jobs, we learned the places to go to that were the most fun. Sometimes we went to the singles' bars. Surprisingly to me, they were nice places where people went to meet each other. Everybody in the city had to meet new friends somehow.

One of the favorite hangouts was City Lights at a big hotel. You dressed up nice to go there . . . high heels, sheer stockings, bracelets, dangling earrings, and perfume.

Allison's girlfriends from the furniture store and my new friends from the telephone company would all get together and go. We couldn't wait for the weekends.

It was really nice at City Lights, intimate lighting

with candles on the tables. The walls were polished wood that reflected the shimmering candlelight. The band played soft music sometimes, along with the fast music. The drinks were pretty expensive, but they were worth it if you sipped on one for a long time.

Best of all, there were men . . . young ones looking for girls like us. They'd come over and talk, sometimes ask us to dance. We got asked out a lot. Sometimes the dates were great.

I began to like one guy named David. He had just moved to Philadelphia and he was the assistant manager at a bank. He was handsome . . . not like Hollywood-handsome or anything, but good looking enough. The first night I went out with him alone was great. We went to dinner at an old train caboose that had been turned into a restaurant. The waiters wore engineer caps, and lights from trains were on the walls. It was also the first time I ever ate oysters. David opened doors for me, and it certainly was a change from dating the boys I'd known at home.

After dinner we went to a movie. I didn't see half of it because David reached over and held my hand. I kept thinking that maybe my hand was sweaty, and that's all I could think about. One time he asked if I wanted popcorn, and I was afraid to say yes because then my hand would be greasy. Strange how little things get so important.

When David drove me home, he came around and opened the car door and walked me to my apartment. I stood there a second, not knowing what to do. I was wondering if I should ask him in, but I was kind of ashamed that we had so little furniture. I was afraid that he would think I was a country girl or something.

Then he took his hand and put it under my chin and leaned down and kissed my lips. That's all. He didn't put his arms around me or anything.

"He is so nice," I told Allison when I got inside the door. "He kissed me, but he didn't try anything. He respects me."

"I know," Allison said. "I was watching through the window." She smiled and I smiled back.

The next day when I got home from work, David called and asked me to dinner at his apartment. I was so happy.

"Help me," I said to Allison. "Will you iron my dress while I take a shower?"

"Anything for love," she said with a dramatic swoosh of her hand.

By the time David rang the doorbell, I was dressed and ready. I hoped he couldn't tell that I was shaking with excitement over having two dates in a row.

When we got to his apartment, I couldn't believe how nice it was. He had expensive furniture, rugs, even pictures on the walls. I could see that he had good taste. He walked over to the stereo and switched it on. Music began playing, soft and low.

"This way, madam," he said, pointing to the table.

It was beautiful. Low candles and silverware by each of our plates. I was so used to hamburgers.

"Sit down, madam, and I will serve you," he said.

First he brought out shrimp cocktail. I thought I would die. I had never eaten shrimp before because they reminded me of little creatures in the creek back home. But I had to eat it. At least I knew to use the tiny fork. It was about all I could do to bite into it, but I did, and it didn't taste too bad at all. Then we had the main course, steak and rice with little mushrooms in it. For dessert there was something chocolate and puffy, and I was too embarrassed to ask the name of it.

After we ate I got up to carry the dishes to the kitchen, but David told me not to . . . that his maid service would clean up in the morning. I was flabbergasted, but I didn't let him know it.

"Come on and sit over here," he said patting the couch he was sitting on.

I felt sort of foolish sitting beside him.

"What are you afraid of?" he asked, sensing that I was nervous. "Here, look at my school yearbook," he said.

Then I sat down, not afraid anymore.

"My picture is on page twenty-five," he said. "Look at it while I get you another glass of wine."

I looked down at the picture, then up at David. He was as handsome then as he was now. I couldn't believe that I was sitting here in the apartment of such a guy.

"Here you are," he said, handing me the wine. He sat down, put his glass on the table, and put his arm around my shoulder. I was so scared. I didn't know what to do because I knew he was going to kiss me.

That time between knowing and getting the kiss seemed like a long time. He slowly put his face to mine, and I closed my eyes. The kiss was long and his lips were warm and tasted like the wine. He put both of his arms around me and pushed me backward against the couch. I put my arms around him, and then he lifted my legs over his.

Suddenly I realized this was going too fast. I wanted him to hold me, yes, but something was wrong.

"Excuse me," I said. "I have to sit up."

"What?" he asked.

"I have to drink my wine," I replied, using that as an excuse.

"Oh," he said. "That's a good idea."

He reached for his glass and then clinked ours together. My wine spilled on my dress. I wondered why he'd hit his glass so hard to mine.

"Oh. I'm sorry," he said, smiling. "Here, go into my bedroom and take your dress off and rinse it out in the bathroom. Wine stains are bad, you know."

It was my good dress. I went into his bedroom and pulled my dress over my head, then I carried it to the bathroom. I held the stained part of my dress under the faucet and then blotted it with a towel. It wasn't really wet then, only damp, and I could put it back on. But when I walked into the bedroom, reaching my arms up to put the dress back on, David was sitting on the bed.

"Come and sit down here," he said. "I want to show you something."

"Wait," I said, starting to go back into the bathroom since I was standing there in my slip.

David jumped up from the bed and grabbed my arm and pulled me onto the bed.

"Wait?" he asked. "Wait for what? I'm not waiting any longer."

He grabbed both my arms and pushed me down. I jerked my knee out from under him and kicked him. I knew where to kick a man when you wanted to hurt him. Every girl knows that.

MY LAST LOVE

David fell backward off the bed onto the floor.

"You little," he began, but I grabbed my dress, putting it on as I ran out the door.

I hurried down the street in the dark, and I kept moving till I found a phone booth to call Allison. She drove right over and picked me up, and by then I was crying.

"I thought he was so nice," I told her.

"Yeah," she said. "Well, some guys are and some guys aren't."

Allison and I decided to start going to other places besides the singles' bars, so one night we went bowling. It was pretty awful. We had barely learned to bowl when we were in high school. Every time I would try to throw the ball down the alley, I would drop it and it would roll off to the side, not even hitting one pin.

"Let us show you how," a man who was bowling in the next lane said.

"It's all in the wrist," the man who was with him added.

They showed us how, gave us a few pointers, and we did improve . . . even though it about killed my arm lifting that heavy ball.

"Want a soda?" the first guy asked us.

We sat down in a booth with them. They seemed nice, though a little older than the guys we'd been dating.

"Maybe they're okay," Allison whispered.

"Well, I work for the phone company, too," the first guy said after I told him where I worked. "I put in phones, but I've never been in the office you work in."

When we were ready to leave, they walked us to

the car. "We want you to be safe," one said.

"I appreciate that," I told him. It was nice to have somebody treating us so kind, not trying to make out with us.

"Can we call you?" one asked.

Allison and I looked at each other, signaling silently that we thought it would be okay. We gave them our number and went home.

"Well, they're not executives, but they seem nice," Allison said.

The next night they didn't call, but we went to the bowling alley again, partly to see them and also to practice. When we went to get a drink, the man who ran the concession stand started talking to us.

"You look like nice girls," he said. "I've got a daughter about your age. I'd want somebody to warn her."

"Warn her about what?" I asked.

"Well, those two jerks you were talking to last night are married. They always come in here to pick up girls. I thought you ought to know that. Both of them have kids, too."

"I swear," I said when we got home, "when are we ever going to meet anybody decent? I mean, we've been here all winter, and we haven't found a good guy yet. Is it too much to ask just to meet a nice guy?"

Spring came and we still went out, except our interest in finding boyfriends grew a little less intense. We learned that it was fun just to go out. We went to parties and learned to enjoy beer over the fruity mixed drinks we always had. We sat by the pool a lot and talked to everybody.

In the fall, Allison and I both got raises at work.

MY LAST LOVE

We bought more furniture for the apartment and painted our bedroom. We learned that sometimes it was fun to stay home. We even got a small color TV.

One evening while we were reading the paper we saw the schedule for the community college in town.

"Maybe we should go to school," I said. "It won't hurt us to learn something new, and maybe we'd meet some interesting men. I'm not giving up yet at the ripe old age of twenty."

We signed up for a typing class, fools that we were. There were no men in the class, not one. We both improved our typing, though. Before class we met some new friends while everybody sat around in the lobby, talking and drinking sodas. We didn't meet any men though because in that part of the building there were all women, going to typing and shorthand classes.

The next time, we decided to take an accounting class. We had walked around and noticed that more men went to those. On the first night we saw that the class was about equal, half women and half men. Again, we sat outside before class and talked to our classmates.

We learned accounting, but we didn't meet any men to take us out.

"At this rate, I can graduate from college and never have a date," I said.

In the spring the telephone company had a huge picnic at a big park. The company was a good one to work for, and the picnic must have cost a lot of money. They had everything . . . barbecue chicken, biscuits, corn, potato salad, and ice cream. At eight o'clock there was going to be a dance with a DJ.

MY LAST LOVE

The manager of our office had asked us to play baseball against the payroll department. We'd practiced for two weeks. I played third base.

Three different teams played at one time, the three fields stretching out beside each other. Our team was losing, five to three.

"Come on, play ball!" our manager yelled.

When it was my turn to bat, I swung and missed the ball twice. On the third try I hit it and ran to first base.

"Hang in there!" the manager shouted.

The next batter from our office hit the ball on the second try and ran to first base as I ran to second. I stopped and looked around and started to sneak to third. All attention was on first base. I started running when—wham!—I was knocked to the ground from behind. My stomach hit the ground first, and I couldn't breathe. Then somebody fell on top of me, and I felt crushed.

"Get up!" our manager hollered. "Get to third."

I tried to get up, but I was just beginning to breathe again.

"Excuse me," a man's voice said.

I rolled over and looked up.

"I think I ran into you," the voice said. A man was standing over me, a ball in his hand.

"You'd better run to third," he said. "Somebody is hollering at you."

I tried to get up, but my knee was bleeding. The man pulled me up, and I started running, my knee aching.

I could hear the shouts from the stands: "Run, run!" Then I felt a hand hit my back. "Out," the umpire called and I looked to see somebody from the other team tagging me out.

I started walking to the bench and looked back at the person who had knocked me down. He wasn't even on the other team, he was playing outfield for another game.

"I'm sorry," he said.

I turned around and yelled, "Look where you're going next time! Play ball in your own field!"

Then I sat down on the bench and somebody washed off my knee and put a bandage on it.

After the game, Allison sat with my friends and I in the tent watching people dance. Guys that I knew came up and asked us to dance, but my knee was too sore.

"Miss?" I heard a voice say as someone tapped my shoulder. I turned and looked up. It was the jerk who'd knocked me down. "I just wanted to say that I'm sorry I ran into you. Would you like to dance?" he asked.

"I have a broken leg," I said hatefully. "and I might have made a home run."

"Would you like some ice cream?" he persisted, like a little boy who was sorry for what he'd done.

I looked at him. He was kind of cute.

"Do you work for the phone company?" I asked.

"Yes," he said. "Do you?" He sat down beside me.

I glanced at his left hand to see if he had on a wedding ring, but he didn't.

"My team lost," he said, shaking his head. "It was because of me. I wasn't watching what I was doing after I ran into you."

"Well, I'm glad." I laughed.

"Does your knee hurt?" he asked, looking down

at it. "Did you get all the dirt out of it?"

We kept talking, and I learned that he worked in design, where they make plans to put up the poles for new lines. He said that he had always lived in Philadelphia. The time seemed to pass so fast as I talked to him. He was sweet. I felt comfortable with him, and I didn't have to play some kind of a game to entertain him.

"See you around," he said when it was time to go home.

I had hoped that he would ask me for my phone number, but he didn't.

"He might have a girlfriend," Allison said when I told her about him later.

When I went to bed, I kept thinking about him. Funny thing, though, he hadn't even told me his name.

When I got up the next morning, I could barely bend my knee. It hurt just awful when I tried to change the bandage. When I got to work, everybody teased me about getting knocked down.

"I guess you don't get a raise this year," the manager kidded.

"Does anybody know who that was that knocked me down? What his name is?" I asked.

"Well, he looked like he was stuck on you when you were talking to him," my friend at the next desk said.

"Really?" I said. "But he didn't even say he'd call."

"He'll just knock you down again," she said, laughing.

Three days went by and my knee got better. I figured there was no use thinking about him anymore.

On the fourth day I was getting ready to go to lunch when my friend at the next desk whispered, "Look who's here. Mr. Bone Crusher."

I jerked my head up and looked. He was coming straight toward my desk.

"How's your knee?" he asked, smiling.

"I'll live," I said.

"I just happened to be in this building and wondered if you'd like to go to lunch. How about hamburgers?"

"I'd love a hamburger," I said.

"By the way," he said, reaching out his hand, "I forgot to tell you that my name is Ryan."

"I'm Dyanne," I told him and smiled.

And so it began. There was finally someone nice, someone decent to go out with because during that lunch he asked me for a date on Saturday night. We went to the drive-in movie the city would set-up during the summers. I hated the idea of going there, afraid that he would try to get fresh, but he didn't.

It was an old Tarzan movie, and we had a great time.

We ate popcorn, and it didn't even matter that my hands were greasy when Ryan held one as we walked to the apartment door. He leaned over, kissed me and said, "Good night, Jane."

I giggled. "Good night, Tarzan."

The next morning I was still in bed when the phone rang.

"Hello," I said in a daze.

"Jane?" a voice asked.

"What?" I said confused.

"It's me, Tarzan," he said.

Then I realized who it was and laughed.

"Are you still in bed?" he asked.

"I was out gathering coconuts for breakfast," I said.

"Tell you what," he said. "Get up and get ready so you come over here for dinner. I want my family to meet you. I'll come for you at twelve. Is that okay?"

"Sure," I said, dumbfounded at the invitation.

I ran to the closet and started digging through it to find the right dress to wear. Not that I wore anything too weird when I went out, but I wanted to look good to meet his family. I was nervous over that.

At noon Ryan rang the doorbell. In his hand he held a coconut. I started laughing.

"I had a hard time finding a store open to buy this," he said.

When we got to his house I was a nervous wreck. Nobody had ever taken me home to meet his family before. My hand shook as I reached out to shake his parents' hands.

"Welcome," his father said. "We're glad to have you here. We've heard a lot about you . . . how Ryan tried to break your leg."

"He didn't mean to," I said. "It was just an accident."

"Lucky accident," Ryan said.

I always felt foolish eating in front of strangers, but somehow I felt comfortable now. Ryan's little sister wanted to show me her rock-star posters, and his folks were just as nice as could be.

Ryan took me back to the apartment before dark.

"We have to get up early, you know," he said. "Have to get to ringing those telephones."

Not many young men would have thought about sleep and work the next day, and I was impressed.

Ryan called the next two nights, and on Wednesday night we went out again. This time we went to an indoor movie. When he walked me to the door, he kissed me again and put his arms around me.

"You know," he said, "I'd climb a telephone pole for you."

I laughed because he was always funny. I put my arms around him. His breath felt warm and exciting on my neck. I pulled his head closer and he nibbled my ear.

I let go laughing, but something stirred inside me something that I hadn't ever felt before. My arms felt like they could float, and my head seemed dizzy. Whatever it was, it was wonderful. Then Ryan kissed my lips, harder this time, and I just wished he'd never let me go.

Suddenly I heard a bell.

"Oh, no, the telephone's ringing," I said, turning to unlock the door. "It might be Allison. She's out tonight."

Ryan followed me inside as I raced to answer the phone.

"Hello?" It was for Allison. "She's not here," I said abruptly.

"Well, come and sit down," Ryan said when I'd hung up.

I went over to the couch and sat beside him. He put his arms around me again. I could smell his shaving lotion, lemon scented, and I would always remember it. He put his hand on my bare knee, and I liked that. His hand was warm like his breath. But something told me to back off. I sat up and pushed him away.

"Maybe you'd better go home now," I said regretfully. I didn't really want him to go.

He didn't call the next day or the day after, and I was a nervous wreck. But on the third day he came into my office.

"Did you miss me?" he asked, kissing my cheek right in front of everybody. "I've been out on a job. Some lines were down because of a storm and I had to go there."

The manager came out of his office. "Anybody who causes our baseball team to lose can't kiss anybody in this office," he said, laughing.

The next month went by like a whirlwind. Everything seemed magical, like it had been at the beach. We didn't go out every night, of course, because sometimes he had to work out of town.

One night Allison was reading the paper and she said, "Cruises are real cheap now. Let's go on one. That might be better than going to the beach. Remember when we went to the beach?"

"I think I'm at the beach now," I told her, "riding a roller coaster."

"You know," Allison said, "a roller coaster hits bottom sometimes. I don't want to see you get hurt."

"Why should you say that?" I asked, my stomach feeling like it had a fist slammed into it.

"No reason," she said, looking sorry for saying anything.

I shrugged, deciding maybe she was jealous because I had a boyfriend. She did get to go out on dates, but nothing special had happened. Her Mr. Wonderful hadn't come along.

For Thanksgiving, Allison and I went home to our small town. I was excited because Ryan was going to come and be with me and my family on Thanksgiving morning. All I'd done before he arrived was talk about him, how wonderful he was, how happy he made me feel.

"You sound like a stuck record," my father said. "Ryan, Ryan, Ryan."

So when the knock on the front door came, my heart nearly stopped. My hands were shaking. I wanted my parents and my sister and brother to like Ryan. But how could they not like him?

He shook hands with Dad, and they sat in the den looking at a football game like they had always been friends.

When Mom and I got the dinner on the table, I was still nervous. I had worked so hard on it, making everything that Ryan liked . . . cranberry relish and pumpkin pie with real whipped cream. Everybody sat down and Dad asked the blessing. I opened my eyes and peeked at Ryan and was thankful that he was my boyfriend.

In the afternoon we went to the parade. I was afraid it would be such a small parade after the big one in Philadelphia that Ryan always saw, but he was excited as a kid and cheered at the last float with Santa Claus on it.

That evening we went to see my old high school girlfriends. I wanted to show off Ryan. He was friendly to all of them and asked about their lives. I was so proud of him.

"Well, what do you think?" I asked one of my friends when we were alone in her bedroom.

"He's certainly nice," she said. "Does he try to get fresh with you? How far have you gone?"

I was embarrassed, but we had always talked in

high school about boys so I knew she meant well.

"You won't believe this," I told her, "but he doesn't push me to do anything I shouldn't. Not much anyway. I have to fight myself, though. I lie in bed at night and think about being up close to him."

That night Ryan went back to Philadelphia. Allison and I were to go back on Sunday night. Friday and Saturday nights seemed like forever. All I could think about was getting back to the apartment, waiting for Ryan to call. On Sunday I talked Allison into going back in the early afternoon.

When we got to the apartment, I took a shower and waited for the phone to ring, for Ryan to call and come over. I hadn't touched him in three days. I just couldn't wait.

Seven o'clock came and went. I walked to the window and pulled back the curtain and looked out at least fifty times. Eight o'clock rolled around and at nine, I called Ryan's house and his mother answered.

"He's not here," she said.

"Oh, I guess he had to go out on a job for the company," I said.

"Well, I don't think so," she replied. "He was here at six, and when he left he wasn't dressed in his work clothes. I'll tell him to call you if he comes in soon."

Ten o'clock came. And a few minutes later the telephone rang and I jumped up from the couch to answer it.

"Hello?" I said, waiting to hear Ryan's voice.

"May I speak to Allison?" the voice said.

"Oh," I said, disappointed. "Just a minute."

"Well, hello," Allison told the person. "What's

new?"

Why did she have to ask that? I wondered. The guy might talk forever about what's new. I walked back and forth from the bedroom through the living room into the little kitchen. I drank cups of tea. I always drank tea when I was nervous, which made me more nervous.

"Please, hurry," I whispered to Allison.

She only talked a few minutes more and then hung up.

"You shouldn't get so nervous," she said. "Ryan probably has a reason for not calling. You aren't married, you know."

Ryan never did call that night, and I stayed awake until two, the caffeine in the tea not helping. I was so tired when morning came and I had to get up and go to work.

All day long I hoped he would come into the office, but he didn't. When I walked into the apartment after work, the phone was ringing. I threw down my purse and ran for it.

"Hi, sweetie," he said. "What's happening?"

"Oh, nothing," I said. I didn't want him to know how anxious I had been. "Did you call me last night? We didn't get back to town until nearly midnight," I lied.

"My mother said you called," he said.

"Oh, that was before I left my hometown," I lied again.

"Well, I went to a friend's party," Ryan said. "You know . . . that guy who works with me? It was his birthday. I sure wish you could have been there. It was a blast. I'll be over tonight, if it's okay."

"Sure," I said, feeling like the sun was shining

again on me.

Christmas was coming, and we had fun shopping. I helped Ryan get a present for his mother. "A woman, even a mother, wants something personal," I told him. "Not a mixer or blender."

The middle part of December we got a Christmas tree for the apartment. Ryan said he knew where there were plenty out in the woods. Allison and I agreed that a tree from the woods felt more like Christmas. Artificial trees weren't the same, and they cost so much.

On Saturday afternoon Ryan came to get Allison and me, and we rode out into the country. The wind was cold, and we had to walk through briars and honeysuckle vines but we found the trees. It was hard deciding which one. We couldn't make up our minds whether we wanted a short one or a tall one. The only thing we knew is that we wanted a fat one. And there it was, not too tall and not too short and fat like Santa Claus.

Ryan lifted up the ax and started chopping. The tree fell, and he dragged it to the car and put it in the trunk. When we got to the apartment, he set it up, and we got out the Christmas decorations Allison and I had been buying. We had red and green balls, silver tinsel, stars, and tattle wooden horses. Ryan stood up on a chair and put the angel on top.

"It's just like you," he said.

We laughed because the angel had a funny look on her face. We drank hot chocolate and talked about how good the tree smelled and wished that we had a fireplace.

I got Ryan a sweater for Christmas, one that I knew he wanted. It took me an hour to wrap it . . .

folding the corners and getting the bow to curl in the right direction.

To make everything even better, Ryan asked me to go to the telephone company party with him. I got a new dress, one that looked like Christmas, sort of shimmery red with silver threads in it and a silver comb to pin my hair back with.

I hoped that all the women in my office wouldn't tease me right in front of him, the way they were beginning to do. It was embarrassing. They would say, "When are you getting married?" Actually, that had crossed my mind, but I wasn't going to get my hopes up, not yet. I was just glad for what I had.

The night of the party Ryan called and told me to meet him there, that he would be late. He didn't explain why, but it didn't matter.

I got to the hotel and went into the ballroom. I saw the people in my office and went and sat down at a table with them. The ballroom was beautiful, red and green ribbons tied around posts and candles with mistletoe on the tables. A giant twinkling ball hung from the ceiling and glittered all over the room. Even the food was beautiful . . . cheese balls covered with nuts and punch bowls full of red punch. It was about the best Christmas in my life. I had gone to the company Christmas party before but somehow things hadn't glittered so much.

"You look nice," a woman who sat at the desk next to mine at work said.

I reached to get a little cracker shaped like a fish.

"Why is Ryan talking to that blond?" the woman asked.

I stopped my hand in midair.

"What?" I asked.

"Over there," she said, pointing across the ballroom to the bar.

Ryan stood facing the bar, his back to us and his arm around the shoulder of a girl.

"Oh, he's just talking. You know he's the friendly type. That's what I like about him so much," I said, putting the cracker into my mouth.

Everybody started talking about work, about the bigger number of phone calls during December, and the extra work we had to do. I talked, too, but my eyes kept watching Ryan. I thought about getting up and going over to him, but I was afraid . . . afraid that he would think I was being possessive. And it was true that he was the friendly type.

I watched him take his hand from the girl's bare shoulder and they laughed. In a little while he turned to leave her and bent down and kissed her on the lips . . . just a peck, not a real kiss, but my heart nearly stopped.

Then he walked among the tables, stopping to talk to people, and then he looked up and saw me.

"Here you are," he said. "I've been looking for you."

I wanted to ask who the blonde was, but I was still afraid, and he didn't say a word. I thought he might say he worked with her or something, but he didn't. I tried to tell myself that he had a right to talk to people. I certainly talked to people, but I wouldn't put my arm around another man.

Then we danced, slow to the soft music. I felt happy, being held by Ryan, being so close. I could smell his lemon shaving lotion, and his breath felt warm against the edge of my hair. I tried to look around the room to see where the blonde was, and

MY LAST LOVE

I saw her dancing with somebody, and I was glad.

The next week was Christmas. Allison and I felt we should go to our hometown and be with our families. Ryan said he would come over to the apartment on Christmas night. It was pleasant being home, being with old friends, and Mom made me my favorite foods, but I was anxious to get back to Philadelphia to be with Ryan.

Christmas morning passed fast, but lunchtime went slowly as I waited for Allison to pick me up.

When we got to Philadelphia, back in the apartment, I kept walking to the frosty window and peeping out, afraid that it would be like Thanksgiving, with Ryan not showing up.

I was looking out the window when I saw the car lights flash. I had watched other cars pass by, but this one stopped, and Ryan got out. I opened the door before he could even ring the bell.

He put his arms around me and kissed me. "Merry Christmas," he said. I looked to see if he had a present for me, but he didn't. I wondered if he didn't buy me one. I went to the tree and picked up the box with his sweater in it.

"Here," I said. "It's your present."

He sat on the couch and opened it.

"Look at this!" he said. "Just what I wanted. You remembered I saw this sweater, didn't you?"

He put it on over his shirt. "Oh, your present. I forgot it," he said, laughing.

"Oh, that's okay," I said, even though it wasn't. I smiled anyway.

"No, I'm just kidding," he said. "Sit down here by me on the couch." He was serious now, which was strange. He was always carrying on and laughing. "I do have a present." He picked up his jacket and reached into the pocket and pulled out a little box.

It was jewelry, I guessed, the necklace I had wanted. Allison probably told him, I thought.

He put it in my hand, and I ripped the paper off the tiny box. I opened it and nearly stopped breathing. It was a ring, a diamond ring! It looked like an engagement ring.

"Try it on," he said. "I know it fits though. Allison told me your ring size."

I put it on my right hand, afraid to put it on my left.

"Wait a minute," he said. "It goes on your left hand. There's where engagement rings go, on the left hand. Of course, you can put it on your right hand. It's up to you. What do you say?"

I put it on the left. I know this sounds corny, but I looked up at the angel on the Christmas tree, and I think she was smiling.

"Allison," I yelled. "Look, look!" I said holding up my hand.

"I know," she said. "I have a bottle of champagne to celebrate with."

We planned a big spring wedding. I couldn't make up my mind at first if it would be someplace in Philadelphia or at home. I finally decided on home, at the old church I had always gone to.

The next thing I did was go shopping for a wedding gown. But they were so expensive, more than two thousand dollars, and that was too much. Mom and Dad didn't have enough money to pay for all of that. Mom could sew really well . . . she had always made our clothes and she said she would make it. She came down to Philadelphia on the bus and spent the night so that we could look at dresses and she could see one to copy. The satin itself cost plenty, twenty dollars a yard. We bought pearls, too—well, tiny fake pearls to sew on the dress, and lace, yards of it.

Then I got the idea about my doll, the bridal doll I'd gotten at Christmas one year when I was a little girl.

Its dress was dirty now and torn, and it was somewhere in a closet. Mom found it and made a wedding gown for it, too, just like the one I would wear. We would put it on the table at the reception.

Ryan decided that we should go to the beach for our honeymoon. It would be warm enough then.

"Well, finally you'll get to kiss on the beach," Allison said, "and you'll get sandy lips."

I felt bad about leaving Allison, but she said a girl at the furniture company would move in with her.

Ryan and I looked for an apartment, too. The one we found was close to the one Allison and I lived in. I was glad to still be near her.

All the women at work gave me a shower . . . pots and pans and towels, and a special gift of a beautiful lacy, sexy nightgown. I showed it to Ryan and he laughed and said, "I can't wait to see you in that . . . and to see you take it off." I was embarrassed to death, but I couldn't wait, either.

The weeks passed quickly. I sent out invitations to just about everybody. Mom finished the dress and started working on the cake for the reception. My friends from Philadelphia would drive up to the wedding.

The week before the wedding Ryan started fixing up the apartment. Allison got us a reduced rate on the furniture. We got a queen-sized bed and a giant soft couch. I bought curtains and put them up.

"Can't we spend the night here before the wedding?" Ryan asked.

"No, it's just a few days," I said.

The wedding was to be on Saturday afternoon, and the weather stayed nice. *Somebody is looking out for me,* I thought. On Friday night we had the final rehearsal, and Ryan had to hurry back to Philadelphia to his bachelor party, given by the guys he worked with.

"My last fling before my neck is in a noose." He laughed.

His family spent the night at my home. Mom had invited them all.

I woke up at six on Saturday morning. The first thing I did was to look out the window to see if the sun was still shining, and it was . . . just peeping over the tops of the trees. I wanted the weather to be good, too, when we got to the beach. We were going to stay in a fancy hotel, not in a ratty apartment like we girls had stayed in before.

I got up and started drinking tea. In a little while everybody else got up and ate breakfast and went to the church to finish putting the candles up and the bows on the pews. Mom took the cake over, and Ryan's mother finished with the tiny sandwiches. At eleven I went to the beauty shop to get my hair fixed.

Ryan would meet us at the church. We were following all the traditions. I wasn't seeing him that day until the ceremony, and I was wearing something old, something new, something borrowed, and something blue. I was carrying an orchid bouquet with long streaming ribbons.

MY LAST LOVE

I went with Dad and Mom to the church at one-thirty and sat in the preacher's office. At a quarter to two the organist started playing "I Love You Truly." I did love Ryan truly. At five minutes to two the minister stuck his head in the door and told me and Allison, who was my maid of honor, that we were to walk around the church and come in and up the aisle. We were standing there waiting for the last guests to go in.

It was just a couple of minutes to two when Reverend Thompson came into the back of the church. "Where's Ryan?" he asked.

"Isn't he here yet?" I asked. My heart started pounding. I was afraid he'd been hurt in a car wreck. My hands started shaking. I looked out the door, waiting for his car to drive up.

Mom came out. "What's wrong?" she asked. "It's time to start the ceremony. Why are you so pale?"

I couldn't move my tongue to talk and answer her.

"Ryan's not here yet," Allison told her. "He'll probably be here in a few minutes."

Another five minutes passed, and it seemed like five years. I peeked inside the church door and people were whispering and looking around.

The minister came back in and put his arm around my shoulder. "Sit down, honey," he said.

"He's dead," I whispered. "He's been killed, hasn't he?"

"No, Ryan's not dead. His friend just called. He's not dead."

"Oh, thank God," I said. "He's hurt but he's not dead."

"No," the minister said. "He's not hurt. Sit down. Here, let me help you."

"What's the matter?" I asked. "What's happening?"

"His friend called . . . He told his friend to call . . . He's not coming. He doesn't want to get married. There won't be a wedding today. I'm sorry, truly sorry," he said, holding my hand.

Suddenly everything got blurry before my eyes. Allison and Mom both put their arms around me. I felt like I was in a movie, some kind of horror movie where everything was black and awful, with a monster running after me.

"I have to announce something," Mom said.

"I'll do it," Reverend Thompson said. "This is the first time I've ever been in such a situation. I'll do it." He turned and walked through the double doors.

"Come on, let's go home," Mom said.

At that moment Ryan's mother came out of the church. "What's going on?" she asked. "Where's Ryan?"

"Your son didn't show up," Mom told her. "The wedding is off. Your son is a—"

"No, Mom," I said. "Don't fuss at her. She can't help what he did."

"Come on," Allison told me. "Let's go to your house."

I felt so weak I could hardly walk. Allison took my hand and pulled me up. She put her arm around my shoulder and helped me to the car.

When we got to the house Mom and Allison told me to take my dress off and lie down. I could feel somebody unbuttoning the back of it. I just let it fall to the floor. It didn't matter what happened to it. I lay down on the bed. My body felt like a rock, like I couldn't move.

"Drink this," Mom said. She put her hand behind my head and held a glass to my lips. It was liquor. "Drink it. It'll make you sleep."

In the fog I could hear Allison whispering, "She hasn't cried yet. I guess she's still in shock."

I went to sleep restlessly, like in a bad dream. I could hear the phone ringing over and over in the distance.

When I finally woke up from my awful sleep, Allison was sitting by the bed.

"Allison," I said, "am I really not getting married?"

"I guess not," she said.

"Where is Ryan?" I asked.

"We don't know," she said. "Why don't you cry? You'd feel better."

"Cry? Cry over what?" I asked.

The night passed and everybody left me alone. I stayed in bed, reliving every moment I had spent with Ryan.

The next morning Allison came back and sat by my bed.

"Allison, maybe he just had cold feet. Maybe he'll come back. I can understand that," I said.

"He wouldn't be worth it," she said.

"But we were supposed to go to the beach," I said.

"You and I will go to the beach soon," she said. "We'll go to Florida or somewhere."

"Where's my cake and the sandwiches and my doll?" I asked.

"Your mother took care of everything," Allison answered. "I'm going back to Philly tonight, and you can stay home and rest all week."

"Why, Allison?" I asked.

"Because I have to go back to work, and you need to rest and straighten out your head."

"No," I said. "Why didn't he come to our wedding?"

"I don't know," she said.

Allison left and my family came into the room, bringing me food. I didn't want to eat. When they all went out of the room I looked out the window and saw the sun going down. I wondered if the sun was shining the same way at the beach. *I'd better cancel the reservations,* I thought. *What if Ryan and I want to go next weekend?* I reached for the phone beside the bed. *We might not get reservations again if we don't show up.*

I dialed the operator.

"Boardwalk Hotel on the Jersey Shore," I said. "I don't know the number."

I could hear the phone ringing. "Good evening," a crisp voice answered. "Boardwalk Hotel. May I help you?"

"I'd like to cancel the reservation for this coming week for room 405. It's in the name of Mr. and Mrs. Ryan Wahl."

"Ma'am, have you made a mistake?" the clerk asked. "Mr. and Mrs. Wahl are in that suite. Would you like me to ring the room?"

"Yes, yes," I said. *Maybe Ryan will want me to come down there,* I thought. Maybe we just got our plans mixed up.

The phone rang and rang, and then there was a hello. It was a girl's voice!

"Ryan?" I asked.

"Just a minute," the girl's voice said. I could hear her giggling. "It's for you," she told him.

I was in shock and hung up before he answered. How could he just leave me at the altar like that? And how could he go on our honeymoon with another woman? I finally cried.

Mom came into the room and saw me crying. "Do you want to talk about it now?" she asked.

"Why?" I kept asking. "What went wrong, Mom?"

The next day I decided to go back to Philadelphia.

"Do you really want to go now?" Mom asked.

"I guess I might as well," I said.

Dad took me back to the apartment Allison and I shared. I went inside, thinking that the things I had moved to the other apartment would be gone. But everything was back and in place, down to my toothbrush in the holder in the bathroom. Allison was a true friend, trying to save me pain. The only thing that was missing was the big eight-by-ten picture of Ryan that had stood on the night table between our twin beds.

"You scared me to death," Allison said when she came in from work, seeing the lights on in the apartment. "How are you?" she asked.

"I'm all right," I said.

"Tell me the truth. I'm your best friend. How do you really feel?"

"My heart is broken, and I'm humiliated. I'll never love anybody again," I said and started crying.

The next day I went back to work at the telephone company. Allison told me to stay in the apartment and take it easy, but the more I sat around, the worse it got. It was hard walking back into the office, even though I knew those people were my friends and everybody cared about me. It was like a little family.

I opened the door and started in. Every type-writer, every machine stopped, and all heads turned toward me. You would have heard a bird's foot-steps. Then everybody smiled and got up and came over to me, asking how I was. I think they were afraid to mention Ryan's name, though.

"Hey," I said, "you can call him a jerk. It's okay to talk about it. He's a jerk, and I'll shout it."

Everyone smiled and hugged me, and we all felt better.

"If he sets foot in this office, I'll call security," my manager said.

"Good," I said. "Do that. I'd laugh." But I knew I wouldn't. I'd cry. I'd cry my heart out.

"You know," my friend at the next desk next to mine said, "I never trusted him. I never wanted to tell you, but I thought he went out on you behind your back. You remember how at the Christmas party he was talking to that blonde? Well, I saw them out together one night after that at a restaurant. It's bet-ter that you learned now what he is than later when you would've been married."

The week passed slowly. Every time the door to the office would open, I'd look up from my desk, afraid it was Ryan and at the same time hoping it was him. I took his diamond ring off my finger and put it in a box.

Every night that week Allison and I went out somewhere . . . to the movies, to a concert.

"There's no way to make it easy," I told her. "I guess it will just take time."

Soon after that, the telephone company had the spring picnic, but I didn't go. I couldn't. I just couldn't face it. And what would I do if I saw him? Several people had told me they had seen him at work, and fortunately the telephone company was big enough that I didn't have to see him. At the picnic I might have seen him, so I couldn't go. The day after, though, the people I worked with told me that they didn't see him there.

So life went on. I didn't die. Nobody dies of a broken heart. My body didn't die, but my heart nearly did. Sometimes a guy would ask me out. Most of the time I didn't want to go, but went anyway. I knew I had to get on with life. I went and was miserable. Most guys never asked me out a second time. I guess I was no fun.

One Sunday Allison and I were reading the paper. I was reading the local section, and Allison was reading the entertainment section. I didn't care much about entertainment.

"Listen to this," she said. "A cruise and two weeks in the Virgin Islands, and it's cheap. Why don't we take a vacation? We have time, you know."

"Yeah, I never did get to the beach on my honeymoon," I said. At least I could joke, laughing on the outside, crying on the inside.

"We might meet somebody on a cruise. It's time you started thinking about that," she said.

"Well, why not?" I agreed. I knew I had to start doing something besides sitting home all the time, moaning and groaning.

"I'll call this agency tomorrow. I can just ask," she said.

I forgot about it then, but the next evening Allison said, "Get out the suntan lotion! We'll be under the palm trees soon."

MY LAST LOVE

I really did want to go. I knew it would do me good. Everybody said I looked pale, that I needed vitamins and to get out in the sun. I began to get excited as the days went by. I didn't expect to find romance but it was somewhere to go, somewhere I had never been. We hoped the ship would be like the one on TV, but I didn't get my hopes up.

We went in late summer. We had to go to the airport, and it was all very exciting. We had never been on a plane before, and we tried to act sophisticated. When the plane took off, we closed our eyes.

"Is anything wrong?" the stewardess asked, and we giggled.

In Miami, we took a taxi to the ship. It was so thrilling, being on a dock. It really was like in the movies. We walked up steps onto the ship and a man told us where our cabins were.

The ship was just like a hotel. We went down one floor on an elevator and found our cabin. It was a little disappointing to see it. It wasn't as big as the ones on TV but it was okay. The bathroom was so small that only one person could walk into it, but it still beat sitting at home.

We hung up our clothes and decided to go upstairs.

"Deck, that's the word," I told Allison.

Land was getting smaller and smaller in the distance. We walked around the deck, just looking. I knew Allison was looking for a romance, but I wasn't.

"You know," she said, "there's not as many young men on board as I thought. I guess it's not exactly like TV."

Then we heard an announcement over a speaker

that dinner would be at six followed by dancing on the upper deck.

"Do you suppose people really wear evening gowns to eat?" I asked. We had each gone out and bought one, a cheap one. We put them on anyway.

When we went into the dining room some people had on dressy clothes and some didn't. We felt better, but we decided not to dress up in evening gowns to eat again. The buffet table was the fanciest I'd ever seen. There was every food imaginable . . . pineapple, salads, and thin roast beef. We filled our plates and sat down.

"Now, on TV somebody is supposed to come over and talk to us," I said. But nobody did.

Later, we walked around the deck. By then the sun was going down over the ocean, and the sky was pink and orange. We went into the bar and ordered coconut drinks. Finally somebody started talking to us, a married couple celebrating their anniversary.

The band began playing at nine, and the four of us went into the small ballroom. It was full of people, and two men came over and asked Allison and I to dance. It was the first time I had danced in a long time. The man pulled me tight up against him, and I pulled away. If the men on the cruise were going to be like that, I would stay away from them.

By eleven, I was ready to go back to the cabin.

"You don't have to come," I told Allison. She was talking to two men at once.

I got in bed, but when I heard the sound of the water hitting the ship, I suddenly felt sad and lonely.

The next morning we put on our bathing suits. Allison just lounged by the pool without diving in.

MY LAST LOVE

She didn't want to mess up her hair. I got on the diving board and dove in. My hands hit the water and then—wham! My body hit another body in the water, somebody who had been underneath when I dived. The breath was knocked out of me. I felt myself sinking, and I tried to move my arms to swim upward to the surface. I wanted to suck in air, but I couldn't.

I felt like a rock, sinking slowly.

Then someone grabbed my hand and pulled me up. My head hit the surface of the water, and I opened my mouth and breathed in. I could kick my legs then and I swam to the edge of the pool and hung on with one hand, wiping the water out of my eyes with the other.

"Are you okay?" a deep voice asked.

I nodded.

"I'm sorry I got in your way like that, under the diving board. I pulled you out as quickly as I could," the voice said.

I shook out my hair and looked around. Beside me in the water was a man with a tiny bit of gray hair at his temples.

"My name is Dylan," he said. "Dylan Jacobs. I'm sorry to meet you this way."

It's not the first time I've met a man by getting knocked down, I thought.

"I'm Dyanne," I told him.

I pulled myself up and sat on the edge of the pool. I was glad to have somebody talk to me. "This pool is too small," I said. "I think the diving board is just for looks, not for real swimmers."

"You're a good diver," he said. "I glanced up as you dove off. Before I got in your way." He laughed and wiped the water off his face with a towel. "Where did you learn?"

"I used to jump off a tree limb into the deep part of the creek," I said.

"You live in the country? I used to live on a farm when I was a little boy," he explained.

It was very nice talking to Dylan. He was comfortable, like an old pair of tennis shoes.

We talked for an hour, laughing and joking. I told him I worked for a telephone company, and he said that his wife had died last year and he came on the cruise as his first vacation in a long time. He had worked so hard, he said, trying to forget, that he just needed a rest.

I understood how he felt after everything with Ryan, but I didn't tell him that.

When lunchtime came, we ate together. Allison was talking to a man, and I was glad not to be left out. All four of us ate dinner together, and at nine we danced. I was glad for a new friend. I was glad to have somebody do something for me, even small things like ordering a drink.

The next two days went like that. When I went to bed at night, I didn't think about Ryan. I thought about Dylan and how happy I was to be on the cruise. He dressed perfectly, too. I was not really used to somebody so well mannered. Ryan was nice, but Dylan had something else, maybe a maturity. But I forced myself to remember that the cruise was temporary and Dylan would go out of my life again. I didn't exactly think of him as only a friend, but I didn't think of him in a romantic way, either.

The next day we docked on an island. We were to stay in a hotel three days so we could explore the island. The first night, Dylan and I walked up and down the streets, looking at things for sale to the tourists, straw hats and necklaces. Dylan bought me a necklace with a green stone in it. We went back to the hotel for drinks and then danced in the dark shadows of the corner of the bar.

The next morning we went to the beach. The sand was pure white, and the palm trees waved in the soft wind. We could see red and yellow and blue sailboats out on the ocean, heading to a little island nearby.

"Do you want to go over there tomorrow?" Dylan asked. "I heard that little island is more native than this one. We can get a boat over there. I'll buy us a picnic lunch in case the food is baked turtle eggs or something weird like that."

Dylan knocked on my door the next morning at eight. We went down to the dock and stepped into a motorboat driven by a native of the island. I had never been in a small boat before, and it bounced up and down. Though I had on a life jacket, I was still afraid. Dylan put his arm around my shoulder and held my hand.

When we got to the other shore, the motorboat driver said, "You be sure to be here at six. Last boat. Storm tonight."

"We'll be here," Dylan told him, handing him money.

We walked up the road to the village. The low buildings were made of cement blocks, not fine and gaudy like the ones on the other big island. Chickens walked across the road.

"This is the real thing," Dylan said. "Let's walk along the beach and collect shells. Maybe we can make you another necklace."

He went to the front of a little store and talked to a woman. She handed him a basket, and he handed her money. Then she pointed toward the sea.

"Now we have something to collect them in," Dylan said.

We started walking along the beach, and it was full of beautiful shells.

"Look at this one," I said. "It's pink on the inside, like pink pearl."

Then we sat down under a palm tree in the shade and ate our lunch. Dylan had brought along a bottle of wine, and we drank it. I had never liked wine much before, but this tasted sweet. The sun was warm and we lay back on the blanket and looked at the sky. "Look at that white cloud," I said. "It looks like a kitten without a tail."

My eyes felt heavy. I looked at Dylan and his eyes were closing, too. It was the sun and the wine, and we went to sleep. I dreamed of riding on soft clouds, and then I felt cold. I opened my eyes, and the white clouds were dark now, and the sun was low.

"Dylan," I said, shaking his shoulder. "Wake up. What time is it? We've got to meet the boat."

He sat up and looked at his watch. "Oh no, it's nearly six," he moaned. "The boat will be gone. Come on, let's go back to the village. Maybe somebody will take us."

We ran along the beach and then up the road to the village. The little stores were closed. A man was leaning on the porch of his house.

"Is there somebody to take us to the big island?" Dylan asked.

"Storm. No boats. Big wind," the man said. "Boat

go morning."

"What are we going to do?" I asked Dylan. "At least Allison knows we came to this island. Maybe she'll guess we're trapped by the storm. But where are we going to sleep?"

"Don't worry," Dylan said, putting his arm around my shoulder.

He turned to the man who was closing down wooden windows. "Is there a hotel?' he asked. "Somewhere we can eat and sleep?"

The man pointed to another house. "That lady has rooms," he told Dylan.

The wind was blowing stronger now, and the clouds were low and darker. The palm trees waved like they were going on a long trip. Drops of rain hit the dust and splattered. A dog yelped and ran under the step of a house.

Dylan grabbed my hand and we ran to the house the man had pointed to. At least it had a porch to shelter us from the rain, and we ran up the steps. Dylan knocked on the door. Nobody came, and he pounded again, this time harder. In a minute a light appeared through the cracks and an old lady with white hair and long earrings cracked open the door a few inches.

"Do you have any rooms?" Dylan asked "We're trapped in the storm and can't get back to the island."

"A fool thing to be in the storm," she said. "But I can help. Come."

She walked to the end of her porch and pointed to a hut. That's just about all it was, a hut. Dylan grabbed my hand, and we ran for it.

"At least it's got a wooden floor," Dylan said.

"Maybe the spiders can't come in."

"Don't say that. That's not funny," I wailed.

There was an oil lamp and a few matches on the table, Dylan lit. There was a table, two chairs, and one big bed with a blanket over the mattress.

"It's not much," Dylan said, "but it's better than sleeping under a palm tree in the rain."

It had really begun to pour then but surprisingly the roof didn't leak.

"Now is the time to talk, with no TV and no dance floor," Dylan said. "Well, I was born, and I had ten fingers and ten toes." He began laughing. "This'll show us we don't need every convenience."

The sky was dark now except for an occasional streak of lightning, and we could hear the waves roll up on the sand at the beach.

"I'm hungry," I complained. "I think I'm more hungry than scared."

Almost on cue, the old woman opened the door. She was wearing a raincoat, but her head was wet. Little beads of water on her white hair looked like diamonds in the lamplight.

"Food," she said, handing over a covered basket. "I'll come back soon and tell fortune." Then she skittered out into the storm.

We lifted the lid and looked inside the basket and started laughing. On a tin plate lay four slices of bread and two slices of bologna. There was also a pull-top can of pork and beans.

"So much for native delicacies," I said making myself a sandwich. "I just wish I had three or four of these."

In a little while the old lady came back in.

"Okay?" she asked, pointing to the empty basket.

"Okay," Dylan told her. "I thank you."

"Now you want to hear your fortune?" she offered.

"Oh, yes!" I said.

"Hold out hands," she ordered.

I put my hands out, and she looked at them for what seemed like a long time. The light flickered on her face, and rainwater dripped down off her forehead.

Finally she said, "You have had much pain in the past, but the sun shines now. Clouds will come, but sun will shine again."

"I hope the sun shines again tomorrow morning," I said.

"Be strong," she continued. "Love will be yours in the end." She turned to Dylan. "Now you," she told him.

She looked at his hands for a longer time than mine. The more she looked, the more she frowned.

"Trouble," she said. "Trouble with your head. But there will be sunshine, too . . . and much happiness."

"Thank you," Dylan told her. "We're waiting for the sunshine, that's for sure."

The old woman nodded, took the money Dylan handed her, and left.

"I guess we should get some sleep," Dylan said. "I'm tired."

The thunder and lightning had stopped and we could see that the sky was solid black like ink, but the wind was still blowing. I walked to the bed and lay down, and Dylan slid down beside me. He put his arms behind his head, looking up, and started talking.

"You know, nobody will believe this, getting caught in a storm on an island. It's almost like Tarzan and Jane."

"Don't say that," I said quickly.

"Say what?" he asked.

"Tarzan and Jane. I hate them," I said.

"You know who I always liked when I was little? Zorro," Dylan said. "I always wanted to ride a horse and be the mysterious hero with a sword."

We talked and laughed. After a while we both got sleepy again. Dylan tried to spread the blanket evenly over both of us.

"Next time I get stranded on a tropical island, I'm going to bring a jacket and long pants," I complained.

Later I woke up suddenly and I was snuggled up close against Dylan's back.

"Dylan?" I whispered, not remembering for a second where I was.

"Everything's okay," he said. "I'm here." He rolled over and put his arms around me.

"I think I was dreaming about spiders," I said.

"Listen," he said.

"To what?" I asked.

"To nothing. The wind has stopped," he answered.

I realized how warm and good it felt to lie up close to Dylan. I could feel his breath on my neck. I turned my face toward his, and he slowly kissed my lips. I reached out my arms and put them around his neck.

"I think I'm beginning to fall in love with you," he whispered.

"Don't tell me that if you don't mean it," I said softly.

"I would never hurt you," he said.

"It's just this island," I said. "It's romantic."

"No," he said, "you're the best thing to happen to me in a long time."

He kissed me again, and I felt something stronger than I'd ever felt for Ryan.

"I think I'm beginning to fall in love with you, too," I whispered.

And so I did with Dylan what I had never done with Ryan. I felt safe and more at ease with Dylan. I felt comfortable in my own skin and that I didn't need to hide my feelings or my needs from him. He was gentle and loving . . . it may have only been a hut with a mattress on the floor, but it was magical and I was glad that I had lost nothing more to Ryan than my heart.

When morning came we were still asleep but the shrill whistle from a boat woke us.

"Dylan," I said, "wake up! A boat is here!"

We jumped up and put on our clothes. I was embarrassed to look at him. He put his arms around me.

"I meant what I said last night. I love you. I really mean that," he said.

We ran out of the hut and down to the dock and got in the boat. Dylan held my hand, but this time I wasn't afraid of the waves.

When we got to the dock on the big island, Allison was waiting for us.

"What happened?" she asked. "I was worried sick. The police were going to look for you, but the storm came up. You both look like you've been in a storm for a month."

"You won't believe this, but we slept in a hut, and this old lady told our fortune and it was the most wonderful night of my life," I explained.

"I can tell," Allison said, looking at me suspiciously.

"Let's have a big breakfast," Dylan said. "About a dozen eggs. I'm starving. I'll order room service."

I went to my room and told Allison everything while I showered. Well, almost everything. Then I put on clean clothes and went to Dylan's room. I was embarrassed and still couldn't look him in the eye. Breakfast was already there, and I started buttering my toast.

"Look at me," Dylan said.

I looked up slowly.

"Any regrets?" he asked.

"I don't know," I said. "I'm just not sure."

"I told you this, and I'll tell you again. I meant what I said. I love you," he said softly. "Do you think I'm too old for you?"

"No," I said. "Do you really love me? You won't leave me?"

"No, I won't leave you. Now eat. We're going on a tour this afternoon, a tour in a carriage. Would you like that?"

The remaining two days sped by. I was at the beach, and it was a thousand times better than I had ever dreamed. And somebody loved me and I loved him.

Then the ship was ready to sail home again. On the last night Dylan and I walked around the deck in the moonlight. "I'll fly out to see you within a week. First, I have to get some business straightened out," Dylan said. "I have to tell my friends about us. It'll be a shock. They thought I was turning into a hermit. I'm glad they wanted me to go on this cruise. I guess it pays to listen to your friends." He kissed me. "And I'll have a present for you, a ring for your finger."

"Do you really mean that?" I asked.

"Why wouldn't I mean it?" He looked puzzled.

I'd never told him about Ryan leaving me at the church.

The next morning we walked down the gangplank together, and all three of us went to the airport. Allison and I got on a plane first, and I sat by the window and watched Dylan get smaller and smaller as the plane slowly moved down the runway to get in line to take off.

I started crying, and Allison asked me why. "You should be happy," she said.

"I am," I said. "That's why I'm crying."

It wasn't long until the plane landed in Philadelphia, and we went to our apartment. It was a hard reality, going back to that world after being in such a glamorous one.

That night I waited for a phone call from Dylan, but then I figured he had a thousand miles farther to go. I knew he would call the next night. When I went to work the next morning, my trip was all I could talk about.

"I hope he doesn't let you down, your new boyfriend," one of the girls said.

"He won't," I said. "This is different." I showed everybody his picture and all of the other pictures Allison and I had taken. I just couldn't quit talking.

That evening when I got home I waited and waited for the phone to ring. I knew there was a time difference, and Dylan would call late. I was so nervous, waiting to hear his voice. But the phone never rang.

I went to pick it up a couple of times to see if it was out of order.

"Are you sure we paid the phone bill?" I asked Allison.

"Maybe he had some kind of business to do," Allison suggested. "He did say that. I heard him."

I knew she was just making excuses.

I went to bed, but I tried to stay awake in case the phone rang. But it never did.

"Well, what did Mr. Wonderful have to say last night?" somebody at work asked.

I tried to change the subject, but there was no way. "He didn't call," I said.

My closest friend there said, "Oh, no, not again. I'm sorry for saying that yesterday, for hurting you. He'll call."

But he didn't. He didn't call all week. Or the next. At least I didn't have so many things to remind me of him like I'd had with Ryan.

"Out of sight, out of mind, I guess," I told Allison. "You know, I'm heartbroken again, but at least I'm used to it."

It was a couple of weeks before I noticed that anything was wrong. It had to be my imagination. On several mornings when I got up I felt sick to my stomach. Allison noticed, too.

"When did this happen?" she asked.

"On that little island. He told me he loved me, and I believed it," I said, tears in my eyes.

The doctor confirmed what I suspected. When I got home I tried to call Dylan's number, but the phone had been disconnected.

"Twice!" I cried. "I've been deserted twice! Why me? What am I going to do? What's wrong with me?"

"There's nothing wrong with you," Allison said. "You just made a mistake. I figure you were just on the rebound from the awful hurt Ryan caused you. You keep on working as long as you can, and then I can pay the rent for a month. We've lived off of peanut butter sandwiches before."

"No, I don't think it was me being on the rebound. I was beginning to love Dylan," I said. "But after the baby is born, then what? What am I going to do?"

"That's up to you to decide. I hope you remember that you must do what's best for the baby," Allison said. "I'll stick with you through whatever you decide."

I was lucky to have a friend like Allison.

A couple of months went by. I was sick in the morning, but it usually subsided by the time I went to work. Then I had to start wearing maternity clothes. I dreaded that because everybody would know my secret.

The first day I went to work wearing them, everybody stopped and stared, but nobody said anything. I just wanted to die. I knew they all felt sorry for me. I could tell it by the looks on their faces.

On the second day I wore the maternity clothes, my friend at the next desk asked, "Was it Dylan?"

"Well, who else?" I said defensively.

"No, no, I didn't mean it that way. Honey, everybody here cares about you. If there's anything we can do, tell us. Everybody's just afraid to say anything," she said.

I knew they cared, and I was happy to have the friends I had. I just wished that the two men I had loved had cared about me.

MY LAST LOVE

The people in my department cared, but I knew that soon talk would be all over the building. I could feel the stares. I quit going to the cafeteria on my breaks.

When Christmas came, Allison and I told our parents that we were going to Atlantic City on vacation. Actually, we stayed in our apartment. Allison was a true friend, sacrificing her Christmas for me. She went out and bought a tiny plastic tree. It wasn't a happy Christmas like the one the year before. The angel on the tree didn't smile for me.

We were almost afraid to answer the phone the few days around Christmas, afraid that it would be our mothers calling, but they must have believed our lie about going to Atlantic City, and they didn't call. When Allison did go home, she told my mother that I had to work seven days a week.

I worked up until the last two weeks of my pregnancy. I was so fat I could hardly walk.

One night Allison said, "That jerk should help pay the hospital bills at least. If I ever get hold of him. . . ."

I'd been going to the clinic at the big public hospital. It was for poor people. I still had to pay something, much more than the others since I had a job, but the whole bill wouldn't be as high.

It was pretty embarrassing going there, with people knowing I wasn't married, but I was not alone. Most of the girls there weren't married. Fools like me, I figured. I even saw another girl from the telephone company, and that made me feel better . . . not because she had problems, too, but because I was not the only one in the world in such a predicament.

MY LAST LOVE

Several weeks before the baby was to be born, a woman from the state adoption agency talked to all of us at the clinic.

"There are many loving and kind couples out there desperately wanting children," she said. "Just think about it. If you choose to let your baby be adopted, it will have a wonderful life."

I was finally going to have to face it. I think I knew all along what I had to do. Giving my baby away was the only thing to do. It had to come first. It couldn't help what its mother had done and be made to suffer for her mistakes. To me, the baby was still an "it," not a boy or a girl yet, not a little person with toes and fingers and a smile. But I still knew it had to have a better life than I could give it.

The pains started one afternoon as I lay on the couch watching soap operas. First it was a dull ache in my lower back and then it got worse, more steady as it came and went. When Allison came home, I told her what I was feeling.

"I guess we'd better go to the hospital," she said.

The nurse in the emergency room sent us to the maternity ward. The pains were stronger now, and I had to hold on to the sides of the wheelchair to be able to stand them.

The nurse in the maternity ward told me to get into a bed in a labor room. She handed me a short gown, and Allison pulled the curtain around me. I put the gown on and crawled up into the bed. In a few minutes a nurse came in and rubbed some kind of lotion on my stomach and then put a big belt over it. Then she reached on the table and flicked on a machine that looked like a little TV, except that the screen just had waving lines. A paper came out of it

324

with wavy lines on it as well.

"This is to monitor the baby's heartbeat," she said. "Don't be alarmed. We do this to everybody."

I could hear the swish, swish, swish of the baby's heart coming loudly from the machine. Somehow that made it become a real baby to me, not just a big lump inside me.

In a little while a doctor came in and examined me. I should have been used to being embarrassed, but I wasn't. I covered up my face with my hands.

The hours went by slowly, and the pains got worse and worse.

"Breathe," Allison said. "Pant like a dog. Remember how we practiced."

The pain would go away, and then it would come back. Every time a pain would hit, Allison would hold my hands. I probably squeezed my fingernails into her arms, but she never said anything.

"Help me," I moaned. "Help me."

"We can give you a shot," a nurse said, "to ease the pain, but it's better if you can stand it as long as you can. That's easier for you and the baby in the long run."

"I wish I had never gone on that cruise," I whispered to Allison. "That storm, the beach. It's a nightmare now."

The doctor came into the room and examined me again. "It's about time," he said, patting my hand.

When he left the room, Allison whispered, "He's got on tennis shoes. Somehow I trust a doctor who wears tennis shoes."

The nurse came back in and said, "This is a busy night. We always have lots of babies born when there's a storm."

"That's all I need to hear," I said to Allison.

"Is there someone to go to the delivery room with her?" the nurse asked.

"I'll go," Allison said.

"Oh," the nurse said.

A pain hit me so hard that I thought my insides were ripping apart. I could feel my bed being pushed into the hall and someone wearing green scrubs and a green shower cap with a surgical mask grabbed my hand.

"It's me," Allison said. "Aren't I cute?"

"Can you stand it?" I asked. "Will you faint?"

Allison just laughed.

The next thing I remembered was being lifted onto a table. Then I screamed, and the lower half of my body seemed on fire. I could see bright lights overhead and I knew I was not dead, not yet. Then my body quit aching suddenly, and I could see somebody holding up a funny-looking baby.

Later, I was put into a bed. The room was dark with only a little lamp on.

"It's a boy," Allison said. "Are you hungry?"

I lifted my head as she held a glass and a straw to my lips. I could see three other beds in the room and three faces staring at me.

In a little while a nurse brought in flowers, a bunch of carnations, and they were for me. The card read, "We love you," and it was signed by everyone at work.

At two o'clock the nurse asked if I wanted to feed my baby. I told her no, I was giving him up for adoption. She didn't ask at six o'clock. I wondered who was feeding him. Suddenly I wanted to walk down the hall. I got to the corner of the hall and then looked down another hall. People were standing in front of the big glass window in front of the nursery.

I tried not to go, but I was drawn, like some big hand was pulling me. I slowly walked toward the glass. People were looking at the babies and smiling. The nurses would pick up a baby and hold it to the window for somebody to look at.

I searched the little cards for the one with my name on it. Finally I spotted it. *Baby Boy Clark,* it read. I slowly raised my eyes and looked at him. His eyes were closed, and he had brown hair. He looked so alone. Nobody was pointing to him. I wanted to rush into the room and pick him up and hold him, but I tried to reason with myself that he would be better off with two parents instead of just me. Tears came to my eyes and I wiped them away angrily.

"Here," somebody said, handing me a handker-chief. "Isn't he beautiful? His daddy's mighty proud of him."

I stood there without moving, listening to the voice. I was almost paralyzed. I couldn't turn around to see who was talking to me. I slowly raised my eyes and looked at the face reflected in the glass. Then I turned and looked at Dylan. He reached out and tried to put his arms around me, but I shoved him away. He was as white as a ghost.

"Why are you here?" I demanded. I hated him.

"Listen!" he said. "Listen to me. Come down the hall where we can talk. People are staring. Please listen."

"I don't want to hear anything you have to say," I said.

"Please listen," he begged, grabbing my hand

and pulling me away from the nursery window. "I'll make it all up to you."

"It's too late. You deserted me. You never even called," I said.

"Not on purpose," he insisted. "I didn't do it on purpose. I've been in the hospital for a long time. Look at my head."

I stared at the hairline above his forehead and there was a scar.

"I was in a bad accident the very day we got home from the cruise," he explained. "I was driving my car home from the airport and a drunk hit me head on. He wasn't even hurt, but I was in a coma most of this time. I would come in and out, but not enough to make sense of anything. It was a miracle that I even lived, the doctors say. But then a few days ago I woke up and could talk. The only reason I can barely walk now is because I was given physical therapy while I was unconscious. Look at the weight I've lost."

I stared at him, and it was true. He looked fifty pounds lighter, and he looked awful.

"Last night Allison called me," he went on. "My phone had been cut off since I was in the hospital and the bills weren't getting paid, but my business associate had just had it turned back on, and he was at my house getting some of my clothes together when Allison called. He would have called you when I was hurt, but he didn't even know about you. The accident happened before I could tell anybody anything. I got on the first plane out today. See that woman down the hall? She's a nurse who's with me. The doctor insisted she had to come."

Suddenly a thought hit me. "Do you remember the fortune-teller on the island?" I asked. "She said we would have pain. And she said something about your head . . . that you'd have trouble."

"Well, there won't be trouble from here on out," Dylan said. "I'm not leaving here until we're married. Then you and the baby and I will go on our honeymoon together . . . maybe to the beach."

"Oh, no," I said. "Not the beach!"

Dylan leaned over and kissed me. "I'm so sorry, Dyanne. You must have gone through so much alone."

"I just felt so hurt," I told him. "I couldn't believe you'd do that to me . . . just disappear." Then I told him about Ryan, how he'd left me at the church.

"Oh, honey," Dylan said softly. "I'll never leave again, I promise."

"I know you won't," I replied.

And so the happy times began for Dylan and me. Fortunately, there were no legal problems about the baby. I hadn't signed any papers giving him up for adoption and Dylan pulled some strings and got his name put on the birth certificate . . . Dylan Louis Jacobs Junior. Maybe our wedding a week later wasn't strictly conventional, with me holding little Dylan in my arms while the nice young minister married us. But it was a wonderful, warm ceremony.

We'll be moving to Dylan's home city soon. Allison and I will miss each other, but she says we're going to be seeing a lot of her. After all, she's Dylan Junior's godmother.

I can't tell you how many times a day I count my blessings: a beautiful little son, a wonderful friend,

MY LAST LOVE

and a husband who's made my every dream come true! THE END

A SPECIAL CHRISTMAS VISIT

I stood alone in the soft evening shadows as they danced across the floor of the den.

"Mama. . . ." her soft voice called. It was so subdued, it was almost a whisper.

I pressed my hands over my ears and closed my eyes. I should have gone away. I should have spent Christmas with Victor. I should have done anything but stay home for Christmas.

"Mama. . . ."

I fell to my knees and buried my face in the soft velvet cushions on the sofa.

"Oh, God!" I cried, and tears burst from my eyes as my mind slipped painfully back to a Christmas two years earlier. . . .

"It's so pretty, Mama!" little Sheryl had cried above the Christmas bells and joyful singing coming from the radio. "It's the prettiest tree on the block, Mama, really it is!"

I had smiled down into my younger daughter's face, and, with a touch of sadness, I'd wished that

A SPECIAL CHRISTMAS VISIT

George was there. But George had chosen to spend Christmas with his other woman and her children. In fact, he'd chosen to spend the rest of his life with them. Why? I didn't know why. I'd only known that he didn't want us anymore. When the divorce became final, our life together would be over.

I'd brushed the feeling of sadness from my mind and scooped up little Sheryl into my arms as I drew Lily, my four-year-old, to my side.

"Well," I'd said, smiling, "I think it's about time Santa started on his rounds, and if he finds you both awake, there'll be no surprises for either of you in the morning."

Lily had laughed with delight, and Sheryl had giggled and squirmed from my arms, running out of the den to the room they both shared.

As I stood in the glow from the tree, my life without George had loomed dim and bleak before me. The lights from the tree had seemed to offer hope for the future as they sparkled and twinkled. That was why I had left them on. Dear God! That was why I had left them on!

I'd sat down in front of the evergreen, my back against the sofa, my feet curled under me, and let my mind drift back to my life with George.

I'd known him most of my life. We'd lived next door to each other and had played together, had grown up together, and had married. It had seemed the natural thing to do. But we'd soon found out that playing house together as children was nothing like the real thing. That wild, thrilling romance we'd seen portrayed on the movie screen just didn't exist, at least, not for us. And, as the years went by, the silent acceptance we had for each other faded.

A SPECIAL CHRISTMAS VISIT

Our life together had been dull, but we'd stayed together. For the children? Maybe. Yet when George found another woman, suddenly I was hurt. As always, I was the last to know.

Ariel, my friend, had avoided telling me the truth about his late nights, but she'd known. She'd told me later how she and Nick had seen him time and again at a local bar, drinking and dancing with the same attractive blonde.

Yes, it had hurt. No woman likes to admit that her marriage is a failure, even though she's living a lie. So, for a short time, I'd tried, unsuccessfully, to rekindle a dying flame.

When George left our home, we'd decided that it would be necessary for me to work. I found a job packing hosiery at a sewing plant, working from eight until four while the children were in a day-care center.

It wasn't long before I missed George. Life may have been dull, but it had never been lonely while we had been together. After he'd left, it was lonely, and I'd found it unbearable. When I realized that he wasn't coming back, I'd made up my mind that I didn't want to remain single for the rest of my life, and I'd begun dating again.

I'd met Victor through Regina and Ned. He was a friend from long ago, who had moved back to town and looked them up. We'd been dating about a month when that last Christmas Eve I had with my children had rolled around.

That Christmas Eve, we'd sat together, Sheryl, Lily, and I, in front of the tree. The lights twinkled in the darkness of the den. I'd retold the story of the birth of Christ, as I'd done every year because I'd vowed that my daughters would grow up knowing the true meaning of Christmas.

Then we'd sat a while and listened to the Christmas music playing on the radio until I'd told them it was bedtime. I'd followed them into their room and tucked them both in the big bed they shared. They laughed happily as they played the guessing game of "What's in Santa's sack?" At last their eyes closed soundly in sleep, and I'd gone back into the den and sat down on the floor with my memories.

It had taken only a few minutes before I was sound asleep, propped up against the sofa. I'd awakened with a headache. With my aching head in my hands, I had gone to the medicine cabinet in the bathroom for some aspirin. I'd found the bottle empty. Groaning, I'd looked at my watch. It would take only a few minutes to drive to a convenience store, and I decided to do so. Regina and Ned were spending Christmas with his folks, or I'd have called them. Instead, I'd gone out.

I'd checked the children before leaving. Both were snug and sleeping soundly beneath the cheerful bedcover that had been George's last gift to them.

I'd never left them alone in the house before, but I'd told myself that no harm would come to them in the little while I'd be gone. I'd stood over them, thinking how much I loved them and not knowing that I was about to say my good-bye to them.

It had been dark and cold outside, and I'd had no heat in my car. It was an older model, but it had served like an old, faithful friend during the years it had been ours. George had left it with me when he'd left, taking our new car for himself.

I'd driven to the nearest convenience store and found it closed, just as I did the next. No one, it seemed, stayed open on Christmas. Reluctantly, I'd decided to go back home, but as I was driving through town, I'd passed Victor's apartment and decided to stop.

"I'll drive you home, Nancy," he said. "I'll bring along the children's gifts, and we'll wake them up and start Christmas early."

"You'll have to help me put their presents under the tree." I'd said, laughing, and the pain in my head was gone.

When we reached my neighborhood, I noticed a fire engine truck. It stood at the end of the block, and a terrible feeling of fear had engulfed me.

The house still stood, hardly touched by the fire, for the fire had remained inside. A neighbor on his way home had glanced into the window, and, instead of seeing the twinkling, pretty lights on the Christmas tree, he had looked into a flame-filled room. He'd been too late to save my children.

Their two small bodies had been found under the fallen tree. Although I was only gone a short time, they had awakened and gone into the den to look at "the prettiest tree on the block." Somehow, they'd caused the tree to come tumbling down on top of them, and the frayed wiring had caused the lights to set fire to the tree.

George had come to the funeral, bringing his new family with him. I'd seen them at the back of the church as Victor had led me down the aisle behind the two small coffins. Victor had taken me home to a silent, empty house with the scent of fire drifting from the den and the presence of death in every room.

A SPECIAL CHRISTMAS VISIT

"Nancy," he'd said, holding me close, "come stay with me until you can begin to think straight."

I'd refused. I couldn't. To me, my babies were still there. The house had been their home, and if I left it, I felt I'd be deserting them.

The toys, unwrapped by little hands and unseen by little eyes, had stayed in the back of the closet, where I'd hidden them from the children. They were a terrible reminder of a Christmas of death, and I couldn't bring myself to touch them.

Days had turned into months. Spring, summer, and autumn had come and gone. Somehow, I'd lived through them. Having Victor at my side had helped ease the pain a little, but it hadn't helped the guilt. If I hadn't gone out that Christmas, if I'd only stayed home—my children would still be alive. Then, the season of Christmas had come around once again, and my children had come back to haunt me!

Just as they had come the year before, they were back again now, their soft, whispering voices reminding me that they had lost their lives through my neglect. I felt their presence with me as I stared at the empty corner of the den. There was no tree standing tall and proud against the large picture window—there never would be. Only the presence of my two little girls remained there.

"Mama . . . Mama. . . ." I heard their voices, soft and subdued, whispering, whispering. . . .

Oh, God! I couldn't take it anymore!

My troubled mind drifted to the bottle of sleeping pills in the medicine cabinet in the bathroom. If I took them all, I could go to sleep and never wake up. Before I could do that, though, the doorbell rang and echoed through the silent house.

I got up from the sofa as if in a dream and went to the door. There, in the gentle glow from the porch light, stood Victor. In his arms, he cradled a small, silver Christmas tree!

"Are you going to let me come in, Nancy?" he teased.

I stepped aside, let him in, and followed him down to the den.

He can't! I thought. *He just can't bring a tree, knowing how I feel!* But I stood silently behind him and watched as he erected the little tree.

"Nancy, come here," he said, pulling me gently toward him and down on the floor by the tree. "Nancy, those voices you hear at Christmas—the voices of your children—I don't think they're blaming you for their deaths. I think they're trying to tell you something else."

I turned my face from him.

"I never got to know the children as well as I'd have liked to, Nancy," he said as if able to read my mind. "But I did know they were good children and wouldn't be blaming you for what was an accident."

He sighed and drew me closer into the circle of his arms. "It was an accident, Nancy, and I think that's what your children are trying to tell you. At Christmas, they know how you blame yourself, and they come back to tell you not to."

He stroked my hair. "Let them rest, Nancy," he begged. "They can't while you grieve the way you do. You taught them the true meaning of Christmas—that Christmas is a season of rebirth, a season of starting anew. You have to give them up and start over."

A SPECIAL CHRISTMAS VISIT

Through a mist of tears, I saw the lonely, bare tree glimmering in the corner. I'd thought he hadn't understood, but he had.

And, as the light from outside caught its branches, I saw their two little faces, smiling and accepting the symbol of Christmas as it stood with its own special pride in the corner. And I heard them—two little voices, laughing with joy and telling me, "It's the prettiest tree on the block, Mama, really it is!"

And, as their dear, precious little faces faded away, and I heard their darling little voices speak to me one last time telling me "good-bye," I lifted my face for Victor's kiss.

I have finally found peace and Victor's been beside me the whole way.   THE END

A BLESSING SAVED MY HUSBAND

Joshua began to talk. "Well, it has been great."

Erica and I laughed. Actually, I guess it had been great. Joshua and Tyrone had watched a football game on TV while Erica and I had sat in the kitchen and talked—after everybody else had left.

Joshua and I had lived there in Shiloh Falls for four years. Then, a little over a year ago, Joshua had changed jobs, and we'd moved about a hundred miles away. We still had a lot of friends in Shiloh Falls, though, and, finally, we'd accepted Erica's invitation to come back and visit.

What a glorious day we'd had! What fun to catch up on everything. We even got a chance to visit our old house. It had been redecorated and looked very different now. The people who'd bought it seemed awfully nice, adding more nice neighbors to what was already one of the nicest neighborhoods we'd ever lived in.

Of course, we should have known better than to plan on leaving by ten P.M. It was now almost eleven-thirty. Erica and Tyrone had asked us to stay over, but even now after more than a year, there were still a million things to catch up on in the new house. Also, although our two little boys loved Joshua's mother, I didn't want them to wake up in the morning and find us not home. I'd read so much about small children feeling deserted and insecure, I didn't want mine to feel that way.

I climbed into the car beside Joshua and sat very close to him. We'd been married six years, and I still looked forward—maybe now even more than when we were first married—to feeling his arms around me in the night.

How frightening the dark used to seem when I was a kid. Both of my parents drank heavily, and I'd lain in my bed, listening to them fight and yell about breaking up. Only they never did break up.

Dad had married Mom because she was pregnant with me—so, of course, in a lot of that yelling, they had blamed me almost as much as they had blamed each other. There were so many times that I'd wanted my mother to be there for me, but she couldn't. Her life seemed to be driven to argue with my dad and drink.

Joshua was quite a guy. When I met him, I was twenty and so scared of men I could hardly talk to him. Oh, how gently, kindly, sweetly, he'd eased me out of my fears! It was more than that, though. When I'd told him, while we were still dating, how much it upset me when he had a drink—even one beer—he'd stopped drinking completely.

Now, six years later, I was a different person. I wasn't always happy, but, most of the time, I was okay. Most of the time, I felt secure, loved, wanted—all the things I'd needed so desperately through all the long, dark, lonely years before I met Joshua.

Of course, I'd never let him know how much I loved him. The truth is, I was afraid I might suffocate him. So, very deliberately, I kept alive interests in other people and other things. Yet I never forgot that comforting sense of being a worthwhile person. I believed that I could be a halfway-decent mother. All of that faith came from Joshua. Maybe someday, that emotional security I drew from Joshua would come from within me, and the healing process that had begun when I met him would be complete. Then I'd be free to love him even more, not with the clinging and dependent love I now tried to hide, but with a love that was open and free like a rushing river.

"Hey that was fun!" he said as he backed the car out of the driveway.

It was a fairly long driveway with no light at the end. I twisted on the seat to make sure no other cars were coming. "Oh, yes," I said. "Let's not make it another year before we do it again." Then, suddenly, I screamed, "Joshua!"

Too late. Metal crunched, glass shattered, and the car spun all the way around. More metal, more glass! The windshield seemed to hurl itself at me. Then it wasn't the windshield but the sidewalk that came at me.

Pain! The door must have been thrown open. All I felt was frigid cold. It was so cold. The sidewalk hit my head. I closed my eyes against the pain.

I heard a groan or the sounds of someone crying. Then I realized the groan was mine.

A BLESSING SAVED MY HUSBAND

Abruptly, I tried to sit up. That was a mistake because the pain brought me right back down again. Below my head was a white pillow. I lay on a white-sheeted hospital bed. Before I could form a complete thought, I felt the pain in my head. It hurt so much. It hurt so much I couldn't concentrate. My head was killing me. It wasn't too bad—if I just didn't move!

Dear God! I was in a hospital! I remembered nothing—nothing except the car. Something had hit the car. Then I had hit the sidewalk. But that was all I remembered.

I heard a voice. At first, it seemed shatteringly loud. Then I realized that it wasn't too loud. It was only a whisper.

"Annette! Are you really awake?"

I moved only my eyes. It was Erica—my former neighbor, my friend. She looked awful.

"Erica," I said. "Hi."

"Oh, thank God you're all right! You were delirious." She rang for the nurse.

"What time is it?"

"Time?" She looked at her watch. "A little after five."

"Five?"

"Almost six hours have passed," she said.

"You were here the whole time?"

Biting back tears, she nodded. Oh, how kind she was to care so much!

"Where's Joshua?" I said.

Somehow, her face seemed to change. She looked careful and guarded. Afraid? No, that was silly. I was still groggy, that was all.

"We'd just stepped inside, and we heard the

crash. The kid who was driving the other car is okay. The police said it wasn't anybody's fault really."

"Police?"

"Sure. Don't you remember? Tyrone and I put a blanket over you. Half the neighborhood must have been there. I kept your purse for you. Oh, and you asked me to call Joshua's mother. You said she was baby-sitting for the boys, and you wanted me to tell her you'd decided to stay a little bit late, so she wouldn't know about the accident and be worried."

It was incredible! "I don't remember any of it. Where's Joshua?"

A nurse walked in. She smiled, but something was wrong about it. Somehow the smile didn't quite touch her eyes.

"Mrs. Millerton," she asked softly, "how do you feel?"

"Dizzy, I guess. And my head hurts. Where's my husband?"

"Your husband's coming along just fine. I'll get you something for the pain. It'll also help you sleep."

"Wait a minute!" I made myself sit up. "What does that mean, 'coming along just fine'? Where is he?"

"He's on the floor below this one, resting. He's still asleep."

"Asleep?" I had been unconscious for more than five hours. "Is he asleep or unconscious? How is he? What happened to him?"

When the nurse didn't answer, Erica did—carefully. "He was thrown about half a block." Then, as if it was supposed to comfort me, she added awkwardly, "He's still alive."

"Still alive? What does that mean? Oh my God! I want to see him!"

Quickly, the nurse slipped to the side of my bed and placed her hands on my shoulders. "I'll give you the injection for pain," she said. "It'll also calm you down."

Panic rose inside me, but I knew I mustn't show it. If I screamed, if I fought her, they'd think I was hysterical and not listen to me.

Very, very quietly, I said, "Take your hands off me. I do not want an injection. I want to see my husband—now."

She hesitated.

I looked over at Erica. "Help me," I whispered.

Erica let out a deep breath. As far as I'm concerned, in that instant, she showed herself to be a real friend, far beyond all the other kind things she'd ever done for me. She treated me like an intelligent adult.

"Joshua's in intensive care," she said. "He's in a coma. His condition is listed as critical. They don't expect him to live through the night."

I just looked at her. The room seemed to be spinning, and everything seemed as though it was out of focus. I looked at Erica's face, and it was wet with tears.

Joshua dead? No! He can't die!

Something happened to me then. Something I can't begin to describe. It was as though Joshua were near me, but I could see him moving away toward some kind of incredibly bright light. In my mind, I called to him, *Joshua, no! Come back. I need you!*

"I want to see him," I said.

Erica hesitated, then looked at the nurse. "Can we get a wheelchair?"

"Absolutely not. She's not well enough to get out of bed!"

"I will take full responsibility," Erica said.

In my heart, I answered, *Thank you, God. Thank you for making Erica the person she was. Thank you for making her as stubborn and as determined as I am. Thank you for love between friends.*

"Now, are you going to help me get a wheelchair," Erica went on, "or do have to steal one?"

Without answering, the nurse marched out of the room.

"Damn!" Erica said. Then she turned to me. "Annette, if you lean on me, can you walk?"

"I'll try."

I threw back the covers and managed to get my legs over the side of the bed. The pain in my head was unbelievable.

For a couple of seconds, I was afraid I might throw up. But I had to see Joshua. I know it probably sounds crazy, but, somehow, I felt that if I could only see him, touch him, hold him, and tell him how desperately I needed him—then he wouldn't leave me, he wouldn't die.

The nurse returned with a man.

Oh no! I thought. *I need help, not another argument!*

"I'm Dr. Bradenton," the man said. "I've got a wheelchair. Don't try to get out of bed by yourself. I'll bring it to you."

"Thank you," I whispered.

A BLESSING SAVED MY HUSBAND

As we reached the intensive care unit one floor below, a high bed on wheels was being pushed out of the room by a nurse and a nurse's aide. Under the sheet was the outline of a human being. The face was completely covered. That meant whoever it was, was dead.

Dear God, no! Not Joshua!

Erica and Dr. Bradenton were with me. Dr. Bradenton looked into the room.

"Your husband's over there," he said, pointing to one of the beds that was curtained off.

They've Joshua in the wrong room, I thought. *The people in this room are dying.*

As we came nearer to that curtained-off bed, I could hear women's voices. One, an older voice, seemed to be instructing someone younger.

"Very good," the older woman said. "And then what?"

"We call—" There was a brief pause. Then the younger voice went on, "We call a doctor to sign the death certificate."

Quickly, Dr. Bradenton stepped behind the curtain. Erica, also, took a couple of steps forward. Then she stopped and just stood there. They'd left me!

I got out of the wheelchair, stumbling, nearly falling. There were other nurses in the room and at least two doctors at another bed with all kinds of equipment. But it was Erica who caught my arm.

"Annette, are you sure—"

She'd heard them, too. Was I sure I wanted to step behind that curtain?

I started to cry. I couldn't help it. At that moment, in my mind, Joshua was alive. A thousand memories came together—all the kindnesses, all the love.

"Yes!" I said.

She helped me.

I only glanced at the figure on the bed. His face was waxen, his eyes open and sightless. An intravenous bottle was still attached to his arm. I looked at Dr. Bradenton instead. "Help him," I said.

Gently, Dr. Bradenton answered, "Everything that could have been done was done."

"Bring him back!" I cried.

"You'll have to leave."

"I won't leave! Bring him back!"

Awkwardly, his hands on my shoulders, supporting me, Dr. Bradenton answered, "I'll see if there is anything else."

"No! That's not enough!"

"I—I'll do some of the things that have already been done—if you'll agree to go back upstairs and take a sedative."

"You'll do it all over again," I said. "Everything! In the sight of God, give me your word."

"I—" To this day, I still wonder whether, until that point, he'd been lying—saying anything he thought might calm me.

Only, when I asked him to swear, he answered. "I give you my word." And I believed him.

Back upstairs, in bed and sedated, I closed my eyes, then opened them. I was startled and concerned. I wondered why someone had turned a bright light on directly over my face.

Only, there wasn't any light.

Again, I closed my eyes and in that drugged,

semiconscious semisleep, I prayed, *Bring him back to me, God.* Over and over, the words ran through my head, *Bring him back! Joshua, come back.*

Erica wasn't there in the morning, but another former neighbor, Tanya Holbrooke, was there.

"Erica had to go home," Tanya said.

"How's Joshua?" I asked.

She smiled. It was a smile that could have lit up the world. "Still in critical condition," she said, "but they're expecting him to pull out of it."

Later, I learned that Dr. Bradenton was supposed to have left the hospital half an hour earlier than he had. Because he'd already signed out, the nurses hadn't known he was still in the building. Another doctor had taken charge of the earlier resuscitation attempts made on Joshua without Dr. Bradenton's knowledge.

I've had friends tell me it must have been a terrible hospital to have been willing to leave Joshua for dead when he obviously was not dead. I don't agree. I believe my husband was dead.

I believe it for many reasons. The report on the failure to bring him around the first time was pretty complete. There was no brain activity, no heartbeat, and no breathing. And, on that first attempt, Dr. Bradenton did tell me the truth. They had done "everything possible." One of the nurses who'd been there was a friend of one of the women in the neighborhood, and the nurse confirmed it. More important, I believe it because of some of the things Joshua had told me.

"There was a sound," Joshua told me. "It was like a whirring or a buzzing, and I felt myself being drawn through a tunnel very fast.

"Then I was in a field, only not like any field you'd ever see on earth. And there was a light. I can't describe the light. I felt it was about to speak to me. And I saw my father."

Joshua's father had died two years earlier.

"Then I saw a fence," Joshua went on. "The light was on the other side. I wanted to reach it, but something told me I couldn't, not this time. This time, I had to go back. I didn't want to go back. Not then. I felt such peace."

I'm not the same person I used to be before the accident, and neither is Joshua. If anything, he is even kinder, more loving, more patient.

And I know that I'm—well, I'm stronger than I used to be, sustained and lifted by a faith I never had before. I now know that we most certainly are God's creatures, that every hurt has its purpose, a purpose that is somehow tied to love and to our need to strengthen our own capacity to love.

For several weeks after Joshua told me about what he'd experienced, I felt guilty and selfish for asking—begging—that he be returned to me. I no longer feel that way. Certainly, we can all ask God for whatever we feel we need, but whether what we ask is granted is God's dominion.

We have two children to raise, friends and neighbors to love, and life to live. Lives that we both hope will prove worthy of this second chance to be together, that God, in His infinite mercy and wisdom, granted us that night my husband died— not "almost" died.

In my heart, I am convinced he did die. He died and came back to us. His work here was not finished. And I feel, somehow, as though my work here—to grow in love, patience, and understanding—has just begun! God granted me a miracle, and I'll be forever grateful. **THE END**